MEN'S MANUAL

VOLUME II

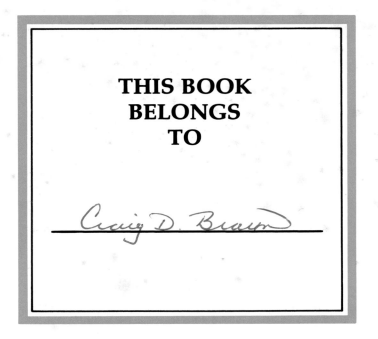

**THIS BOOK
BELONGS
TO**

Craig D. Brown

*"For the eyes of the Lord run to and
fro throughout the whole earth, to shew
himself strong in the behalf of them
whose heart is perfect toward him. . . ."*
II Chronicles 16:9

Printed by Rand McNally and Company
1985

INSTITUTE IN BASIC YOUTH CONFLICTS, INC.   BOX ONE   OAK BROOK, ILLINOIS 60521

Printed in the United States of America

Fourth Printing, February 1985

ISBN 0-916888-09-6

Library of Congress
Catalog Card Number: 79-88994

FINANCIAL FREEDOM

"HOW LONG HALT YE BETWEEN TWO OPINIONS?"

The great prophet Elijah thundered this challenge to the wavering multitudes of his day: *". . . If the Lord be God, follow him: but if Baal, then follow him. And the people answered him not a word"* (I Kings 18:21).

Elijah proposed a test. Two altars would be built. The prophets of Baal would call on their god, and Elijah would call on his God. Whichever one answered by fire would be the one whom they would serve. (See I Kings 18:17–40.)

In every age God's supernatural power will be tested against man's ability to work out his own solutions. One of the most important tests will involve our finances. God's challenge to us is to *". . . prove me now herewith [with tithes and offerings], saith the Lord of hosts, if I will not open you the windows of heaven, and pour you out a blessing, that there shall not be room enough to receive it"* (Malachi 3:10).

God is looking for men who will obey His principles of finance and demonstrate to a skeptical, unbelieving world that He lives and that He is a rewarder of them that diligently seek Him. (See Hebrews 11:6.)

Men of such Scriptural convictions will not only influence the history of our own day, but will raise up the foundations of many Godly generations. (See Isaiah 61:4.)

LET'S ALLOW GOD TO SHOW HIMSELF STRONG!

TEN SCRIPTURAL CONVICTIONS

. . . which every man must teach his family in order to protect them from the destructive influences of wrong desires, false philosophies, and evil companions.

1. God alone is sovereign, and the Bible is His inspired Word and the final authority for my life.

2. My purpose in life is to seek God with my whole heart and to build my goals around His priorities.

3. My body is the living temple of God and must not be defiled by the lusts of the world.

4. My church must teach the foundational truths of the Bible and reinforce my basic convictions.

5. My children and grandchildren belong to God, and it is my responsibility to teach them Scriptural principles, Godly character, and basic convictions.

6. My activities must never weaken the Scriptural convictions of another Christian.

7. My marriage is a life-long commitment to God and to my marriage partner.

VOLUME II

8. My money is a trust from God and must be earned and managed according to Scriptural principles.

9. My words must be in harmony with God's Word, especially when reproving and restoring a Christian brother.

10. My affections must be set on things above, not on things in the earth.

CONTENTS

TWENTY ESSENTIAL GOALS
TO GAIN FINANCIAL FREEDOM

NEBUCHADNEZZAR
One of the greatest rulers of all time

PRIDE AND BONDAGE

". . . Is not this great Babylon, that I have built for the house of the kingdom by the might of my power, and for the honour of my majesty? . . . And he was driven from men, and did eat grass as oxen . . ." (Daniel 4:30, 33).

1 LEARN WHAT IT REALLY MEANS TO BE FINANCIALLY FREE

"Beware that thou forget not the Lord thy God . . . And thou say in thine heart, My power and the might of mine hand hath gotten me this wealth. But thou shalt remember the Lord thy God: for it is he that giveth thee power to get wealth . . ." (Deuteronomy 8:11, 17–18).

FREEDOM BY HUMILITY

"Now I . . . praise and extol and honour the King of heaven, all whose works are truth, and his ways judgment: and those that walk in pride he is able to abase" (Daniel 4:37).

TO WHAT DEGREE ARE YOU FINANCIALLY FREE?

PERSONAL EVALUATION:

YES NO

1. This morning, did you consciously ask God for the things you would need to get through this day? (See Matthew 6:9–15.) ☐ ☐

2. Can you list three of God's basic purposes for money? (See I Timothy 6:8; Malachi 3:10; II Corinthians 8:14–15.) ☐ ☐

3. Does a man need more than careful planning and hard work to be wealthy? (See Deuteronomy 8:18.) ☐ ☐

4. Has your study of God's Word increased since your last financial crisis? (See Haggai 1:9.) ☐ ☐

5. Have you ever lost money, a promotion, a job, or a friend because you refused to compromise your convictions? (See Proverbs 29:25.) ☐ ☐

6. Are you consistently giving at least ten percent of your income to your church? (See Malachi 3:10.) ☐ ☐

7. Have you paid all of your debts? (See Romans 13:8.) ☐ ☐

8. Does God intend for victorious Christians to suffer financial need? (See Philippians 4:12.) ☐ ☐

9. When you read a sales catalog, do you always check the price before studying the product? (See Luke 14:28.) ☐ ☐

10. If someone were to offer you a quick way to legally make a large amount of money, would you tend to turn it down? (See Proverbs 28:22.) ☐ ☐

11. Have you ever researched items in a consumer guide or consumer report? (See Proverbs 14:15.) ☐ ☐

12. Do you have accurate records for all of your expenditures? (See I Corinthians 4:2.) ☐ ☐

13. Is it your policy to refuse to co-sign for anyone? (See Proverbs 6:1–2.) ☐ ☐

14. Do you believe that mothers are able to accomplish more for the family's finances from within the home than outside of the home? (See Proverbs 31:10–31.) ☐ ☐

15. Have you ever kept a verbal promise even though it was costly to do so? (See Psalm 15:4.) ☐ ☐

16. Can you recall three instances in which you received money, goods, or services in answer to specific prayer? (See John 16:24.) ☐ ☐

17. Have you avoided business partnerships, especially equal partnerships? (See Matthew 6:24.) ☐ ☐

18. Is it wise for a man to work beyond retirement age as long as he is physically able? (See Luke 12:19–20.) ☐ ☐

19. Have you ever avoided an unwise business decision because you listened to the cautions of your wife? (See Proverbs 31:11, 26.) ☐ ☐

20. Have you ever sacrificially given a large sum of money to God? (See Matthew 6:19–20.) ☐ ☐

TOTAL CORRECT ☐

EVALUATION SCORE:

20 correct = Financial freedom
19–15 correct = Financial danger
14–10 correct = Financial confusion
9–0 correct = Financial bondage

Answers:

The answer to each question is yes.

8

BASIC FACTORS OF FINANCIAL FREEDOM

FINANCIAL FREEDOM

1. GIVING

- Giving to God (tithes and offerings—Malachi 3:10)
- Giving to the poor (the necessities of life—Proverbs 19:17)
- Giving to Christians (Romans 12:13)

2. RECEIVING

- Receiving through diligent labor (II Thessalonians 3:12)
- Receiving through creative resourcefulness (Proverbs 31:13)
- Receiving through answers to prayer (Philippians 4:6)

3. MANAGING

- Building sales resistance (Proverbs 20:14)
- Looking for the best buys (Proverbs 31:16)
- Being prompt in paying bills (Proverbs 3:28)

1. GIVING

Financial freedom begins with Scriptural giving. Giving activates the work of God in our financial affairs. *"Give, and it shall be given unto you . . ." (Luke 6:38).*

Giving must begin with tithes and offerings to God. No Christian can afford to neglect tithing or giving *". . . as God hath prospered him . . ." (I Corinthians 16:2).* If we give to God and His work, He will *". . . open you the windows of heaven . . ." (Malachi 3:10).*

By giving, we invest treasures in heaven *". . . where thieves do not break through nor steal" (Matthew 6:20).*

Giving increases our love for God, because *". . . where your treasure is, there will your heart be also" (Matthew 6:21).*

2. RECEIVING

In response to our giving, God opens up opportunities to receive provisions directly or indirectly from His hand. He gives the ability to create employment or to secure and hold an existing job.

He provides motivation to be resourceful and to conserve what He has already given. He gives specific promptings to pray for food, clothing, or other items of need; and He answers that prayer in precise ways and with supernatural timing.

To the degree that we give we receive. *". . . He which soweth sparingly shall reap also sparingly; and he which soweth bountifully shall reap also bountifully" (II Corinthians 9:6).*

3. MANAGING

Our once-a-week worship experience of giving to God is a powerful reminder of the fact that we are stewards and not owners of what God has entrusted to us.

We are accountable to God for how we use each hour of our day and each dollar that we have. Accordingly, we cannot make final decisions without checking with God's Word. Every financial decision must be in harmony with the principles of Scripture.

God's Word warns us to flee from those who would waste our time and take our money. He instructs us to use great care in purchasing and to pay our bills promptly. As we wisely manage small amounts, God will entrust us with greater amounts. (See Luke 16:10.)

WHAT IT REALLY MEANS TO BE FINANCIALLY FREE

1. Financial freedom is realizing that true prosperity comes only from God.

If we think that we can get rich by our own efforts, we will become the victims of our own schemes. *". . . For it is he [God] that giveth thee power to get wealth . . ." (Deuteronomy 8:18).*

2. Financial freedom is committing ourselves to God's purposes for money.

The purpose of money is not to free us from daily dependence on God, but to demonstrate God's love and power in our lives. *". . . If God so clothe the grass of the field, which to day is, and to morrow is cast into the oven, shall he not much more clothe you, O ye of little faith" (Matthew 6:30).*

3. Financial freedom is recognizing and rejecting false financial concepts.

An ad that reads "Be Your Own Boss" implies that financial freedom comes by working for ourselves. True freedom begins by accepting Scriptural restraints, whether we work for someone else or for ourselves. *"For he that is called in the Lord, being a servant, is the Lord's freeman: likewise also he that is called, being free, is Christ's servant" (I Corinthians 7:22).*

4. Financial freedom is responding to God's reproofs for wrong financial decisions.

If we fail to fully apply God's principles of finances, God allows riches with sorrow or the devouring of our assets. *"Ye looked for much, and, lo, it came to little; and when ye brought it home, I did blow upon it. Why? saith the Lord of hosts. Because of mine house that is waste, and ye run every man unto his own house" (Haggai 1:9).*

5. Financial freedom is choosing to serve God rather than money.

The needs of daily provision cause most men to build their lives and affections on temporal things rather than on eternal riches. The only escape from slavery to money is to decide to serve God, for *"no man can serve two masters . . ."* (Matthew 6:24).

6. Financial freedom is giving God tithes and offerings.

Poverty is the result of following our natural inclinations. On the other hand, God's increase comes by developing a spirit of generosity according to God's direction. *"Honour the Lord with thy substance, and with the firstfruits of all thine increase: So shall thy barns be filled with plenty, and thy presses shall burst out with new wine"* (Proverbs 3:9–10).

7. Financial freedom is keeping out of debt.

Most debt is the result of disregarding God's limitations or rejecting God's opportunities to show Himself strong on our behalf. The basis of debt is presumption: assuming that we can pay back tomorrow what we borrow today. But God warns that all such presumption is evil. We are instructed, *"Boast not thyself of to morrow; for thou knowest not what a day may bring forth"* (Proverbs 27:1).

8. Financial freedom is learning how to abound and how to suffer need.

God did not intend that wealth or poverty should be permanent positions in life, but rather stages in the development of the true riches of inward character. Toward this end Paul said, *"I know both how to be abased, and I know how to abound . . . to be full and to be hungry . . ."* (Philippians 4:12).

9. Financial freedom is having sales resistance.

Impulse buying is the sure way to financial bondage. The marketplace and the road to it are carefully designed to trap the undisciplined shopper; but God wants us to have the discernment which Eve failed to have in the Garden of Eden. We must reject that which appeals to the lust of the flesh, the lust of the eyes, and the pride of life. (See I John 2:16.)

10. Financial freedom is recognizing and rejecting swindlers.

The shrewdest businessmen in history have fallen prey to swindlers. The swindler gives very few evidences of his deception. He is usually very personable and enthusiastic about how we can make a large amount of money. He keeps our focus on the business deal, but God wants to teach us to focus on warning signals. Only then will He be able *"to deliver thee from the way of the evil man . . ."* and *". . . from the strange woman . . ."* (Proverbs 2:12, 16).

11. Financial freedom is getting the best buy.

Getting a good buy requires taking the time and effort to do research; and it means walking away from purchases which do not measure up to predetermined standards. It means knowing exactly what we want and what questions to ask in order to get it. Developing a good relationship with the seller helps to secure the best in quality and service. Good buys are the result of disciplined living and inner contentment. *"But godliness with contentment is great gain"* (I Timothy 6:6).

12. Financial freedom is keeping accurate and useful records.

If a venture is to prosper, it must be preceded by wise planning, diligent working, and accurate record keeping. One's record-keeping system, however, must be functional in form and clear in reinforcing God's purposes for funds: *". . . Moreover it is required in stewards, that a man be found faithful"* (I Corinthians 4:2).

13. Financial freedom is refusing to lend or co-sign.

If borrowing money makes us a servant to the lender, lending money to a friend forces that one to become our servant. If a person is truly needy, God expects us to give to that one's needs. Co-signing means bondage to the one for whom we signed and also potential bondage for us when circumstances do not turn out the way we had planned. "... *If thou be surety for thy friend, if thou hast stricken thy hand with a stranger... deliver thyself*..." (Proverbs 6:1–3).

14. Financial freedom is developing the full potential of the home.

Many costly services which are performed by others were designed by God to be done by the family in the home. These include early education, medical recovery, care of elderly family members, and partial production of food and clothing. The key to such a home program is a wise, Godly, and virtuous woman. "... *Her price is far above rubies*" (Proverbs 31:10).

15. Financial freedom is choosing a good name rather than great riches.

Broken vows, secret sin, cheating of widows, dishonoring parents, and returning evil for good are a few of the violations which cause God to withhold funds. When Israel experienced famine, King David discovered and removed the cause. (See II Samuel 21.) In the same way, God wants us to search our ways so that He is free to "... *open you the windows of heaven, and pour you out a blessing, that there shall not be room enough to receive it*" (Malachi 3:10).

16. Financial freedom is knowing how to receive funds through prayer.

God delights in having His children trust Him for their daily needs. When riches increase, however, it is easy to cease depending upon the Lord; and when we feel that we do not need the Lord, we lose our love for Him. To remedy the situation, God brings unexpected needs which force us to His Word and prayer. (See II Chronicles 7:13–14.) He then delights in giving us our daily bread and also doing "... *exceeding abundantly above all that we ask or think*..." (Ephesians 3:20).

17. Financial freedom is having the courage to avoid partnerships.

A man must purpose ahead of time to reject any financial gain which comes as a result of violating Scriptural principles. Once he makes this decision, he must reject pressures which would cause him to do wrong. The basis of secular humanism is the thinking that the end justifies the means. In contrast to this, Daniel purposed in his heart that he would do what was right, regardless of the cost. (See Daniel 1:8.)

18. Financial freedom is detecting and conquering slothfulness.

Trying to live without working is rebellion against God's order. He has determined that provision must come by the sweat of the brow. (See Genesis 3:17–19.) His one remedy for laziness is hunger. "... *If any would not work, neither should he eat*" (II Thessalonians 3:10). Any financial concept that appeals to slothfulness must be identified as not being from God and then must be rejected. One example is the false notion that we should work for a life of ease. Those who do this are usually met with unexpected pressures or disillusionments, such as the rich man who said to his soul, "... *Thou hast much goods laid up for many years; take thine ease*..." (Luke 12:19).

19. Financial freedom is listening to the cautions of your wife.

Many financial disasters can be avoided by listening to your wife's cautions about a financial decision before it is made. God designed the wife to be "an help meet." As such, she has special abilities to sense dangers which are often overlooked by her husband. "*A wise man will hear, and will increase learning*..." (Proverbs 1:5).

20. Financial freedom is knowing how to pass on an inheritance which insures a Godly and responsible heritage.

An inheritance is God's way of passing on a heritage to children and grandchildren. God's primary purpose through the inheritance is to strengthen the larger family unit. Vital functions, such as the education of the children, health care, home provision, care of the elderly, and resources for business are some of the responsibilities which God intended for the family to meet. There are also dangers in an inheritance; thus God gives both a challenge and a warning. "*A good man leaveth an inheritance to his children's children*..." (Proverbs 13:22). "*An inheritance may be gotten hastily at the beginning; but the end thereof shall not be blessed*" (Proverbs 20:21).

God promises a blessing to those who honor their father and mother, but He warns that those who reject the Scriptural counsel of their parents will be cursed. If a man does not learn to be under authority at home, he will have conflicts in his employment. He may then be drawn into the false conclusion that he should be his own boss, but this will only produce new pressures from God to teach him to properly respond to authority. (See Ephesians 6:1–3; Proverbs 3:33.)

- ### CLEAR CONSCIENCE

Lack of clear conscience in one area will give the incentive to lower God's standards in other areas. Once this happens, compromise will cause that man to make shipwreck of his faith, and he will begin to trust his own judgment in financial decisions. He may also try to compensate for guilt by the inappropriate use of funds. (See I Timothy 1:19.)

- ### A FORGIVING SPIRIT

A man who has a forgiving spirit is conscious of the great debt that he owes to God. He is willing to release others from the debts which they owe him. (See Luke 16:1–12.) However, a man who has a bitter, unforgiving spirit will find that it will adversely affect his business relationships and his personal health. (See Hebrews 12:15–17.)

- ### YIELDING RIGHTS

One who yields his rights to God is a meek person. God promises that the meek will inherit the earth. (See Matthew 5:5.) A meek person works to earn a hearing rather than demanding one. Such a person is assured of good judgment in financial matters. *"The meek will he guide in judgment: and the meek will he teach his way"* (Psalm 25:9).

- ### MORAL FREEDOM

A man who violates God's moral laws will become prey to immoral women. These women will bring him to poverty, and others will exploit the labors of his hands. *"Remove thy way far from her, and come not nigh the door of her house: Lest thou give thine honour unto others, and thy years unto the cruel: Lest strangers be filled with thy wealth; and thy labours be in the house of a stranger"* (Proverbs 5:8–10).

- ### LIFE PURPOSE

When a man commits himself to God's purposes for his life, he has the clearest basis for making wise financial decisions. He knows which purchases will assist him in reaching his goal and which ones will hinder God's purpose for his life. (See Matthew 6:33.)

HOW SCRIPTURAL PRINCIPLES AFFECT FINANCIAL FREEDOM

God has established certain universal, non-optional principles of life. Failure to live by these principles will directly affect our attitude toward money.

- ### SELF-ACCEPTANCE

A man who rejects the way that God made him will experience strong feelings of inferiority. To compensate for these feelings, he will often buy expensive items which he does not need and cannot afford. (See Isaiah 45:9–10; Matthew 6:27.)

- ### RESPONSE TO AUTHORITY

It is natural to want to be independent. However, God emphasizes the importance of being under the protection and direction of proper authority.

KNOW THE EVIDENCES OF FINANCIAL BONDAGE

- **INSECURITY**

    Insecurity is the by-product of building our lives around persons, positions, or possessions which we know can be taken from us.

- **FEAR**

    Fear occurs as we become aware of all of the possible ways in which we could lose our most cherished possessions.

- **ANXIETY**

    Anxiety is the physical and emotional tension which results when we think about financial problems.

- **LOSS OF SLEEP**

    Worry and pressure from financial cares become greater at night and remove the possiblity of peaceful sleep.

- **UNGRATEFULNESS**

    Financial cares and concerns decrease our ability to appreciate or enjoy the many benefits that God and others provide for us.

- **ENSLAVEMENT**

    Money and possessions have built-in demands for protection and maintenance. Thus, the things that we own soon own us.

- **ENVY**

    Envy is desiring to have what someone else has. It is the by-product of comparison. It robs us of our ability to enjoy what God has given to us.

- **BITTERNESS**

    Bitterness is evidence that we love money and possessions more than we love God, because it is God who allows our possessions to be taken or destroyed so that He can build the character of Christ in our lives.

- **DISILLUSIONMENT**

    When we attempt to use money to fulfill all of our dreams, we discover that what we thought would make us happy and fulfilled only brings temporary pleasure and unseen disappointments.

Personal Commitment to Financial Freedom

Based on the Scriptural warning that the borrower is servant to the lender, and on the command to owe no man anything but love, I purpose to work toward gaining and maintaining financial freedom.

Projected date to achieve financial freedom:

Present date: _____   _____

CAN YOU DEFINE BASIC FINANCIAL TERMS?

Choose the best definition for each term.

1. FINANCIAL FREEDOM

- ☐ **A.** Having the ability to buy whatever you want
- ☐ **B.** Not having financial needs
- ☐ **C.** Being content with food and clothing

2. FINANCIAL BONDAGE

- ☐ **A.** Having many expenses
- ☐ **B.** Working hard for money
- ☐ **C.** Owing money to other people

3. A RICH MAN

- ☐ **A.** One who has a large amount of money
- ☐ **B.** One who is in the process of collecting wealth
- ☐ **C.** One who gets a large salary

4. A POOR MAN

- ☐ **A.** One who has little money
- ☐ **B.** One who cannot pay his bills
- ☐ **C.** One who cannot buy food and clothing

5. A WEALTHY MAN

- ☐ **A.** One that has more money than he needs
- ☐ **B.** One who looks for good investments
- ☐ **C.** One who lends money to others

6. INDEBTEDNESS

- ☐ **A.** Not being able to pay bills
- ☐ **B.** Borrowing money with interest
- ☐ **C.** Borrowing money without interest

7. CO-SIGNING

- ☐ **A.** Going into a business partnership
- ☐ **B.** Guaranteeing that a check is good
- ☐ **C.** Guaranteeing that another's loan will be repaid

8. FINANCIAL SUCCESS

- ☐ **A.** Earning a large amount of money
- ☐ **B.** Achieving the financial goals that I have set
- ☐ **C.** Fulfilling the right purposes for funds

Answers: 1.C 2.C 3.B 4.C 5.B 6.A 7.C 8.C

15

HOW DOES GOD ILLUSTRATE FINANCIAL FREEDOM?

A. Nebuchad-
nezzar

B. Elijah

C. Abraham

D. Elisha

E. Paul

F. Joshua

G. Cornelius

H. David

I. Moses

J. Peter

Match the following clues with the person that they best describe.

☐ **1.** He served a man who taught many to trust the Lord for daily provision. When he became the leader, he led those same people into great prosperity. With prosperity came new dangers, so he warned them to serve only the Lord and not money.

☐ **2.** He was such an upright and generous man that he was highly respected by everyone. His worshipful giving to God's work and to God's people was so sincere that God personally rewarded him with a special messenger of spiritual truth.

☐ **3.** He was offered a valuable reward, but he knew that it was not appropriate to receive it. His servant despised the wisdom of his decision, claimed the reward for himself, and experienced God's severe reproof.

☐ **4.** He pronounced judgment on leaders who violated God's principles to gain wealth. They sought to kill him, but God protected him and demonstrated how He could provide daily needs in supernatural ways.

☐ **5.** He was exposed to a life of wealth and luxury as a boy; however, he also saw the traps and disillusionment that come with such a life. As a result, he chose a life of discipline and hardship, but through it he led many others out of bondage.

☐ **6.** He left a prosperous area to follow the Lord. God made him a wealthy man. He gave generously to God and to others and wisely rejected gain from evil men so they could not claim that they made him wealthy.

☐ **7.** He had something money could not buy. He met a man who wanted to buy what he had. He recognized the wrong character in this man and sternly rebuked him for evil motives.

☐ **8.** He worshiped gold and he forced others to worship gold. He achieved man's greatest dream, that of ruling the world. God broke his pride, took all that he had, and then returned it when he proclaimed to the world that God alone gives power to get wealth.

☐ **9.** He wanted to do something extra special for God, but it required more money than he had. Instead of borrowing the money or forcing people to give, he spent the rest of his life in gathering the funds and training his son to achieve his goal.

☐ **10.** He had the best education money could buy. He had great influence with people and collected large sums of money for others, but he refused to take any of it for himself. He understood that security and freedom come by contentment in God, regardless of how much or how little he had.

Answers: 1.F 2.G 3.D 4.B 5.I 6.C 7.J 8.A 9.H 10.E

HOW DOES GOD ILLUSTRATE FINANCIAL FREEDOM?

Match the following clues with the person that they best describe.

K. Solomon

L. Ezra

M. Nehemiah

N. The Ideal Wife

O. Zacchaeus

P. Caleb

Q. Daniel

R. Samuel

S. Joseph

T. Jacob

☐ **11.** This person lost all material possessions, but he developed a servant's heart. He gained favor with God and man. This resulted in increased responsiblity, even to the point of governing an entire nation.

☐ **12.** He knew that many people disliked him because of his past business dealings. One day he decided to earn a good name even if it would cost him a great deal of money to do so.

☐ **13.** This person is admired by God and man as an example of diligence, frugality, generosity, resourcefulness, and careful money management. The wise planning and self-discipline demonstrated in this person's life brought prosperity to others and won public praise and acclaim.

☐ **14.** He was trained by slothful men, but he never lost sight of the Godly heritage of his parents. As a result, he was used of the Lord to bring about proper discipline and turn a nation back to God's ways.

☐ **15.** He had great riches because he did not seek them. They were the by-product of what he did seek. His responsibilities involved international buying and selling, and his astonishing success brought prosperity to everyone around him.

☐ **16.** He did not always do things right. In fact, he made some very serious mistakes. He knew what it was to earn wealth and lose wealth; but throughout his life he developed a valuable heritage of experience, understanding, and power with God.

☐ **17.** He was entrusted with a great treasure. He realized that it belonged to the Lord. He set up a very precise accounting system, and with it he was able to bring the Lord's treasure to its proper destination.

☐ **18.** He lost everything he had except food and clothing. However, this prompted him to give complete trust and commitment to God. The peer pressure to compromise was very strong, yet he was willing to even reduce his food to stay true to God.

☐ **19.** He lived with wealth, but he was concerned for the welfare of God's people. While he was busy working for them, unscrupulous associates put them in bondage with loans and mortgages.

☐ **20.** He saw beautiful property and asked God to give it to him and his descendants. God answered his prayer, but it required patience to wait forty-five years and courage to conquer the giants who possessed it.

Answers: 11. S 12. O 13. N 14. R 15. K 16. T 17. L 18. Q 19. M 20. P

ELIJAH
A great example to a backslidden nation

PROVISION

"... I have commanded the ravens to feed thee ..." (I Kings 17:4).

DIRECTION

"And it came to pass after a while, that the brook dried up ..." (I Kings 17:7).

FELLOWSHIP

"... I have commanded a widow woman there to sustain thee" (I Kings 17:9).

2 KNOW GOD'S FOUR PURPOSES FOR MONEY

"For the eyes of the Lord run to and fro throughout the whole earth, to shew himself strong in the behalf of them whose heart is perfect toward him . . ." (II Chronicles 16:9).

DEMONSTRATION

"Elias was a man subject to like passions as we are, and he prayed earnestly . . ." (James 5:17).

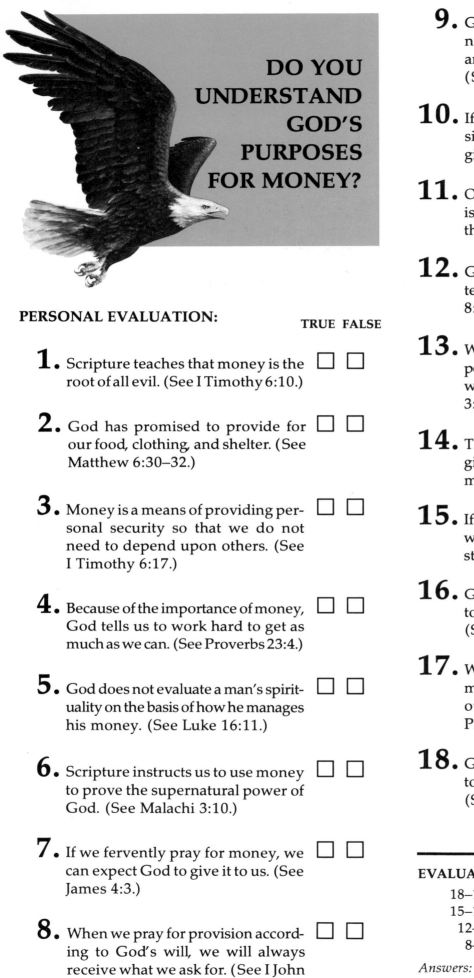

DO YOU UNDERSTAND GOD'S PURPOSES FOR MONEY?

PERSONAL EVALUATION:

                                                   TRUE FALSE

1. Scripture teaches that money is the root of all evil. (See I Timothy 6:10.) ☐ ☐

2. God has promised to provide for our food, clothing, and shelter. (See Matthew 6:30–32.) ☐ ☐

3. Money is a means of providing personal security so that we do not need to depend upon others. (See I Timothy 6:17.) ☐ ☐

4. Because of the importance of money, God tells us to work hard to get as much as we can. (See Proverbs 23:4.) ☐ ☐

5. God does not evaluate a man's spirituality on the basis of how he manages his money. (See Luke 16:11.) ☐ ☐

6. Scripture instructs us to use money to prove the supernatural power of God. (See Malachi 3:10.) ☐ ☐

7. If we fervently pray for money, we can expect God to give it to us. (See James 4:3.) ☐ ☐

8. When we pray for provision according to God's will, we will always receive what we ask for. (See I John 5:14–15.) ☐ ☐

9. God's purpose in giving us financial need is to increase our love for Him and our dependence upon Him. (See John 16:24.) ☐ ☐

10. If we ask God for money or possessions that will harm us, He will not give them to us. (See Psalm 106:15.) ☐ ☐

11. One of God's purposes for money is to unite Christians. (See II Corinthians 8:14–15.) ☐ ☐

12. God intends for welfare to be on a temporary basis. (See II Corinthians 8:14.) ☐ ☐

13. Withholding food from any hungry person is not a Scriptural or Christian way to act. (See II Thessalonians 3:10.) ☐ ☐

14. The amount of money that God gives to a person is based on how much faith he has. (See James 2:5.) ☐ ☐

15. If we desire to do a work for God, we should not let a lack of funds stop us. (See Luke 14:28.) ☐ ☐

16. God uses financial loss as one way to discipline a sensual Christian. (See Proverbs 6:26.) ☐ ☐

17. When it comes to managing our money, God expects us to use our own common sense. (See Proverbs 3:5.) ☐ ☐

18. God uses a lack of funds as a signal to stop and get clearer direction. (See I Thessalonians 5:24.) ☐ ☐

TOTAL CORRECT ☐

EVALUATION SCORE:

    18–16 correct = Clear understanding
    15–13 correct = Fair understanding
    12–9 correct = Poor understanding
    8–0 correct = Lack of understanding

Answers:
1. False 2. False 3. False 4. False 5. False 6. True 7. False 8. True 9. True 10. False 11. True 12. True 13. False 14. False 15. False 16. True 17. False 18. True.

THE SECRET OF KNOWING GOD'S PURPOSES FOR MONEY

In Scripture, God explains the difference between a "natural mind" and a "spiritual mind." A man with a natural mind uses human reasoning before he decides to obey God's Word. A man with a spiritual mind begins by obeying a Scriptural command. After he obeys, he then understands the hidden wisdom and purpose behind the command.

The tragedy of a man with a natural mind is that he is not able to understand the wisdom of God. Instead, he resorts to his own understanding and experiences the destruction and disillusionment that go along with it. (See I Corinthians 2:14–15.)

- **PROVIDING NEEDS**
- **DEMONSTRATING SUPERNATURAL POWER**

Elijah was commanded by God to flee to a brook in the wilderness. He obeyed God, and as a result he was protected from the wrath of wicked Queen Jezebel. God then miraculously fed Elijah by ravens every morning and evening. (See I Kings 17:1–6.)

The purposes of God's command were only understood by Elijah after he obeyed. During those months by the brook he overcame severe depression. He found rest for his body and mind. He enjoyed intimate fellowship with the Lord, and he experienced the daily evidence of God's miraculous provision during a time of severe famine.

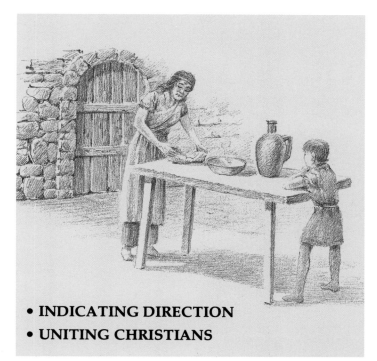

- **INDICATING DIRECTION**
- **UNITING CHRISTIANS**

Soon, however, the brook dried up; and although God could have miraculously provided more water, He used this lack of provision as a signal for Elijah to change direction. God commanded him to go to Zarephath. Again Elijah obeyed God, and later he understood God's purposes for the move.

God has promised to give special care to widows and fatherless children. (See Psalm 68:5.) The widow of Zarephath had only enough food for one more meal. God directed Elijah to instruct her to make a meal for him first. She obeyed, and because she did, God miraculously multiplied her food. God's provision lasted for over a year, until the famine ended.

The widow's obedience allowed her to discover and understand an important principle: When we give of our assets to God first, He causes the remainder of our assets to meet our needs.

The widow also discovered the rewards of thanksgiving and fellowship that come through meeting the needs of others. (See II Corinthians 9:8.)

FOUR BASIC PURPOSES FOR MONEY

Financial bondage is an immediate consequence of misunderstanding God's purposes for money. The purposes for money are not to provide security, establish independence, or create power and influence. God's purposes are:

1. TO PROVIDE BASIC NEEDS

Only a few things, such as food, clothing, and shelter, are necessary to maintain life.

God demonstrates His loving care by providing the resources for these items. *"Behold the fowls of the air: for they sow not, neither do they reap, nor gather into barns; yet your heavenly Father feedeth them. Are ye not much better than they?*

"And why take ye thought for raiment? Consider the lilies of the field, how they grow; they toil not, neither do they spin: And yet I say unto you, That even Solomon in all his glory was not arrayed like one of these. . . . Shall he not much more clothe you, O ye of little faith?" (Matthew 6:26, 28–30).

". . . Having food and raiment let us be therewith content."

I Timothy 6:8

God's wisdom in this purpose

- *To establish daily dependence on Him*

    Since the beginning of time, mankind has attempted to become independent of God. There is within each one of us a desire to be self-sufficient so that we can be our own boss. We tend to pray: "Give us riches for our future needs," or "Give us this month our monthly paycheck." However, God taught us to pray, *"Give us this day our daily bread" (Matthew 6:11).* He knows that daily needs produce daily dependence.

- *To deepen our love for the Lord*

    When we fail to recognize our need for a person, we tend to lose our love for that person. God created us to need Him. We are only complete in Christ, and apart from Him we can do nothing at all. (See Colossians 2:10; John 15:5.)

    When the Israelites were in the wilderness, God taught them to look to Him for daily food. Every man, whether rich or poor, must recognize his daily dependence upon God.

- *To develop a spirit of gratefulness*

    Gratefulness is a delightful by-product of contentment with basics. However, we begin to lose our contentment when we compare what we have with what others have. Expectations then dominate our focus. To the degree that our expectations increase, our gratefulness decreases.

- *To teach us to live within our means*

    Contentment with basics equips us to resist the continuous barrage of advertising which seeks to convince us that we are not able to really enjoy life unless we buy some new gadget or service. On the contrary, a contented person feels wealthy because he knows that he already possesses more than he needs for daily living. *". . . Godliness with contentment is great gain" (I Timothy 6:6).*

- *To help us enjoy our possessions*

    Discontent destroys our ability to enjoy the things that God has given to us, since our focus is on the things that we think He should have given us rather than on what we do have. Therefore God warns us not to be covetous but to ". . . *be content with such things as ye have . . ." (Hebrews 13:5).*

2. TO CONFIRM DIRECTION

God will use the supply of money or the lack of it to confirm His direction for many of the decisions we must make in our lives.

If we think that we should buy a car but do not have the money for it, we can safely assume that until God does provide the funds, it is not His will for us to buy a new car.

If we have half of the funds needed for a new car, and a car is urgently needed, we can assume that God wants us to buy a lower priced car, unless He directs otherwise.

In order to get a driver's license, we must learn to recognize all of the road signs. In order to be in a leadership position, we must learn to recognize God's signals through the provision or lack of finances.

> *"Rest in the Lord, and wait patiently for him: fret not thyself because of him who prospereth in his way. . . ."*
>
> Psalm 37:7

God's wisdom in this purpose

- ### To build our faith and vision

  Faith is discerning what God wants to accomplish in and through our lives. *"By faith Noah, being warned of God of things not seen as yet, moved with fear, prepared an ark . . ."* (Hebrews 11:7).

  Every one of us should visualize how we can advance the work of God. What can we allow God to accomplish through our lives that will build up Christians and benefit the Kingdom of God?

  We can be certain that if God gives us clear direction that is confirmed by Scripture, He will provide whatever is necessary to carry out that direction.

In contrast to faith, presumption is deciding what we want to accomplish and trying to get God to do it for us.

- ### To determine who is the lord of our life

  It is easy to claim that Jesus Christ is the Lord of our life. However, His Lordship is only confirmed when we are obedient to the promptings and limitations which He places on our daily decisions.

  A person who has unlimited funds will find it more difficult to detect God's leading through finances. Because of this, God gives special warnings to the rich. *"Charge them that are rich in this world, that they be not high-minded, nor trust in uncertain riches, but in the living God..."* (I Timothy 6:17).

- ### To protect us from harmful items

  It seems that no matter how much God gives to us, we still want more. God gave Adam and Eve everything that they needed to enjoy life, yet Satan tempted them to desire something more. How clear and true God's warnings are on this point. *". . .They that will be rich fall into temptation and a snare, and into many foolish and hurtful lusts, which drown men in destruction and perdition (I Timothy 6:9).*

- ### To teach us patience

  Patience is an essential quality for maturity in life. It is so important that God assures us that it is worth going through tribulation in order to obtain it. (See Romans 5:3.) Having to wait for God to provide funds is one valuable way to perfect patience. *"Knowing this, that the trying of your faith worketh patience. But let patience have her perfect work, that ye may be perfect and entire, wanting nothing"* (James 1:3–4).

- ### To concentrate on true riches

  As Paul matured in his Christian life, he came to the important discovery that temporal things tend to compete with eternal riches and to obscure the priceless knowledge of our inheritance in Christ. With this in mind, he wrote this testimony: *"But what things were gain to me, those I counted loss for Christ. Yea doubtless, and I count all things but loss for the excellency of the knowledge of Christ Jesus my Lord: for whom I have suffered the loss of all things, and do count them but dung, that I may win Christ"* (Philippians 3:7–8).

3. TO GIVE TO CHRISTIANS

Our generosity will determine how much spiritual light we have within our being. If we have a greedy eye, our whole being will be filled with spiritual darkness. But if we have a generous eye, our whole being will be filled with spiritual light.

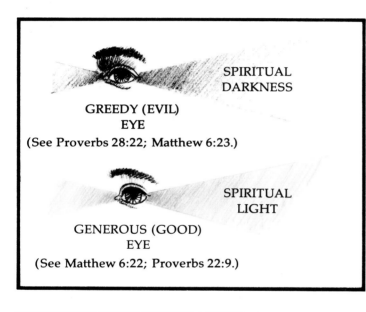

SPIRITUAL DARKNESS

GREEDY (EVIL) EYE
(See Proverbs 28:22; Matthew 6:23.)

SPIRITUAL LIGHT

GENEROUS (GOOD) EYE
(See Matthew 6:22; Proverbs 22:9.)

> "Distributing to the necessity of saints; given to hospitality."
>
> Romans 12:13

God's wisdom in this purpose

• To unite Christians

In the early days of the Church, the Jews had no social dealings with the Gentiles. When a severe famine caused many Jewish Christians to suffer, the Apostle Paul urged every Gentile church to collect an offering for these Jewish Christians.

That offering was an important means of tearing down barriers between Christians and building bonds of genuine Christian love. The basis for this kind of giving is explained in II Corinthians 8:14. *"... That now at this time your abundance may be a supply for their want, that their abundance also may be a supply for your want. ..."*

• To demonstrate the mark of a Christian

The mark of a true Christian is a zealousness for good works. This is one of the purposes for which Christ redeemed us, *"Who gave himself for us, that he might redeem us from all iniquity, and purify unto himself a peculiar people, zealous of good works"* (Titus 2:14).

God gives special desire and power to a generous Christian so that he is able to multiply his good works. *"And God is able to make all grace abound toward you; that ye, always having all sufficiency in all things, may abound to every good work"* (II Corinthians 9:8).

• To initiate spontaneous thanksgiving

Giving to the needs of fellow Christians means that many will thank God. Spirit-directed gifts not only meet practical needs, but result in an overflowing tide of thanksgiving to God and to the giver. *"Being enriched in every thing to all bountifulness, which causeth through us thanksgiving to God"* (II Corinthians 9:11).

Praise and thanksgiving are the bases of dynamic, growing Christians and churches.

• To multiply the potential for giving

God likens giving to planting a harvest. *"... He which soweth sparingly shall reap also sparingly; and he which soweth bountifully shall reap also bountifully"* (II Corinthians 9:6).

The potential multiplication of planting and harvesting is seen in the following diagram.

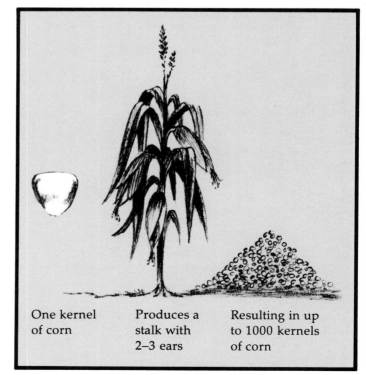

| One kernel of corn | Produces a stalk with 2–3 ears | Resulting in up to 1000 kernels of corn |

THE LAW OF THE HARVEST

4. TO ILLUSTRATE GOD'S POWER

God is a supernatural God. He wants to demonstrate His reality and power to both Christians and non-Christians. One means by which He has chosen to do this is through the miraculous provision of money.

A miracle is a supernatural or natural event with precise timing to bring glory to God.

When a Christian prays about a special financial need, and an unexpected and unsolicited gift is handed to him by one who did not know about the need, the supernatural power of God is demonstrated.

> "... Prove me now herewith, saith the Lord of hosts, if I will not open you the windows of heaven, and pour you out a blessing. ..."
>
> Malachi 3:10

God's wisdom in this purpose

• To cause Christians to trust Him

In the day of Elijah the nation of Israel tried to worship God and serve Baal at the same time. Elijah knew that this would only bring God's judgment, so he proposed a test.

The test involved building two altars, one for God and one for Baal. Whichever god answered by supernatural power was the one whom they would worship.

The prophets of Baal cried out to their god all day long and nothing happened. Then Elijah prayed. God sent fire from heaven which consumed the offering, the altar, and the water around it. (See I Kings 18:21–40.)

• To mock the false gods of our age

One of the false gods of our day is money. It has become an idol because people expect from it what only God can give. As the world seeks after money, God wants to prove that those who seek after Him will not lack any good thing. Seeking after God involves building our lives, motives, affections, and activities around Him and His will for us.

• To purify our lives and motives

A prerequisite in experiencing God's supernatural power is actively seeking Him with a pure heart and unselfish motives. God has warned us that if we regard iniquity in our heart, He will not hear us. (See Psalm 66:18.) The need for God's miraculous intervention in our financial affairs is a powerful motivation for us to examine our own lives.

• To bring non-Christians to salvation

When Christians are in right relationship with the Lord and each other, and when they are experiencing God's miraculous provision in their lives, non-Christians are drawn to Christ and to the local church.

This cause-and-effect sequence is well documented in the early Church. The greatest explosion of church growth occurred when the believers demonstrated God's supernatural power. (See Acts 5:12–14.)

• To glorify God

God is glorified when His people praise Him for His mighty acts. He does great things for us so that we can report them to each other and to our children and our grandchildren. *"And call upon me in the day of trouble: I will deliver thee, and thou shalt glorify me"* (Psalm 50:15).

APPLY GOD'S PURPOSES FOR MONEY

1. If we need money for time payments on a car, can we expect God to provide them?

Answer: No.

A car is not a basic need, nor is it Scriptural to buy one on time payments. (See James 4:13–17.)

2. If we are rich, will we have greater difficulty in loving God than if we are poor?

Answer: No.

A rich man is tempted to deny God, but a poor man is tempted to curse Him. (See Proverbs 30:8–9.)

3. If the tuition for one school is $1000 more than a comparable school, should we choose the less expensive school unless God provides an unexpected $1000?

Answer: Yes.

When either choice is right, it is proper to ask God to confirm the more expensive one. (See Judges 6:36–40.)

4. Should we buy an exceptional bargain if it would require a second job to pay for it?

Answer: No.

God's instruction is to use only what we have to buy bargains. (See Matthew 13:44–46.)

5. If, after working hard and being successful, our boss refuses to pay us enough to meet our obligations, should we look for a new job?

Answer: Yes.

". . . The labourer is worthy of his hire. . ." (Luke 10:7).

6. If a poor Christian needs money for food and clothing, should we lend it to him?

Answer: No.

God wants us to give to the poor. (See Proverbs 19:17.)

7. If we ask God to provide $500 by a certain date and it arrives three days after the deadline, should we reconsider our decision?

Answer: No.

Unless God gives additional confirmation, we can trust Him to provide money the day it is needed. (See Jeremiah 32:27.)

8. If our taxes are used for immoral purposes, should we refuse to pay them?

Answer: No.

God commands us to pay all taxes. Even Christ paid taxes to the government that eventually had Him put to death. (See Romans 13:7.)

Personal Commitment to God's Purposes for Money

My financial decisions will be based on being content with food and clothing, waiting patiently for God to provide, distributing to the necessities of the saints, and proving God with tithes and offerings.

My wife and I have prayed and agreed together on this goal.   Date: _____

CAN YOU IDENTIFY BASIC NEEDS?

God states that certain items are basic to a life of contentment. Check which ones would be on God's list.

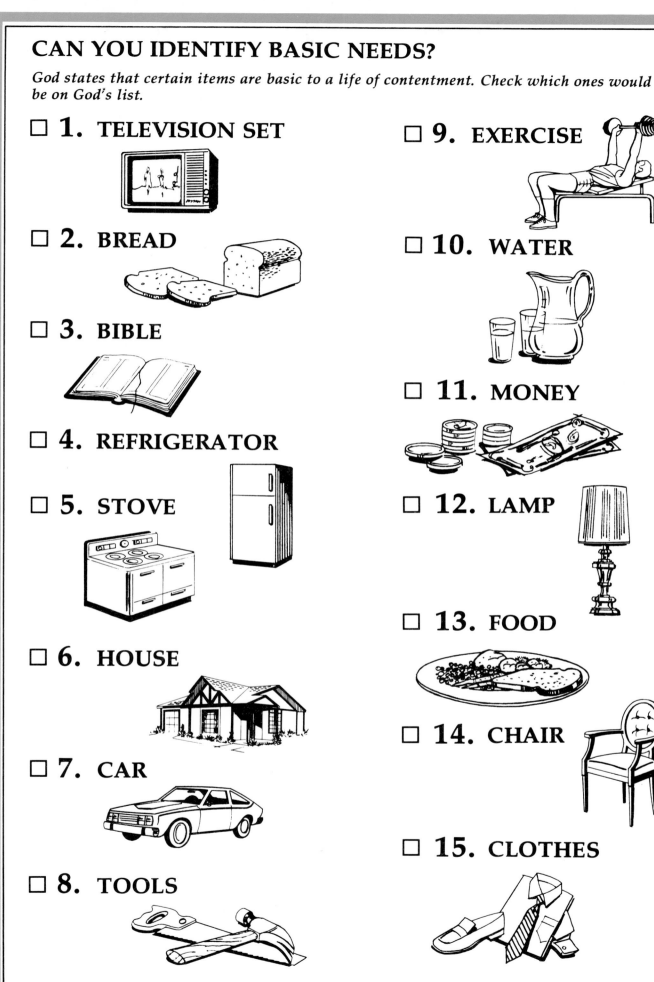

☐ **1. TELEVISION SET**

☐ **2. BREAD**

☐ **3. BIBLE**

☐ **4. REFRIGERATOR**

☐ **5. STOVE**

☐ **6. HOUSE**

☐ **7. CAR**

☐ **8. TOOLS**

☐ **9. EXERCISE**

☐ **10. WATER**

☐ **11. MONEY**

☐ **12. LAMP**

☐ **13. FOOD**

☐ **14. CHAIR**

☐ **15. CLOTHES**

Answers: 2, 3, 10, 13, 15

WHO ILLUSTRATES GOD'S PURPOSES FOR MONEY?

A. Peter
(Matt. 17:27)

B. Cornelius
(Acts 10)

C. Paul
(II Cor. 9)

D. Boaz
(Ruth)

E. Joseph
(Genesis 41)

F. Elijah
(I Kings 17)

G. Elisha
(II Kings 4)

H. Abraham
(Genesis 13)

Match the following statements with the right persons.

☐ **1.** God directed his life, his family's location, and his children's future by creating a need for basic provisions and then supplying the provisions to meet that need.

☐ **2.** He fulfilled the proverb that a good name is rather to be chosen than great riches. He had both. His generosity brought him praise from men and from God.

☐ **3.** An improper tax was levied against him and the One whom he served. In order not to offend the tax collectors, he was instructed how to get the money in a miraculous way.

☐ **4.** When he experienced a time of deep depression, God took special care of him, miraculously providing two meals each day.

☐ **5.** He knew that generosity and love went together, so he used his personal influence to promote generosity; and he achieved remarkable unity among those who previously did not keep company with each other.

☐ **6.** He was involved in a "welfare program" that allowed people to keep their self-respect. His just treatment and generous spirit won him a place in the genealogy of Christ.

Answers: 1. E 2. B 3. A 4. F 5. C 6. D

CAN YOU APPLY GOD'S PURPOSES FOR YOUR MONEY?

Indicate your response to the following situations.

YES   NO

1. If you bought a car on time payments and suddenly lost your job, would it be proper to expect God to supply this need on the basis of Philippians 4:19: *"But my God shall supply all your need . . ."?* ☐ ☐

2. Is it true that it is harder to love God if you are wealthy than if you are poor? ☐ ☐

3. If you are accepted at two equally-rated schools but the tuition for one is $1000 more than the other, would you go to the less expensive one unless God provided an extra $1000? ☐ ☐

4. If you found an exceptional bargain but were not able to fully pay for it, would you buy it and then get a second job to pay for it? ☐ ☐

5. If you worked hard and successfully on a job but were not paid enough to meet your financial obligations, would you look for a new job? ☐ ☐

6. If you met a Christian family that was in financial need, would you lend them money to buy food and clothing? ☐ ☐

7. If a sign for which you had prayed did not arrive until three days after you had to make a business decision, should you accept that sign as an answer to prayer? ☐ ☐

8. If you discover that your taxes are being used for immoral purposes, should you stop paying them? ☐ ☐

"Consider the ravens: for they neither sow nor reap; which neither have storehouse nor barn; and God feedeth them: how much more are ye better than the fowls?" (Luke 12:24).

Answers: See page 26.

ABRAHAM
A great obtainer of unseen riches

REJECTING ENTANGLEMENTS

"... I will not take any thing that is thine, lest thou shouldest say, I have made Abram rich" (Genesis 14:23).

3 IDENTIFY AND REJECT FALSE FINANCIAL CONCEPTS

"For my thoughts are not your thoughts, neither are your ways my ways, saith the Lord" (Isaiah 55:8).

YIELDING AFFECTIONS

". . . Now I know that thou fearest God, seeing thou hast not withheld thy son, thine only son from me" (Genesis 22:12).

CAN YOU IDENTIFY FALSE FINANCIAL CONCEPTS?

PERSONAL EVALUATION:

TRUE FALSE

1. If you think, act, and look successful, you will become successful. ☐ ☐

2. There is no excuse for poverty. ☐ ☐

3. Every man can determine his own financial destiny. ☐ ☐

4. Whatever your mind can conceive and believe, you can achieve. ☐ ☐

5. You should make it your goal to become financially independent so that you do not have to look to other people for help. ☐ ☐

6. The things that you will be able to provide for your family will more than compensate for whatever sacrifices your job requires. ☐ ☐

7. You can borrow your way to financial success. ☐ ☐

8. The ultimate financial goal is to be the president of your company or to own your own business. ☐ ☐

9. You have the right to determine how you will use the money that you earn. ☐ ☐

10. To be successful you must learn how to overcome every obstacle that is between you and your financial goals. ☐ ☐

11. You can build a successful business with a good advertising program. ☐ ☐

12. You can measure your success by the amount of money that you make. ☐ ☐

13. Those who reach the top of the "success ladder" are usually self-made people. ☐ ☐

14. In order to succeed in the business world, you must be willing to compromise. ☐ ☐

15. To be promoted in a big company, it is not what you know but whom you know that really counts. ☐ ☐

16. There is no real virtue in being poor. ☐ ☐

TOTAL CORRECT ☐

EVALUATION SCORE:

16 correct = You are wise
15–13 correct = You have insight
12–9 correct = You need insight
8–0 correct = Study the following pages

Answers:

The answer to each question is false.

LEARN THE DANGERS OF FALSE FINANCIAL CONCEPTS

To allow error to remain in your mind is like allowing poison to remain in your body. God instructs us to be actively involved in "casting down imaginations, and every high thing that exalteth itself against the knowledge of God, and bringing into captivity every thought to the obedience of Christ" (II Corinthians 10:5).

1. *If you think, act, and look successful, will you become successful?*

No. This concept causes a person to believe that he, rather than God, is the source of power to get wealth. God warns us not to say in our heart *". . . my power and the might of mine hand hath gotten me this wealth. But thou shalt remember the Lord thy God: for it is he that giveth thee power to get wealth . . ." (Deuteronomy 8:17–18).*

2. *Is it true that there is no excuse for a person's being poor?*

No. This statement sounds true, but it is Scripturally false. *"The rich and poor meet together: the Lord is the maker of them all" (Proverbs 22:2).* God has a number of methods and purposes for causing various types and lengths of poverty. For this reason, He warns us not to mock the poor or to take advantage of them; because in so doing, we reproach their Maker, and we will receive God's punishment.

3. *Can every man determine his own financial destiny?*

No. This idea causes a man to be self-centered rather than God-centered. It gives him the idea that whatever destiny he chooses will be right. However, money gained contrary to God's principles will bring sorrow with it. (See Proverbs 10:22; Psalm 16:4.)

4. *Can you achieve whatever your mind can conceive and believe?*

No. This concept is based on the false idea that a man can achieve financial independence and true happiness apart from God. It puts confidence in human ability rather than giving proper recognition to God's enablement. God has given special power to man, but it must be used in accordance with Scriptural principles. (See Romans 8:7.)

5. *Should you make it your goal to become financially independent so that you will not have to look to other people for help?*

No. This goal encourages just the opposite of God's warning not to trust in uncertain riches. (See I Timothy 6:7, 17.) Although it is not wrong to prepare for the future, God does not want us to develop a spirit of independence from Him or from others. The very fellowship among believers involves a sharing during times of need. *". . . Now at this time your abundance may be a supply for their want, that their abundance also may be a supply for your want . . ." (II Corinthians 8:14).*

6. Do the material things that you provide for your family make up for any sacrifices that a job requires?

No. If a man's wife or children feel that his job is more important to him than they are, they will despise him and look at the things he provides as attempts to buy their affections.

The real needs of a family are not material things but spiritual leadership. No amount of money can restore time and relationships which are lost because of wrong priorities. (See Luke 12:15; Malachi 4:6.)

7. Can a person borrow his way to financial success?

No. A person may increase his assets by borrowing during a time of rising inflation. However, financial success is not measured by assets, but by freedom from greed, worry, and bondage.

Borrowing is based on the false assumption that things will be better tomorrow than they are today. This assumption disregards the warning of James 4:13–14. This concept also overlooks the fact that the borrower becomes the servant of the lender. (See Proverbs 22:7.)

8. Is being the president of your own business the ultimate financial goal?

No. This concept runs counter to the very spirit of Christ's teaching on both serving and being successful in business. The goal is not to become the "boss" but to become the servant of all. (See Matthew 23:11–12.) When the focus is on serving, it may well lead to an executive position or ownership of a company. Such leadership is then the by-product of helping others become successful. It is not a goal to be sought after.

9. Do you have the right to decide how you will spend the money that you earn?

No. This concept is totally opposite of God's teaching. The money that we have does not belong to us. We are only stewards of that which God has entrusted to us. We demonstrate our stewardship each week by tithes and offerings. (See Malachi 3:10–11.)

10. In order to be successful, must you overcome every obstacle that is between you and your financial goals?

No. God wants us to recognize that some obstacles are given by Him as reproofs. He designs these obstacles so that we will turn from our ways and follow His direction. (See Proverbs 1:23; 13:8.)

11. Can you build a successful business with a good advertising program?

No. A successful business must be built on word-of-mouth promotion by satisfied customers. The better and more vital the product, the less advertising is needed. The Scriptural counsel is that we should not praise ourselves, but that we should let others praise us instead. (See Proverbs 27:2.)

12. Can you measure your success by the amount of money that you earn?

No. This is a false picture of success and of life. It is based on the assumption that one's emotional needs, such as peace, security, happiness, acceptance, and fulfillment, will be met through money. This assumption is untrue, because these needs are only satisfied through a right relationship with God. If we expect to gain from money the things that only God can give, then we make money our god. (See I Timothy 6:10.)

13. Are those who reach the top of the "success ladder" usually self-made people?

No. This prideful idea totally overlooks the fact that it is God who "... *putteth down one, and setteth up another*" *(Psalm 75:7)*. It also discounts all the investments which parents and others have made in our lives. Those who believe that they are fully responsible for their own success will soon experience the reaction of the ones who helped them reach it.

Pride is believing that we achieved what, in reality, God and others have done for us and through us.

14. Must you be willing to compromise if you want to succeed in the business world?

No. Just the opposite is true. If we compromise basic Scriptural convictions for financial gain, our "success" will be short-lived and there will be trouble with the money we gain.

Daniel is one of God's choice examples of how to succeed in a job by not compromising, whatever the cost. Daniel's dedication to his job and to God's moral standards brought him even higher promotions and recognition, in spite of every pressure and plot to get him to compromise. *(See Daniel 1:8.)*

15. In order to be promoted in a big company, is whom you know more important than what you know?

No. The quality of your work will bring you to the attention of the right people. "*Seest thou a man diligent in his business? he shall stand before kings; he shall not stand before mean men*" *(Proverbs 22:29)*.

Trying to gain favor or influence with the rich is condemned by God. *(See Proverbs 23:1–8.)*

16. Is it true that there is no real virtue in being poor?

No. However, this answer is based on the right definition of virtue and the right understanding of poverty.

Virtue is the positive, moral influence which we have on the lives of others.

Poverty comes in at least four different forms. There is real virtue in two of these forms and there can be virtue in the other two, depending on our response to it.

TYPE OF POVERTY	CAUSE	VIRTUE
1. Chastening poverty	Violating God's principles (Samson)	Influences others to obey God
2. Testing poverty	Learning God's character (Job)	Helps others not to trust in riches
3. Redemptive poverty	Giving wealth for others (Christ)	Prompts others to praise God
4. Attitude poverty	Realizing our need for God (Moses)	Encourages others to be humble

Christ was rich, yet for our sakes He became poor that we through His poverty might be rich. (See II Corinthians 8:9.)

GOD CONTROLS WEALTH

An example of God's control of circumstances is seen in II Kings 6 and 7. Because of God's judgment on Samaria, there was a famine in the land. At the same time, the Syrians were besieging Samaria so that food supplies could not get into the city. As a result, a donkey's head had a value of eighty pieces of silver. In one day's time God delivered the people of Samaria. Food was suddenly in abundance, and a donkey's head became worthless.

WHY WE MUST TRACE WEALTH TO ITS TRUE SOURCE

- *All wealth is ultimately in God's hands, since He controls the basic factors which affect it. These factors are as follows:*

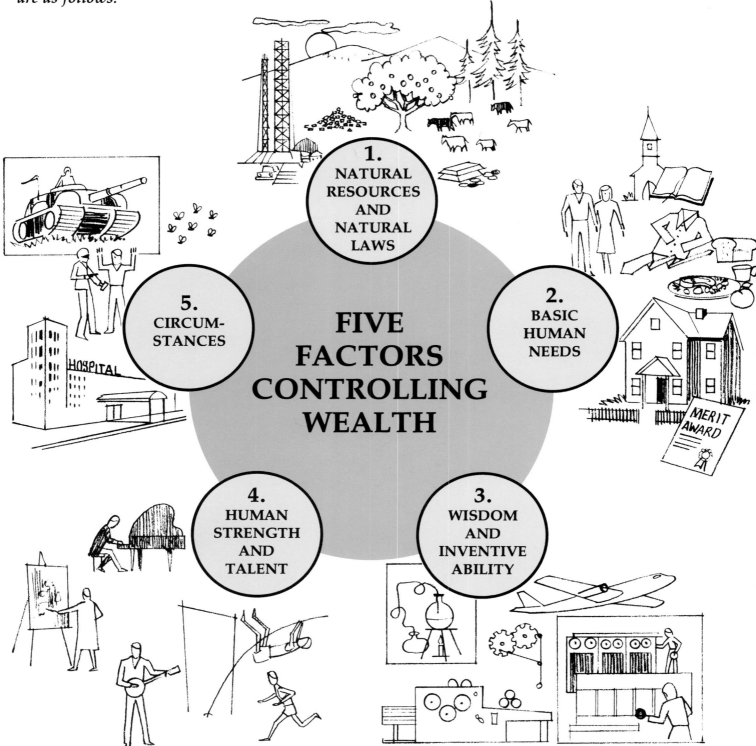

FIVE FACTORS CONTROLLING WEALTH

1. NATURAL RESOURCES AND NATURAL LAWS

2. BASIC HUMAN NEEDS

3. WISDOM AND INVENTIVE ABILITY

4. HUMAN STRENGTH AND TALENT

5. CIRCUMSTANCES

- *If a man believes that wealth comes from natural resources, human ability, or a successful company, he will attach loyalties and devotion to them rather than to God. His trust will be misplaced, and his priorities will be out of balance. In the end he will be disillusioned.*

Security : THE REWARD OF TRACING ALL WEALTH TO GOD

5.
God controls
CIRCUMSTANCES

"Ye looked for much, and, lo, it came to little; and when ye brought it home, I did blow upon it . . ."
(Haggai 1:9).

1.
God created
NATURAL RESOURCES AND NATURAL LAWS

"In the beginning God created the heaven and the earth"
(Genesis 1:1).

GOD

4.
God sustains
HUMAN STRENGTH AND TALENT

"For who maketh thee to differ from another? and what hast thou that thou didst not receive? . . ."
(I Corinthians 4:7).

2.
God designed
BASIC HUMAN NEEDS

". . . Your heavenly Father knoweth that ye have need of all these things"
(Matthew 6:32).

3.
God gives
WISDOM AND INVENTIVE ABILITY

"I wisdom dwell with prudence, and find out knowledge of witty inventions"
(Proverbs 8:12).

• *By tracing all wealth to God, we free ourselves to find true security and true riches in our relationship with Him, for He can never be destroyed or taken away.*

> "... He that is greatest among you shall be your servant. And whosoever shall exalt himself shall be abased; and he that shall humble himself shall be exalted."
>
> *Matthew 23:11–12*

REJECT FALSE CONCEPTS

God's Way to Financial Success	*Man's Way to Financial Success*
1. Focus on submission	**1.** Focus on power and position
2. Emphasis on personal responsibility	**2.** Emphasis on rights and freedom
3. Desire to meet the needs of others	**3.** Desire to gain for self
4. Concern for lasting achievement	**4.** Concern for immediate fulfillment
5. Yearning for the approval of God	**5.** Yearning for the praise of men
6. Aspiration to serve others	**6.** Aspiration to be served
7. Need for patience	**7.** Need for pushing ahead
8. Striving to follow God	**8.** Striving to lead men
9. Interest in cooperation	**9.** Interest in competition
10. Motivation for God's glory	**10.** Motivation for self-glorification

Personal Commitment to God's Financial Concepts

For me, success in finances means learning how to be successful in God's character, faith, wisdom, self-control, gentleness, and love.

I hereby acknowledge that any funds that I have or will receive are from God's hand and must be earned and managed according to the principles of His Word.

Date _____

HOW DID GOD ILLUSTRATE HIS CONTROL OVER WEALTH?

A. SOLOMON
(I Kings 3:9)

B. LOT
(Genesis 19:19)

C. JOB
(Job 1:21)

D. HEZEKIAH
(Isaiah 39:8)

Match the descriptions with the right persons.

☐ **1.** I was the wealthiest man in the country, but in a few minutes' time I became the poorest.
I said, *". . . Naked came I out of my mother's womb, and naked shall I return thither: the Lord gave, and the Lord hath taken away; blessed be the name of the Lord."* Who am I?

☐ **2.** I lost all of my wealth because I did not obey the command to avoid evil people.
I said, *". . . Thou hast magnified thy mercy, which thou hast shewed unto me in saving my life. . . ."* Who am I?

☐ **3.** I received riches because I did not ask for them.
I said, *"Give therefore thy servant an understanding heart to judge thy people, that I may discern between good and bad. . . ."* Who am I?

☐ **4.** I encouraged evil men to steal all of my wealth, because I unwisely showed it to them.
I said, *". . . Good is the word of the Lord. . . ."* Who am I?

Answers: 1.C 2.B 3.A 4.D

WHO FOLLOWED FALSE FINANCIAL CONCEPTS?

Match each description with the correct name.

☐ **1.** They founded a community based on the concept that whatever the mind can conceive it can achieve. The result was confusion. (See Genesis 11:1–9.)

☐ **2.** He tried to look and act successful by getting chariots and horses and having fifty men run ahead of him to announce his coming. His pride caused his death. (See II Samuel 15–18.)

☐ **3.** He had the philosophy that he was the master of his own destiny. He was able to convince one-third of those around him to follow his example. Both he and his followers were condemned by God. (See Isaiah 14:12–17.)

☐ **4.** He purposed to make financial independence his goal. On the day that he achieved it, God called him a fool. (See Luke 12:16–20.)

☐ **5.** This group borrowed money when financial pressures increased. They expected things to improve, but instead they got worse, causing this group great anguish. (See Nehemiah 5:1–5.)

☐ **6.** He believed that his money belonged to himself and used it as he saw fit. This included lavish living. After his death, he realized how foolish he had been. (See Luke 16:19–31.)

☐ **7.** He reached financial success only to discover that it lacked fulfillment. He became a prisoner of temporal gain and lost out on eternal rewards. (See Matthew 19:16–26.)

☐ **8.** He listened to the advice of inexperienced counselors and decided to be harsh with those who stood in the way of his success. He lost most of what he had. (See I Kings 12:1–24.)

A. The rich farmer

B. The rich young ruler

C. Wall builders

D. Absalom

E. Rehoboam

F. Builders of Babel

G. Rich man

H. Satan

The tower of Babel represents the world's system of Humanism.

Answers: 1.F 2.D 3.H 4.A 5.C 6.G 7.B 8.E

CAN YOU IDENTIFY DECEPTIVE FINANCIAL CONCEPTS IN ADVERTISING?

Match each false financial concept with the corresponding advertising slogan.

☐ **1.** If you think, act, and look successful, you will be successful.

☐ **2.** You are the master of your own destiny.

☐ **3.** Whatever your mind can conceive you can achieve.

☐ **4.** Make financial independence your goal.

☐ **5.** Bigger wages will compensate for family sacrifices.

☐ **6.** Borrow your way to success.

☐ **7.** Be your own boss.

☐ **8.** The money that you earn is yours to use as you see fit.

☐ **9.** Overcome any obstacle in the path of success.

☐ **10.** Build a successful business with good advertising.

☐ **11.** The more money that you earn, the more successful you will be.

A. We will put your product before the public.

B. Show your wife you love her—buy her a Cadillac.

C. Start saving now for your retirement.

D. You owe it to yourself to vacation in Hawaii.

E. We will teach you how to dress for success.

F. For as little as $20,000 you can start your own company.

G. Our graduates shape the future.

H. Work with other people's money.

I. Discover the hidden powers within yourself.

J. Remember that you are only in business to make money.

K. Let us solve your management and marketing problems.

ELISHA

A powerful reprover of unjust riches

GIFTS REFUSED

". . . [Naaman] said, . . . take a blessing of thy servant. But he [Elisha] said, As the Lord liveth... I will receive none . . ." (II Kings 5:15–16).

4 RECOGNIZE GOD'S REPROOFS FOR WRONG WAYS TO RICHES

"How long, ye simple ones, will ye love simplicity? and the scorners delight in their scorning, and fools hate knowledge? Turn you at my reproof . . ." (Proverbs 1:22–23).

GREED REBUKED

". . . Is it a time to receive money, and to receive garments, and oliveyards, and vineyards, and sheep, and oxen, and menservants, and maidservants? The leprosy therefore of Naaman shall cleave unto thee, and unto thy seed for ever . . ." (II Kings 5:26–27).

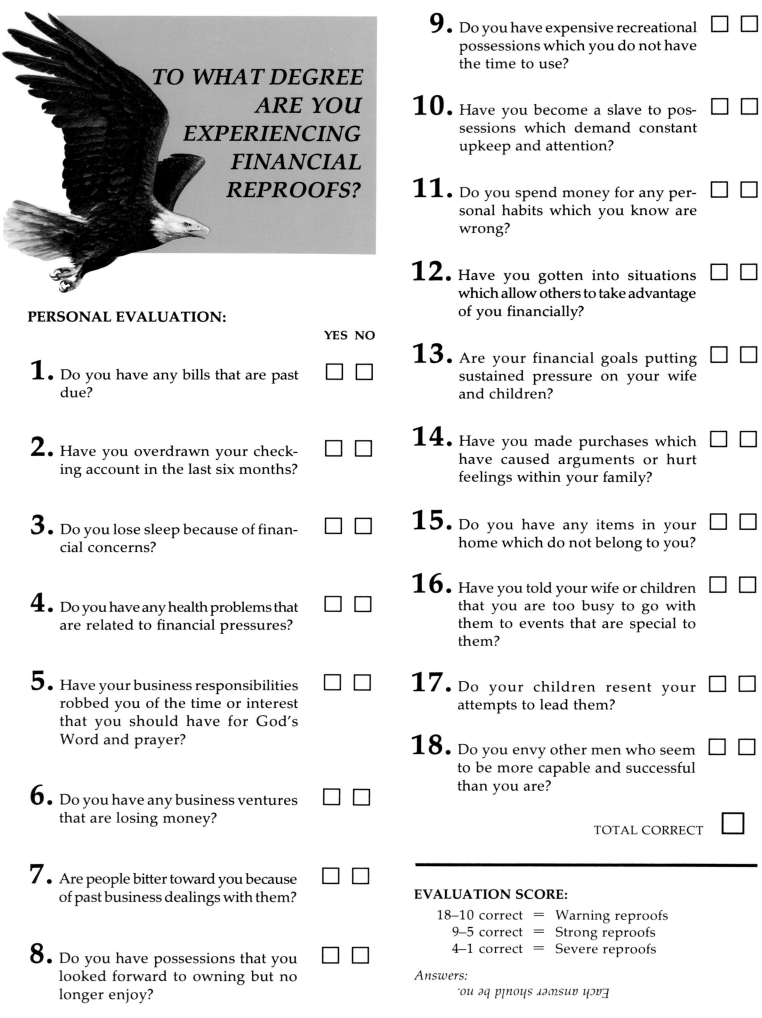

TO WHAT DEGREE ARE YOU EXPERIENCING FINANCIAL REPROOFS?

PERSONAL EVALUATION:

YES NO

1. Do you have any bills that are past due? ☐ ☐

2. Have you overdrawn your checking account in the last six months? ☐ ☐

3. Do you lose sleep because of financial concerns? ☐ ☐

4. Do you have any health problems that are related to financial pressures? ☐ ☐

5. Have your business responsibilities robbed you of the time or interest that you should have for God's Word and prayer? ☐ ☐

6. Do you have any business ventures that are losing money? ☐ ☐

7. Are people bitter toward you because of past business dealings with them? ☐ ☐

8. Do you have possessions that you looked forward to owning but no longer enjoy? ☐ ☐

9. Do you have expensive recreational possessions which you do not have the time to use? ☐ ☐

10. Have you become a slave to possessions which demand constant upkeep and attention? ☐ ☐

11. Do you spend money for any personal habits which you know are wrong? ☐ ☐

12. Have you gotten into situations which allow others to take advantage of you financially? ☐ ☐

13. Are your financial goals putting sustained pressure on your wife and children? ☐ ☐

14. Have you made purchases which have caused arguments or hurt feelings within your family? ☐ ☐

15. Do you have any items in your home which do not belong to you? ☐ ☐

16. Have you told your wife or children that you are too busy to go with them to events that are special to them? ☐ ☐

17. Do your children resent your attempts to lead them? ☐ ☐

18. Do you envy other men who seem to be more capable and successful than you are? ☐ ☐

TOTAL CORRECT ☐

EVALUATION SCORE:

18–10 correct = Warning reproofs
9–5 correct = Strong reproofs
4–1 correct = Severe reproofs

Answers:
Each answer should be no.

44

KNOW THE TWO WAYS TO GET RICHES

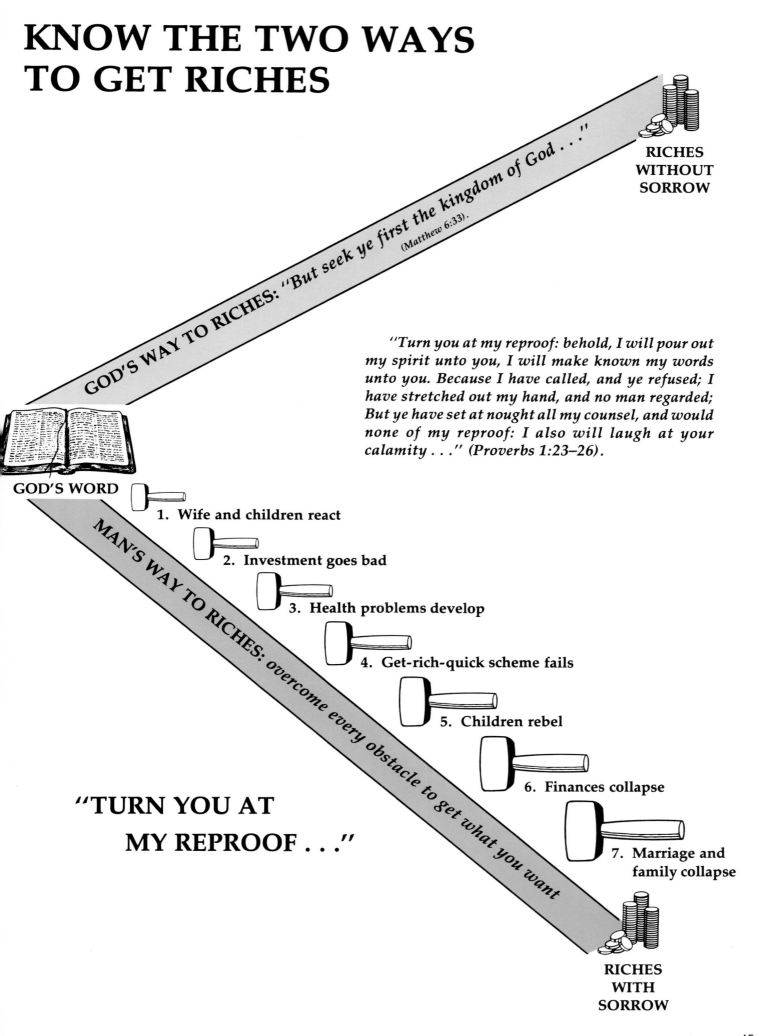

GOD'S WAY TO RICHES: "But seek ye first the kingdom of God . . ." (Matthew 6:33).

RICHES WITHOUT SORROW

"Turn you at my reproof: behold, I will pour out my spirit unto you, I will make known my words unto you. Because I have called, and ye refused; I have stretched out my hand, and no man regarded; But ye have set at nought all my counsel, and would none of my reproof: I also will laugh at your calamity . . ." (Proverbs 1:23–26).

GOD'S WORD

MAN'S WAY TO RICHES: overcome every obstacle to get what you want

1. Wife and children react
2. Investment goes bad
3. Health problems develop
4. Get-rich-quick scheme fails
5. Children rebel
6. Finances collapse
7. Marriage and family collapse

"TURN YOU AT MY REPROOF . . ."

RICHES WITH SORROW

HOW REPROOFS DEVELOP IN MARRIAGE

Financial Reproofs from Self-Rejection

Husband's Actions	Wife's Responses
1. INFERIORITY When a man fails to understand and accept unchangeable features in himself or in his family, he develops deep feelings of inferiority.	**INSECURITY** His wife needs to admire her husband and to depend upon him for wise and consistent leadership in the marriage and the family.
2. EXTRAVAGANCE A husband who does not accept himself often attempts to improve his self-image through expensive clothing, cars, furnishings, and other status symbols. In order to buy these, he may go into debt.	**FEAR** His wife does not understand his need to go into debt for these expensive items. She outwardly accepts them but inwardly develops fears and insecurity because of the debt.
3. WRONG PRIORITIES The husband commits himself to financial goals. He is motivated by the need for approval. In order to reach his goals, he encourages or allows his wife to begin working outside of the home.	**DIVIDED LOYALTY** His wife goes to work and soon finds herself in two worlds. She discovers that needs which were not met by her husband can be at least partially fulfilled through her job.
4. REJECTION The husband who expects his wife to help support the family surrenders part of his God-given responsibility as provider. This only deepens his feeling of inferiority. He then projects onto his wife and children the same attitude of rejection which he has toward himself.	**RESENTMENT** His wife reacts to his rejection. She feels a growing resentment to the tight budget that they must follow because of his financial decisions. She begins to look to other people for fellowship and encouragement.
5. REACTION The husband reacts to his wife's independent spirit. Financial pressures cause him to be quick-tempered and irritable. He expects his wife to have patience while he works through problems. However, the problems become greater.	**SEPARATION** His wife loses confidence in his leadership as she sees the pressures mounting. She tries to give him counsel, but she does not understand his motivation. Convinced that he is proud and stubborn, his wife then decides that she must look out for her own interests.

Financial Reproofs
from Moral Impurity

Husband's Actions		Wife's Responses
1. LACK OF SELF-CONTROL Before their marriage, the husband was attracted to his wife on a physical level. During their courtship he violated God's moral standards with her.		**GUILT AND DOUBT** His wife lowered her standards to accept his physical affection before marriage. This damaged her self-respect and planted destructive seeds of guilt and doubt in her.
2. SENSUAL FOCUS The husband began marriage by expecting his wife to fulfill his sexual needs. However, he was insensitive to her real needs because of his sensual expectations.		**COOLNESS** His wife's seeds of guilt and doubt began to grow. She wondered if he really loved her or if he was only using her to gratify his own desires. This fear caused her to be physically cool toward him.
3. REACTION The husband now reacts to his wife's coolness toward him. He begins to make demands that she meet his physical needs.		**COLDNESS** His wife now sees his demands and his continued insensitivity as confirmation that he does not love her. She becomes physically cold toward him.
4. ATTEMPTS TO PROVE LOVE The husband senses that his wife has been offended. However, he does not realize how deep the wounds really are. He believes that buying her some expensive gifts will solve the problem.		**EXTRAVAGANCE** His wife feels insecure and inadequate. She tries to find security in temporal things, so she accepts his gifts and buys more on her own as well. This leads to financial bondage.
5. OVEREMPHASIS ON WORK The husband realizes that his gifts did not restore his wife's broken spirit. He tightens the budget and expects her to cooperate in order to get out of debt. He spends more time at work or gets additional work. This further hinders him in meeting his wife's real needs.		**SEPARATION** His wife turns from him and concentrates on her own vocation, the children, or the fantasy world of television; or she looks for sympathy and understanding from the people with whom she works.

RECOGNIZE FINANCIAL REPROOFS

☐ **1.** **The need to borrow money**

"Only if thou carefully hearken unto the voice of the Lord thy God, to observe to do all these commandments . . . thou shalt lend unto many nations, but thou shalt not borrow . . ." (Deuteronomy 15:5–6).

☐ **2.** **Overdue bills**

"Say not unto thy neighbour, Go, and come again, and to morrow I will give; when thou hast it by thee" (Proverbs 3:28).

☐ **3.** **Speculative losses**

"He that hasteth to be rich hath an evil eye, and considereth not that poverty shall come upon him" (Proverbs 28:22).

☐ **4.** **Sleepless nights**

"The sleep of a labouring man is sweet, whether he eat little or much: but the abundance of the rich will not suffer him to sleep" (Ecclesiastes 5:12).

☐ **5.** **Unexpected losses**

"Ye looked for much, and, lo, it came to little; and when ye brought it home, I did blow upon it . . ." (Haggai 1:9).

☐ **6.** **Inability to enjoy what you have**

"There is an evil which I have seen under the sun, and it is common among men: A man to whom God hath given riches, wealth, and honour, so that he wanteth nothing for his soul of all that he desireth, yet God giveth him not power to eat thereof, but a stranger eateth it: this is vanity, and it is an evil disease" (Ecclesiastes 6:1–2).

☐ **7.** **Spiritual barrenness**

". . . The care of this world, and the deceitfulness of riches, choke the word, and he becometh unfruitful" (Matthew 13:22).

☐ **8.** **Family pressures**

"He that is greedy of gain troubleth his own house . . ." (Proverbs 15:27).

☐ **9.** **Health problems**

"There is a sore evil which I have seen under the sun, namely, riches kept for the owners thereof to their hurt" (Ecclesiastes 5:13).

☐ **10.** **Lawsuits**

"Now therefore there is utterly a fault among you, because ye go to law one with another. Why do ye not rather take wrong? why do ye not rather suffer yourselves to be defrauded" (I Corinthians 6:7).

My present reproofs are:

_____

_____

_____

_____

Personal Commitment to Turn at God's Reproofs

I do accept my financial pressures and problems as God's reproofs for violating His financial principles. I will learn the reasons for these reproofs and take the proper Scriptural steps to resolve them.

I will begin by reading the chapter of Proverbs each day that corresponds to the day of the month.

Date _____

CAN YOU RECOGNIZE GOD'S FINANCIAL REPROOFS?

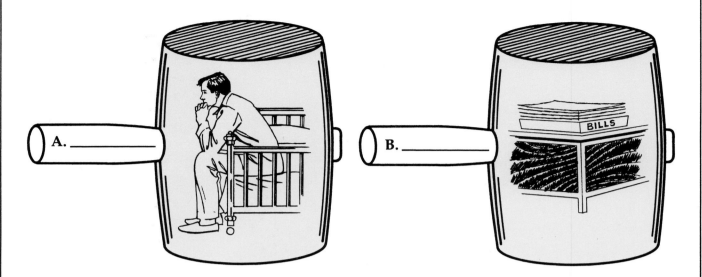

Put one Scripture reference in the handle that best illustrates the verse.

1. **Romans 13:8**

"Owe no man any thing, but to love one another. . . ."

2. **Matthew 13:22**

". . . The deceitfulness of riches, choke the word, and he becometh unfruitful."

3. **Ecclesiastes 5:12**

". . . The abundance of the rich will not suffer him to sleep."

4. **Proverbs 22:7**

". . . The borrower is servant to the lender."

5. **I Corinthians 6:7**

"Now therefore there is utterly a fault among you, because ye go to law one with another. . . ."

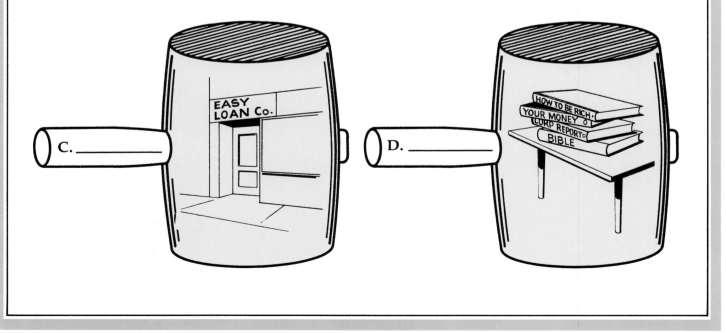

Answers: A.3 B.1 C.4 D.2

WHOM DID GOD REPROVE FOR UNSCRIPTURAL RICHES?

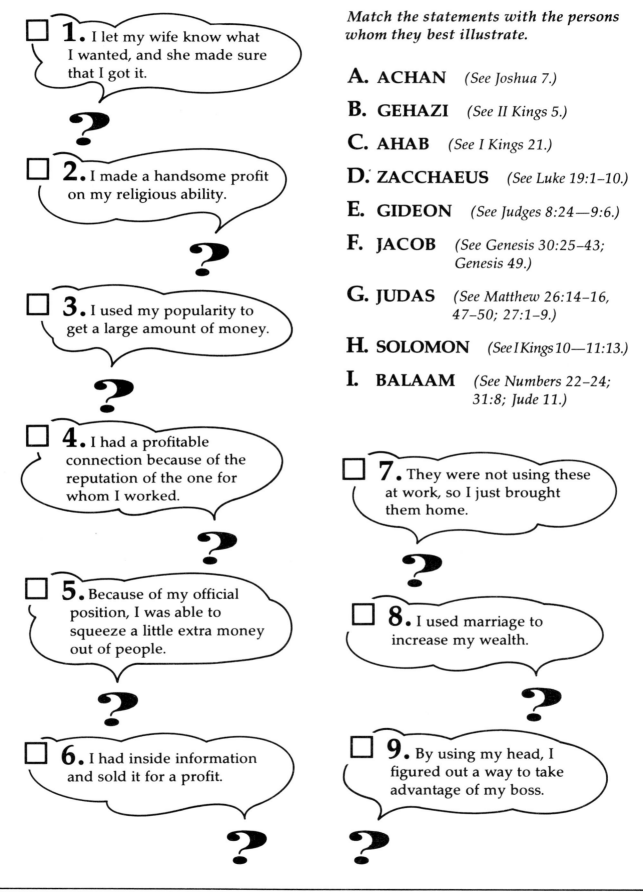

☐ **1.** I let my wife know what I wanted, and she made sure that I got it.

☐ **2.** I made a handsome profit on my religious ability.

☐ **3.** I used my popularity to get a large amount of money.

☐ **4.** I had a profitable connection because of the reputation of the one for whom I worked.

☐ **5.** Because of my official position, I was able to squeeze a little extra money out of people.

☐ **6.** I had inside information and sold it for a profit.

Match the statements with the persons whom they best illustrate.

A. ACHAN   *(See Joshua 7.)*

B. GEHAZI   *(See II Kings 5.)*

C. AHAB   *(See I Kings 21.)*

D. ZACCHAEUS   *(See Luke 19:1–10.)*

E. GIDEON   *(See Judges 8:24—9:6.)*

F. JACOB   *(See Genesis 30:25–43; Genesis 49.)*

G. JUDAS   *(See Matthew 26:14–16, 47–50; 27:1–9.)*

H. SOLOMON   *(See I Kings 10—11:13.)*

I. BALAAM   *(See Numbers 22–24; 31:8; Jude 11.)*

☐ **7.** They were not using these at work, so I just brought them home.

☐ **8.** I used marriage to increase my wealth.

☐ **9.** By using my head, I figured out a way to take advantage of my boss.

Answers: 1.C 2.I 3.D 4.B 5.D 6.G 7.A 8.H 9.F

WHAT WERE GOD'S REPROOFS FOR WRONGFUL GAIN?

Match the men in column one with the way in which they wronged others (column two) and then with the consequences they received (column three).

MEN WHO GAINED WRONGFULLY	HOW THEY WRONGED OTHERS	CONSEQUENCES THEY RECEIVED
1. ACHAN *See Joshua 6–7.*	☐ **A.** He cheated citizens out of their money by false accusations.	☐ **J.** He lived in sorrow because his family followed his example.
2. GEHAZI *See II Kings 5.*	☐ **B.** He wronged the nation and his family by establishing ungodly alliances.	☐ **K.** He and his entire family were stoned to death.
3. AHAB *See I Kings 21.*	☐ **C.** He caused a nation to lust after a material possession.	☐ **L.** He was killed along with the enemy of Israel with whom he had chosen to live.
4. ZACCHAEUS *See Luke 19:1–10.*	☐ **D.** He shamed an entire nation and caused thirty-six deaths.	☐ **M.** His family was persecuted, and all but one of his sons were killed by an illegitimate brother.
5. GIDEON *See Judges 8.*	☐ **E.** He wronged his family by his crafty example.	☐ **N.** He and his entire family were destroyed by violent deaths.
6. JACOB *See Genesis 27–34.*	☐ **F.** He caused a nation to be defeated by planting seeds of immorality.	☐ **O.** He committed suicide.
7. JUDAS *See Matthew 26–27.*	☐ **G.** He lied to the one whom he served and damaged the message that he was trying to give.	☐ **P.** He returned four times the amount that he had wrongfully gained, and he gave half of all that he had to the poor.
8. SOLOMON *See I Kings 10–11.*	☐ **H.** He violated the trust of those who elected him to office.	☐ **Q.** His heart was turned from the Lord, and his descendants lost the wealth which he had gained.
9. BALAAM *See Numbers 22–24.*	☐ **I.** He killed a Godly man and his innocent family.	☐ **R.** He became diseased with leprosy.

Answers: A4 B8 C5 D1 E6 F9 G2 H7 I3 J6 K1 L9 M5 N3 O7 P4 Q8 R2

51

JOSHUA

A great conqueror with singleness of heart

DECISION REQUIRED

"... Choose you this day whom ye will serve ...
but as for me and my house, we will serve the Lord"
(Joshua 24:15).

5 CHOOSE TO SERVE GOD RATHER THAN MONEY

"No man can serve two masters: for either he will hate the one, and love the other; or else he will hold to the one, and despise the other. Ye cannot serve God and mammon [money]" (Matthew 6:24).

PROTECTION SECURED

"And ye have seen all that the Lord your God hath done unto all these nations because of you; for the Lord your God is he that hath fought for you" (Joshua 23:3).

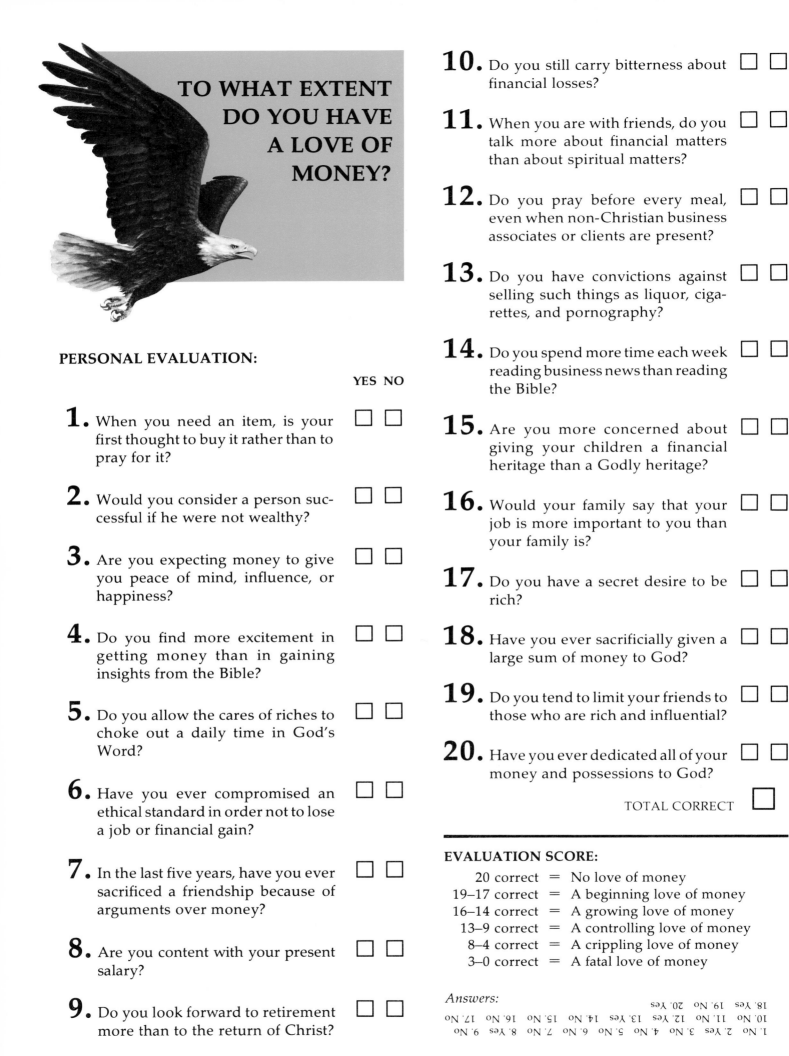

TO WHAT EXTENT DO YOU HAVE A LOVE OF MONEY?

PERSONAL EVALUATION:

YES NO

1. When you need an item, is your first thought to buy it rather than to pray for it? ☐ ☐

2. Would you consider a person successful if he were not wealthy? ☐ ☐

3. Are you expecting money to give you peace of mind, influence, or happiness? ☐ ☐

4. Do you find more excitement in getting money than in gaining insights from the Bible? ☐ ☐

5. Do you allow the cares of riches to choke out a daily time in God's Word? ☐ ☐

6. Have you ever compromised an ethical standard in order not to lose a job or financial gain? ☐ ☐

7. In the last five years, have you ever sacrificed a friendship because of arguments over money? ☐ ☐

8. Are you content with your present salary? ☐ ☐

9. Do you look forward to retirement more than to the return of Christ? ☐ ☐

10. Do you still carry bitterness about financial losses? ☐ ☐

11. When you are with friends, do you talk more about financial matters than about spiritual matters? ☐ ☐

12. Do you pray before every meal, even when non-Christian business associates or clients are present? ☐ ☐

13. Do you have convictions against selling such things as liquor, cigarettes, and pornography? ☐ ☐

14. Do you spend more time each week reading business news than reading the Bible? ☐ ☐

15. Are you more concerned about giving your children a financial heritage than a Godly heritage? ☐ ☐

16. Would your family say that your job is more important to you than your family is? ☐ ☐

17. Do you have a secret desire to be rich? ☐ ☐

18. Have you ever sacrificially given a large sum of money to God? ☐ ☐

19. Do you tend to limit your friends to those who are rich and influential? ☐ ☐

20. Have you ever dedicated all of your money and possessions to God? ☐ ☐

TOTAL CORRECT ☐

EVALUATION SCORE:

20 correct	= No love of money
19–17 correct	= A beginning love of money
16–14 correct	= A growing love of money
13–9 correct	= A controlling love of money
8–4 correct	= A crippling love of money
3–0 correct	= A fatal love of money

Answers:
1. No 2. Yes 3. No 4. No 5. No 6. No 7. No 8. Yes 9. No
10. No 11. No 12. Yes 13. Yes 14. No 15. No 16. No 17. No
18. Yes 19. No 20. Yes

THE WITNESS OF GOD AGAINST THOSE WHO TRIED TO SERVE GOD AND MONEY

NO MAN CAN SERVE TWO MASTERS

1. Using religion for gain

Balaam was a prophet during the early days of the nation of Israel. He had a special power. Those whom he cursed were cursed, and those whom he blessed were blessed. The king of Moab hired Balaam to curse Israel; but God warned Balaam not to curse His people, so he blessed them instead. This angered the king of Moab. Balaam appeased the king and collected his money by teaching the king how to morally corrupt the people whom he could not curse. Later, Balaam lost his money and his life when Israel conquered Moab. (See Numbers 22–24; Jude 11; Revelation 2:14.)

BALAAM

LOT

JACOB

2. Compromising with evil

Lot was the nephew of Abraham. He went with Abraham to the land of Canaan, where his flocks and herds increased so much that there was not enough land for his flocks and Abraham's flocks together. Lot separated from Abraham and chose to live near Sodom, an area that was very fertile. Lot's business dealings caused him to compromise in his choice of associates. He tried to be an example to them, but ultimately he lost all of his possessions and most of his family. (See Genesis 12–14, 19.)

3. Mixing faith and self-effort

Jacob was assured by God that he would be blessed, but he felt that he had to help God work out the blessing. He talked his brother out of the birthright, stole his brother's blessing, and cleverly worked to get his father-in-law's flocks. God brought Jacob to a crisis when his brother Esau came with four hundred men to get revenge for being cheated. Jacob first made restitution and then spent a night wrestling with God. Through that experience he demonstrated a new trust in God, but the seeds of destruction took a heavy toll with his wife and children. (See Genesis 27–34.)

ACHAN

4. Yielding to covetousness

Achan had fought in Joshua's army and had helped to conquer Jericho. He knew of God's promise to give victory and certain spoils of the land to Joshua and his army. In his service for God, however, Achan was exposed to the corrupt things of the enemy. Rather than treating them with Godly contempt, he determined how they would benefit his life; and then he took the forbidden treasures in violation of God's clear command, "... *Keep yourselves from the accursed thing, lest ye make yourselves accursed...*" *(Joshua 6:18)*. God judged Achan by having him and his entire family stoned to death. (See Joshua 7.)

GIDEON

5. Commercializing religion

Gideon was used of God to conquer the Midianites and to free Israel from their oppression. The men of Israel asked Gideon to be their king. He refused this honor but requested instead that he be given all of the golden earrings of the enemy. From these earrings he made a golden ephod, a richly-embroidered outer vestment worn by Jewish priests. This ephod became a national tourist attraction; and although it was used for religious worship, it caused "... *all Israel [to go] ... a whoring after it ...*" *(Judges 8:27)*. Gideon had many wives and seventy sons. After he died, God judged his family through the son of a concubine. This son killed sixty-nine of his half-brothers and seized the kingship which his father had refused. (See Judges 8:24—9:6.)

GEHAZI

6. Cashing in on another's ministry

Gehazi was the servant of the prophet Elisha. When Naaman, the captain of the Syrian army, came to Elisha to be cured of leprosy, Elisha instructed Naaman through Gehazi. Naaman was miraculously healed of his leprosy, and he wanted to give Elisha a valuable reward. Gehazi listened as Elisha clearly refused it. After Naaman left, Gehazi ran after him and, through deception, got some of the reward for himself. He was sharply rebuked by Elisha, and the leprosy of Naaman came upon Gehazi. (See II Kings 5.)

THE RICH YOUNG RULER

7. Trying to worship Christ and money

The rich young ruler possessed more than riches. He had character qualities that were outstanding. He showed diligence in coming to Jesus, he demonstrated honor to Jesus, he had a teachable spirit, and he was morally upright from his youth. Jesus detected only one major flaw in this young man—he loved money. Jesus instructed him to sell all that he had, give it to the poor, and then follow Him. Upon hearing this, the rich young ruler walked away sorrowfully, for he had great riches. Jesus used this incident to explain how difficult it is for a rich man to enter into the kingdom of heaven. (See Luke 18:18–30.)

8. Selling inside information

Judas was the most trusted of the disciples. He was the only one among the disciples to hold an office. Perhaps he was appointed treasurer because his interest in money was obvious. He evaluated events on the basis of monetary gain for the treasury and for himself. Consequently, he totally missed the message and significance of Mary's anointing of Jesus' feet. He determined that the ointment which she used could have been sold for 300 pence and given to the poor. It is possible that the information he sold to the religious leaders was designed to enrich his pockets while giving Christ another opportunity to escape death. When he saw that he had betrayed innocent blood, Judas returned the money and hanged himself. (See Matthew 26–27.)

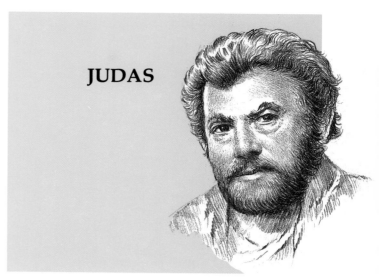

JUDAS

9. Purchasing public praise

Ananias and Sapphira were involved in the social concerns of the early Church. When Barnabas sold his property and gave the money to the Church leaders, Ananias and Sapphira saw the admiration and encouragement that he received. They decided to follow Barnabas' example, but they secretly agreed between themselves to keep back part of the money. In this way they planned on getting public recognition while still maintaining private resources. However, their deception failed to elude the spiritual alertness of Peter. When they lied about the amount of the sale, Peter rebuked them. Immediately after being rebuked by Peter, both Ananias and Sapphira fell dead at his feet. (See Acts 5.)

ANANIAS
AND
SAPPHIRA

10. Trying to buy spirituality

Simon was a converted sorcerer. Before his salvation he had been a very powerful person. He had kept the people spellbound with his magic and experienced their continual admiration. When Simon saw Peter transmitting the power of the Holy Spirit by the laying on of hands, he immediately recognized this as being more effective than any of his magic. He visualized the personal gain and admiration which he could have with this power, so he offered Peter money to buy it. Peter sharply rebuked Simon for his carnal approach to spiritual ministry. In his rebuke, Peter exposed Simon's root problems, saying that Simon was in the gall of bitterness and bound with his own iniquity. (See Acts 8:9–24.)

SIMON

CHOOSE YOU THIS DAY
WHOM YOU WILL SERVE

HOW TO SERVE GOD RATHER THAN MONEY

Genesis 22

Most Christians, if asked, would claim that they are serving God. They would deny that they have a greater love of money than of God. However, God knows our hearts. He searches out our motives. He is aware of how many of the following steps we have actually taken.

1 NAME THE THINGS THAT YOU LOVE THE MOST

". . . Take now thy son, thine only son Isaac, whom thou lovest . . ." (Genesis 22:2).

God will always start with the things that we love the most. He will direct us to name the people or possessions which have captured our affections.

Unless the objects of our strongest love are dedicated to Him, they will become objects of our worship and sources of future sorrow. In the end, we will lose the very things that we refused to give to God.

Who or what, if taken from you, would give you the greatest inward pain:

☐ Your Wife   ☐ Your Parents
☐ Your Son   ☐ Your Reputation
☐ Your Daughter   ☐ Your Money
☐ Your Home   ☐ Your Friends
☐ Your Job   ☐ Your Possessions
☐ Your Health   ☐ Your Skills
☐ Your Sisters or Brothers
☐ Your Freedom

• Present them completely to the Lord

". . . Offer him there for a burnt-offering upon one of the mountains which I will tell thee of" (Genesis 22:2).

God's way of doing business involves a specific time and place. He wants us to make definite decisions that we will remember.

Just as Abraham built his altar, we can also get alone with the Lord and "build our altar."

Abraham was confident that the God who told him to offer his only son was also able to raise him up again. We can be sure that whatever we give to God He can protect and bless and restore. *". . . I know whom I have believed, and am persuaded that he is able to keep that which I have committed unto him against that day" (II Timothy 1:12).*

By giving our most cherished objects of affection to the Lord, we are saying: "From this moment on these things belong to You. I give them to You. I have no more rights to them or claim on them."

• Die to them in your human emotions

"And Abraham stretched forth his hand, and took the knife to slay his son" (Genesis 22:10).

The action of dedicating our most cherished possessions to the Lord is not complete until we die to them in our human emotions.

This means that we *thank God ahead of time* for whatever He allows to happen to the things that we gave to Him.

Be prepared to thank God if He allows the things that you gave to Him to be taken from you; and be prepared to thank God if they are entrusted back to your care.

Abraham never could have lifted the knife over his son if he had not first "died to him" in his human emotions. Without this emotional break, the offering is only a meaningless ritual.

Realize that God will test your sincerity with whatever you give to Him.

2 EXPECT GOD TO SHOW HIS SUPERNATURAL POWER THROUGH THAT WHICH YOU GIVE TO HIM

"... Lay not thine hand upon the lad.... Because thou ... hast not withheld thy son ... I will bless thee ..." (Genesis 22: 12, 16–17).

Abraham learned that the real sacrifice takes place in the heart, not in the act of sacrifice itself.

Abraham also illustrates that once we emotionally let go of our most treasured possessions, God will be able to show His miraculous power through them. They will become the basis of our service to God and the means through which He works.

Abraham gave his son to God, and God made of him a great nation. Moses gave his rod to God, and God worked through it to lead the nation of Israel out of bondage.

☐ Give your marriage to God, and He will give you love that surpasses human understanding. (See Ephesians 3:19.)

☐ Give your family to God, and He will raise up the foundations of many Godly generations. (See Isaiah 61:4.)

☐ Give your home and possessions to God, and you "... *shall receive an hundredfold now in this time ... and in the world to come eternal life*" (Mark 10:30).

☐ Give your friendships to God, and He will allow you to experience true fellowship. (See I John 1:7.)

☐ Give your reputation to God, and He will lead you to make right decisions in order to protect His reputation. (See Psalm 23:3.)

THE PRECISE STEPS WHICH A FATHER TOOK IN TRANSFERRING OWNERSHIP TO GOD

I PICTURED MYSELF KNEELING BEFORE GOD'S ALTAR

"I knew that I had failed in managing the money that God had entrusted to me. My deep indebtedness was daily evidence of that fact. After hearing about dedicating everything I had to God, I went into my bedroom and got down on my knees.

"I pictured everything that I loved and owned behind me—my wife, children, home, car, job, and every other item that I could think of. One by one I pictured myself taking each item from behind me and placing it on God's altar.

"I prayed, 'God, I give You my wife, whom I love. From now on, she belongs to You. If You allow something to happen beyond my control, I will thank You for it. And if You allow me to continue to enjoy her love and fellowship, I will thank You for that. Lord, here is my job. I give You the rights to it. If You continue to allow me to have the job, I will accept the responsibility of working as unto You.'

"I continued praying in this manner until every single item was taken from behind me and placed on the altar. When I finished, I felt an inner freedom that I had never experienced before. That dedication became the turning point in my finances. It released me from the pressure of doing things my way and freed me to learn how to do things God's way.

I WAS ABLE TO TEACH MY CHILDREN TRUTHS THAT HAD BECOME REAL TO ME

"Once I experienced the freedom and blessing of dedicating everything I had to God, I was able to include the family in any new dedication of a possession. One day we bought a camper. I said to my wife and children, 'Let's go out in the camper and dedicate it to God.' We prayed, 'Lord, You gave us the funds for this camper and the direction to buy it. We now give it back to You. You are free to do with it whatever You want. If You allow us to use it, we purpose to use it to bring glory to You.' This time of prayer was especially significant to my young son, and the camper became a means for God to teach valuable lessons to our family."

NOTE: Several of the personal illustrations in this volume are from the growing "life message" of this father.

CHOOSE TO SERVE GOD

THE FIRST STEP IS TO RECEIVE JESUS CHRIST AS SAVIOR

1. *"As it is written, There is none righteous, no, not one. . . . For all have sinned, and come short of the glory of God" (Romans 3:10, 23).*

2. *"For the wages of sin is death; but the gift of God is eternal life through Jesus Christ our Lord" (Romans 6:23).*

3. *"For God so loved the world, that he gave his only begotten Son, that whosoever believeth in him should not perish, but have everlasting life" (John 3:16).*

4. *"For by grace are ye saved through faith; and that not of yourselves: it is the gift of God: Not of works, lest any man should boast" (Ephesians 2:8–9).*

5. *"That if thou shalt confess with thy mouth the Lord Jesus, and shalt believe in thine heart that God hath raised him from the dead, thou shalt be saved. For with the heart man believeth unto righteousness; and with the mouth confession is made unto salvation" (Romans 10:9–10).*

6. *"He that believeth on the Son hath everlasting life: and he that believeth not the Son shall not see life; but the wrath of God abideth on him" (John 3:36).*

7. *"The Spirit itself beareth witness with our spirit, that we are the children of God" (Romans 8:16).*

8. *"These things have I written unto you that believe on the name of the Son of God; that ye may know that ye have eternal life, and that ye may believe on the name of the Son of God" (I John 5:13).*

NICODEMUS

"YE MUST BE BORN AGAIN"

Nicodemus was a religious ruler. He came to Jesus one night and listened as Jesus said to him, *". . . Verily, verily, I say unto thee, Except a man be born again, he cannot see the kingdom of God" (John 3:3).*

Personal Commitment to the Lord Jesus Christ

"Thank You, God, for loving me, a sinner, and for sending Your Son to pay the penalty of my sin. Right now I put my trust in His death and resurrection for my salvation, and I receive the eternal life that You offer me through Him. Thank You for hearing this prayer, cleansing all my sin through Christ's blood, and accepting me now as Your child. Teach me and direct me through Your Word and Your Spirit to discover Your purpose and will for my life. Amen."

Date _____

Personal Commitment to Serve God Rather Than Money

As a Christian, I now give the ownership and rights to all of my money, possessions, and time to God. I purpose that the principles of His Word will now be my final authority for earning and managing whatever God entrusts to me.

Date _____

WHAT DOES IT MEAN TO TRANSFER OWNERSHIP TO GOD?

Use the words at the right to complete each statement.

1. Transferring ownership to God means that every decision as to how my money will be earned or used will be based on _____.

2. After I dedicate my money to God, I must view myself as a _____ rather than an owner.

3. Once I transfer ownership to God, He has the right to _____ those funds as He sees fit.

4. By giving God the ownership of my money, I allow Him to work _____ through it.

5. God will require me to follow His _____ once I transfer ownership of my money to Him.

6. One day I must give _____ as to how I managed all the funds that God entrusted to me.

7. God usually asks for the object of my most cherished affection _____.

8. Giving God the rightful ownership of my possessions means that I _____ to them.

9. The actions of _____ in Scripture provide an excellent example to me of how to transfer ownership of my possessions to God.

10. I have purposed this date to serve _____ rather than money.

A. Commands

B. Supernaturally

C. The Lord

D. First

E. Scriptural principles

F. Abraham

G. Steward

H. An account

I. Take or leave

J. Die emotionally

WHOSE CHOICES FREED GOD TO WORK SUPERNATURALLY?

Match each statement with the best answer.

☐ **1.** God asked me to take what was in my hand and give it to Him. He then gave it back to me and worked through it to show His supernatural power. Who am I?

☐ **2.** I willingly offered what was in my hand to the Lord. He took it, broke it, blessed it, and performed a great miracle through it. Who am I?

☐ **3.** My son and I were one meal away from starvation, and God's servant asked me for that meal. I gave it to him, and God fed us for three years. Who am I?

☐ **4.** I gave a thousand offerings but could not outgive God. He had me name my greatest wish, and He miraculously fulfilled it. Who am I?

☐ **5.** I gave my rights and expectations of marriage and children to God. He marvelously provided a husband and descendants who became world famous. Who am I?

☐ **6.** I surrendered to God what I longed for the most. He took what I gave Him, but He gave me fivefold in its place. Who am I?

☐ **7.** I sold what I had and gave all the money to the Lord. He used it to encourage the entire Church, and He gave me a special ministry. Who am I?

☐ **8.** I gave the little I had to the Lord, but He saw the motive of my heart and used my gift to teach an important truth about sacrificial giving. Who am I?

A. The widow of Zarephath
(See I Kings 17:8–16.)

B. The widow at the treasury
(See Mark 12:41–44.)

C. Ruth
(See Ruth.)

D. The lad with the loaves and fishes
(See John 6:1–14.)

E. Barnabas
(See Acts 4:32–37.)

F. Solomon
(See I Kings 3:4–15.)

G. Moses
(See Exodus 4:2–5.)

H. Hannah
(See I Samuel 1:10—2:21.)

Answers: 1.G 2.D 3.A 4.F 5.C 6.H 7.E 8.B

WHOSE LIFE GOALS WERE GREATER THAN MONEY?

Match each statement with the best answer.

☐ **1.** He learned that God's people were in great distress, because their enemies could easily torment and afflict them. His goal was to build a protective wall around them.

☐ **2.** He wanted to encourage worship and praise to the God of heaven and earth. He dedicated the rest of his life to making preparations to build a house of praise and prayer.

☐ **3.** He saw his people suffer under the cruel treatment of the heathen rulers. He purposed to make whatever sacrifices that were necessary to lead them out of bondage.

☐ **4.** He realized that God's judgment would soon overwhelm the wicked people of his day. He invested everything that he had into what became both a warning to his generation and an escape for him and his family.

☐ **5.** He lived among a nation that refused to obey God's Word. He saw the inevitable consequences and committed his life to giving persistent warnings of coming judgment.

☐ **6.** He had an outstanding education, practical skills, and influential friends. He turned his back on them all in order to proclaim the Gospel to those who had never heard it.

☐ **7.** He had specialized training and could have made a comfortable living. Instead, he used his life and skills to serve one of God's greatest leaders.

☐ **8.** He followed the goals which his parents gave him for serving God. This involved rejecting evil companions and wrongful gain. He provided wise leadership during a time when this was lacking among God's people.

A. Luke
(See Colossians 4:14.)

B. Noah
(See Hebrews 11:7.)

C. Nehemiah
(See Nehemiah 1.)

D. Samuel
(See I Samuel 1–3.)

E. Moses
(See Hebrews 11:24–29.)

F. Paul
(See Philippians 3:4–8.)

G. David
(See II Samuel 7:4–11.)

H. Jeremiah
(See Jeremiah 1.)

Answers: 1.C 2.G 3.E 4.B 5.H 6.F 7.A 8.D

CORNELIUS
A man whose generosity was greatly rewarded by God

CORNELIUS GAVE TO GOD

"There was a certain man in Caesarea . . . which gave much alms to the people, and prayed to God alway" (Acts 10:1–2).

6 ESTABLISH THE TITHE AS A WEEKLY REMINDER

"Will a man rob God? Yet ye have robbed me. But ye say, Wherein have we robbed thee? In tithes and offerings. Ye are cursed with a curse. . . . Bring ye all the tithes into the storehouse, that there may be meat in mine house, and prove me now herewith, saith the Lord of hosts, if I will not open you the windows of heaven . . ." (Malachi 3:8–10).

GOD GAVE TO CORNELIUS

". . . Thy prayers and thine alms are come up for a memorial before God. And now send men to Joppa, and call for one Simon, whose surname is Peter . . . he shall tell thee what thou oughtest to do [to receive salvation]" (Acts 10:4–6).

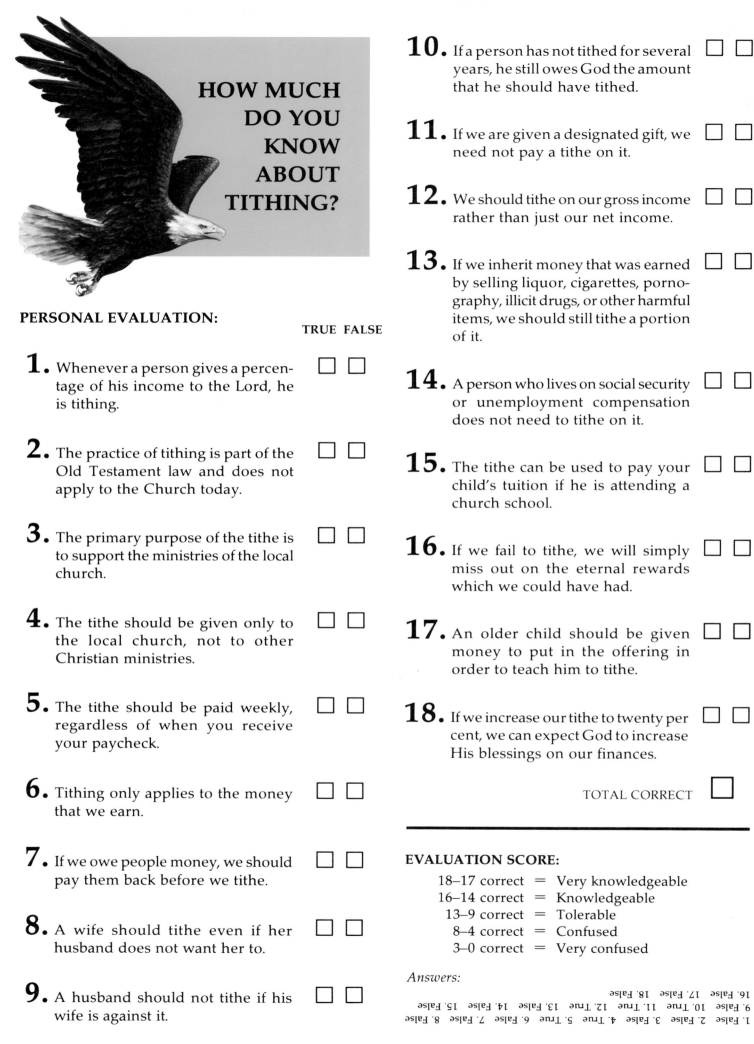

HOW MUCH DO YOU KNOW ABOUT TITHING?

PERSONAL EVALUATION:

TRUE FALSE

1. Whenever a person gives a percentage of his income to the Lord, he is tithing. ☐ ☐

2. The practice of tithing is part of the Old Testament law and does not apply to the Church today. ☐ ☐

3. The primary purpose of the tithe is to support the ministries of the local church. ☐ ☐

4. The tithe should be given only to the local church, not to other Christian ministries. ☐ ☐

5. The tithe should be paid weekly, regardless of when you receive your paycheck. ☐ ☐

6. Tithing only applies to the money that we earn. ☐ ☐

7. If we owe people money, we should pay them back before we tithe. ☐ ☐

8. A wife should tithe even if her husband does not want her to. ☐ ☐

9. A husband should not tithe if his wife is against it. ☐ ☐

10. If a person has not tithed for several years, he still owes God the amount that he should have tithed. ☐ ☐

11. If we are given a designated gift, we need not pay a tithe on it. ☐ ☐

12. We should tithe on our gross income rather than just our net income. ☐ ☐

13. If we inherit money that was earned by selling liquor, cigarettes, pornography, illicit drugs, or other harmful items, we should still tithe a portion of it. ☐ ☐

14. A person who lives on social security or unemployment compensation does not need to tithe on it. ☐ ☐

15. The tithe can be used to pay your child's tuition if he is attending a church school. ☐ ☐

16. If we fail to tithe, we will simply miss out on the eternal rewards which we could have had. ☐ ☐

17. An older child should be given money to put in the offering in order to teach him to tithe. ☐ ☐

18. If we increase our tithe to twenty per cent, we can expect God to increase His blessings on our finances. ☐ ☐

TOTAL CORRECT ☐

EVALUATION SCORE:

18–17 correct = Very knowledgeable
16–14 correct = Knowledgeable
13–9 correct = Tolerable
8–4 correct = Confused
3–0 correct = Very confused

Answers:

1. False 2. False 3. False 4. True 5. False 6. False 7. False 8. False 9. False 10. True 11. True 12. True 13. False 14. False 15. False 16. False 17. False 18. False

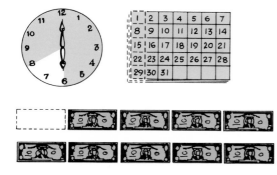

KNOW WHAT GOD SAYS ABOUT TITHING

1. *What is the tithe?*

The tithe is the first ten per cent of our income. This belongs to the Lord. There is also encouragement to give offerings to special needs, but offerings are above and beyond the tithe. In the New Testament, tithes and offerings are combined in the instruction to give as the Lord has prospered. (See II Corinthians 9:6–8.)

2. *Is tithing a part of the law that does not apply to us today?*

No. Tithing was established before the law was given by Moses. (See Genesis 14:20.) It was reaffirmed by Christ in the New Testament. (See Matthew 23:23.)

3. *What is the real purpose of the tithe?*

The tithe serves the practical functions of supporting vital church ministries. However, the underlying purpose of the tithe is to learn to fear the Lord. God has promised to give wisdom and blessing to those who fear Him. *"Thou shalt truly tithe all the increase of thy seed . . . of thy corn, of thy wine, and of thine oil, and the firstlings of thy herds and of thy flocks; that thou mayest learn to fear the Lord thy God always"* (Deuteronomy 14:22–23).

4. *Where is the tithe to be given?*

The tithe of money is to be given to support the local church. God has designed the Church to carry out vital social functions among Christians, as well as getting out the Gospel to non-Christians. These functions include caring for the widows, distributing to the necessity of the saints, ministering to the sick, giving to the poor, and teaching families to care for themselves. If the Church fails to carry out these functions and they are taken over by others, the Church will lose its effectiveness and become despised by the world. (See Matthew 5:13–16.)

5. *When should we pay the tithe?*

The tithe is to be paid on the first day of each week. *"Upon the first day of the week let every one of you lay by him in store, as God hath prospered him, that there be no gatherings when I come"* (I Corinthians 16:2).

6. *Does the tithe include more than money?*

Yes. We are to give God the firstfruits of all that He gives to us. Christ commended those who tithed each part of their harvest. At the same time, He warned them not to neglect such important items as justice and the love of God. (See Luke 11:42.) This means that we should give God the firstfruits of our time: the first day of each week, and the first part of each day. *"Honour the Lord with thy substance, and with the firstfruits of all thine increase: So shall thy barns be filled with plenty, and thy presses shall burst out with new wine"* (Proverbs 3:9–10).

7. *Should a man tithe if he is in debt?*

Yes. The debt itself is often a witness that tithing is not taking place. It should, therefore, be a motivation to begin tithing in order to allow God to show His power in gaining financial freedom. As a practical matter, special arrangements should be made with all creditors so that they continue to receive some payment and the promise of more as funds increase. (See Matthew 6:33.)

8. Should a wife tithe if her husband does not want her to?

No. A wife's spiritual decisions, other than salvation, are under the protection of her husband. *"But if her husband disallowed her on the day that he heard it [her vow]; then he shall make her vow which she vowed, and that which she uttered with her lips, wherewith she bound her soul, of none effect: and the Lord shall forgive her"* (Numbers 30:8). However, this does not mean that a wife cannot give the equivalent of a tithe in other ways, with her husband's permission.

One wife, whose husband did not want her to give money, asked if she could give items that they were no longer using. He agreed to this. She then organized a garage sale with some other women, and she raised $1000 for the Lord's work. This was more money than they would have tithed, and the husband was proud of his wife and pleased with the outcome.

Other wives have received permission to make items to sell, or they have prepared food to give to those in need. God gives an example of this through the ministry of Dorcas. (See Acts 9:36–43.)

9. Should a husband tithe if his wife does not want him to?

Yes. However, her objections to tithing should be a signal to him that he may not be meeting her needs, either materially or spiritually. It would be important for this husband to find out the real reasons why his wife does not want him to tithe. If any material needs have been neglected, the husband should fulfill them; and then he should discuss with his wife God's Scriptural admonition on tithing. God holds a man responsible for teaching his wife the Word. (See Ephesians 5:26.)

10. What if I have not tithed for several years?

Each Christian must come to his own decision as to how far back he should go in paying tithes.

Catching up on past tithes will give us a clear conscience toward God, a conscience that is free of any guilt of robbing Him. (See Malachi 3:8.)

God wants us to be cheerful givers, and He promises that the more we give to Him the more He will give to us. *"... He which soweth bountifully shall reap also bountifully"* (II Corinthians 9:6).

11. Should a person tithe on a designated gift?

No. The person who receives a designated gift accepts an implied trust to use it for the purpose for which it is intended. The receiver should report back to the giver that the gift was properly used. However, this does not mean that the receiver cannot use other moneys to express his gratefulness to the Lord for unexpected provision.

12. Should we tithe on our gross income or our net income?

Whether we have simple or complicated earnings, we should always tithe on our gross income. If a builder spends $100,000 to construct an office complex and sells it for $120,000, the $20,000 difference is his actual income from which he would figure his tithe. This is consistent with the command to *"honour the Lord ... with the firstfruits of all thine increase"* (Proverbs 3:9). Gross income is determined before taxes, social security, and other deductions, since we are to give Him the "firstfruits" of all our increase.

13. Should we tithe on an inheritance that was gained by selling harmful items?

No. These harmful items would include such things as liquor, cigarettes, and pornography. God does not want ill-gotten gain brought into His house, and it would be wise for us to also refuse it for our own personal use. *"Thou shalt not bring the hire of a whore ... into the house of the Lord thy God ..."* (Deuteronomy 23:18). Pornography is wholesale prostitution. It is an abomination to the Lord. As such it carries a curse to those who engage in it or profit from it. The same would be true for money gained from liquor, illicit drugs, or any other means which damage the lives of others. (See Habakkuk 2:15.) The wisest use of such an inheritance would be to establish a fund to bring restitution and spiritual benefit to the groups of people whose lives were damaged. *"He that by ... unjust gain increaseth his substance, he shall gather it for him that will pity the poor"* (Proverbs 28:8).

14. Should a person tithe from his social security check?

Yes. Jesus commended and honored the widow in the temple who gave all that she had to the Lord. (See Luke 21:1–4.) God will also observe and reward the Christian who gives from his income, whether it be social security, unemployment compensation, or regular earnings.

15. Can the tithe be used to pay the tuition at a church school?

No. This is contrary to the spirit of giving, since there would be personal benefit derived from the gift. There are also legal complications for such a practice. Funds given in this manner do not qualify as a charitable deduction.

16. Are there only eternal consequences for not tithing?

No. There are also temporal consequences. If we fail to give tithes and offerings, God will not "rebuke the devourer," and then we will suffer unnecessary financial loss. (See Malachi 3:8–11.)

17. Should an older child be given money to put in the offering plate in order to teach him to tithe?

No. A child who is able to earn money should be taught to tithe out of the money he earns, not out of money that is simply given to him. It is the faith of sacrifice that needs to be taught, since that is what God has promised to honor. (See Hebrews 11:6.)

18. If we increase our tithe, will God increase our financial reward?

No. The tithe is only ten per cent. Anything beyond this would be offerings. We should not give with the expectation of financial reward, even though God will often give it. Our motives should be advancing God's kingdom, meeting needs, laying up treasures in heaven, and growing in personal faith.

THE CONSEQUENCES OF ROBBING GOD

A farmer received a $100,000 profit on the sale of some land. He was encouraged to give a tithe to his church, but he decided not to do it. Shortly thereafter, he was burning some brush on the back of his property. A strong wind came and blew the fire over his fence and into his neighbor's field. The neighbor sued for damages. The total cost to the farmer was $10,000.

A successful Christian businessman listened as his neighbor explained how sick their baby was, how their car had broken down, and how a series of other unexpected expenses had come upon them. The businessman asked this Christian neighbor, "Are you tithing?"

The neighbor replied, "We can't afford to tithe. We are barely meeting our bills now."

The businessman encouraged him to make the following analysis: "Why don't you add up all of the unexpected bills that you received during the past months and see if they don't equal the tithe that you have not been paying."

The neighbor checked over his expenses of several previous months. He itemized all of the unexpected bills. To his amazement, he discovered that it was almost exactly the same amount that his tithe would have been.

This neighbor was experiencing the truth of God's principles regarding the tithe. If we fail to give tithes, God will simply not rebuke the devourer. (See Malachi 3:11.)

PURPOSE NOT TO ROB GOD

"Will a man rob God? Yet ye have robbed me. But ye say, Wherein have we robbed thee? In tithes and offerings. Ye are cursed with a curse. . . . Bring ye all the tithes into the storehouse. . . . And I will rebuke the devourer for your sakes, and he shall not destroy the fruits of your ground . . ." (Malachi 3:8–11).

1. When did you become a Christian? Date _____

2. Since you became a Christian, have you kept accurate records of all of your income? YES ☐   NO ☐

3. Are you an active member of a church that honors and obeys the Bible as the inspired, infallible Word of God? YES ☐   NO ☐

4. Have you given your tithes to your local church? YES ☐   NO ☐

5. Have you kept records of your tithing? YES ☐   NO ☐

6. Based on your own records, is there tithe money that you have not given to God? YES ☐   NO ☐

Amount _____

7. During times that you did not tithe, did you experience the devouring of your funds through unexpected losses? YES ☐   NO ☐

Amount _____

8. Have you honored God by regularly giving Him His day each week? YES ☐   NO ☐

Personal Commitment to Scriptural Tithing

I have confessed my sin of robbing God, and I claim the forgiveness He promises in I John 1:9. From this day forward, I purpose to give God tithes and offerings of my time and money.

Date _____ This week's tithe _____

WHAT WOULD YOU TITHE?

Supply the following situations with the correct answer.

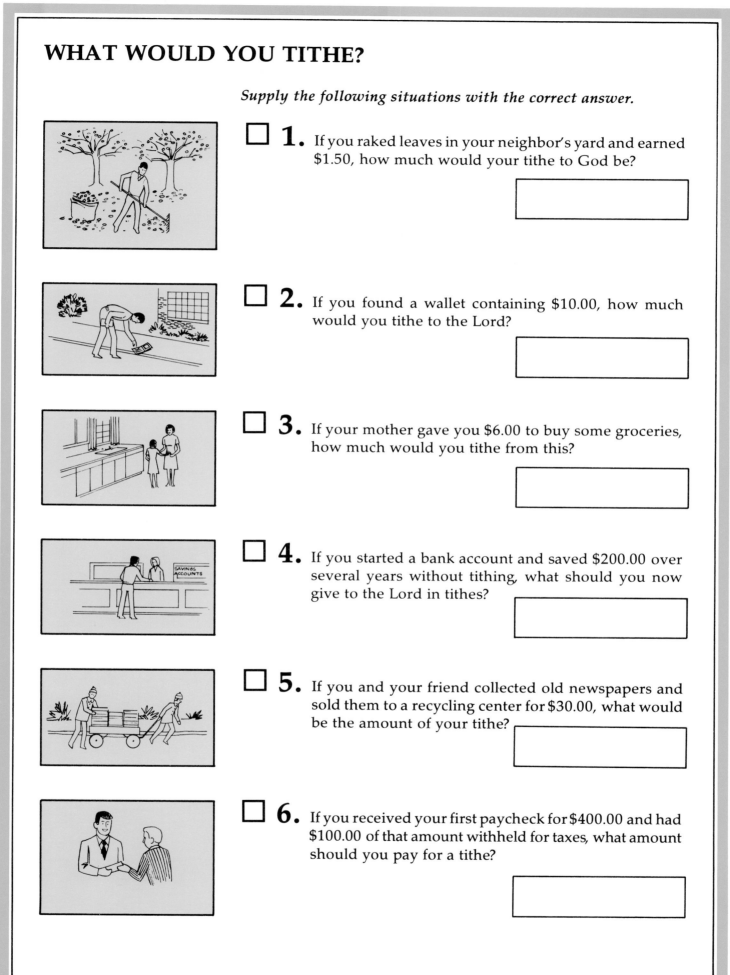

☐ **1.** If you raked leaves in your neighbor's yard and earned $1.50, how much would your tithe to God be?

☐ **2.** If you found a wallet containing $10.00, how much would you tithe to the Lord?

☐ **3.** If your mother gave you $6.00 to buy some groceries, how much would you tithe from this?

☐ **4.** If you started a bank account and saved $200.00 over several years without tithing, what should you now give to the Lord in tithes?

☐ **5.** If you and your friend collected old newspapers and sold them to a recycling center for $30.00, what would be the amount of your tithe?

☐ **6.** If you received your first paycheck for $400.00 and had $100.00 of that amount withheld for taxes, what amount should you pay for a tithe?

HOW DID GOD HONOR THOSE WHO GAVE TITHES AND OFFERINGS?

Match God's rewards to the following individuals.

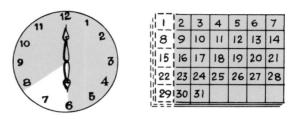

☐ **1.** Abraham tithed ten per cent of all the spoils which he had won in his battle against King Chedorlaomer. (See Genesis 14–15.)

☐ **2.** Solomon gave a thousand burnt offerings to the Lord after becoming king. (See I Kings 3:4–15.)

A. God gave to him and his family salvation and the power of the Holy Spirit.

B. He was given the promise of a son.

☐ **3.** Jacob offered to God ten per cent of all he received back from the Lord. (See Genesis 28:22.)

C. God stopped the plague that was destroying the nation.

☐ **4.** Cornelius, a Roman Centurion, gave generously to the needs of the Jews. (See Acts 10.)

D. God promised that He would never again repeat the judgment he had seen.

☐ **5.** David gave an offering to the Lord, and this offering required personal sacrifice on his part. (See II Samuel 24:18–25.)

E. He received twenty years of financial success.

F. He was given public honor and a special ministry from the Lord.

☐ **6.** Barnabas sold his land and gave the money to the Church. (See Acts 4:36–37.)

G. God gave him riches and honor and long life as well as wisdom.

☐ **7.** Noah gave an offering to the Lord immediately after coming out of the ark. (See Genesis 8:20–22.)

Answers: 1.B 2.G 3.E 4.A 5.C 6.F 7.D

72

CAN YOU MATCH TITHING QUESTIONS TO SCRIPTURAL TESTIMONIES?

Check the person who most clearly illustrates God's answers on tithing.

1. Is tithing a part of the Mosaic Law and therefore not applicable to us today?

- ☐ Noah
- ☐ Abraham
- ☐ David

2. Should the tithe be given to the local church?

- ☐ Stephen
- ☐ Peter
- ☐ Barnabas

3. How do we know that the real purpose of the tithe is to learn the fear of the Lord?

- ☐ Joshua
- ☐ Naaman
- ☐ Cornelius

4. Who says that the tithe should be paid on the first day of the week?

- ☐ Paul
- ☐ Matthew
- ☐ John

5. Can the tithe involve something other than money?

- ☐ Luke
- ☐ Jonah
- ☐ Abraham

6. Should I decide to tithe even if I do not have any money?

- ☐ Jacob
- ☐ Joseph
- ☐ Lot

7. What if I have failed to tithe for several years?

- ☐ Nicodemus
- ☐ Zacchaeus
- ☐ Cornelius

8. Should a husband tithe without his wife's approval?

- ☐ Abraham
- ☐ Isaac
- ☐ Jacob

9. How do we know that we should not tithe from a designated gift?

- ☐ Ananias
- ☐ Barnabas
- ☐ Paul

10. Is it true that God even honors the tithes of a non-Christian?

- ☐ Saul
- ☐ Silas
- ☐ Cornelius

Answers: 1. Abraham 2. Barnabas 3. Cornelius 4. Paul 5. Abraham 6. Jacob 7. Zacchaeus 8. Abraham 9. Paul 10. Cornelius

73

DAVID
A man after God's own heart

FINANCIAL RESPONSIBILITY

"... I will surely buy it of thee at a price: neither will I offer burnt offerings unto the Lord my God of that which doth cost me nothing . . ." (II Samuel 24:24).

7 PURPOSE TO KEEP OUT OF DEBT

"Owe no man any thing, but to love one another: for he that loveth another hath fulfilled the law" (Romans 13:8).

FINANCING BEFOREHAND

"Now I have prepared with all my might for the house of my God the gold for things to be made of gold, and the silver for things of silver . . ." (I Chronicles 29:2).

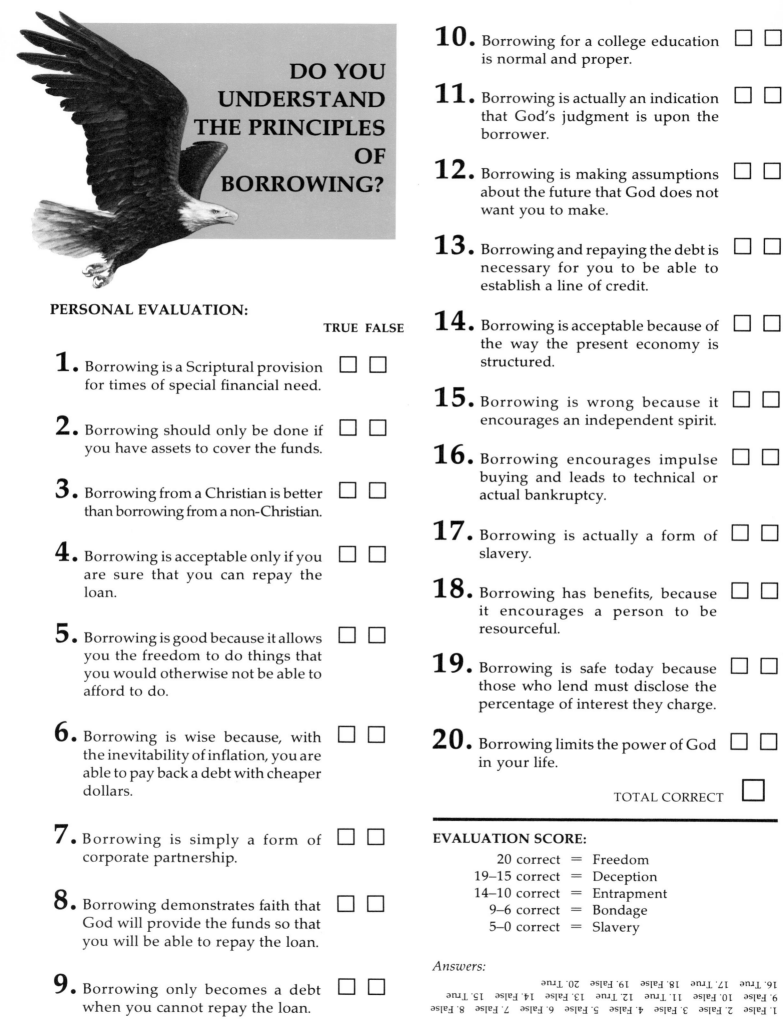

DO YOU UNDERSTAND THE PRINCIPLES OF BORROWING?

PERSONAL EVALUATION:

TRUE FALSE

1. Borrowing is a Scriptural provision for times of special financial need. ☐ ☐

2. Borrowing should only be done if you have assets to cover the funds. ☐ ☐

3. Borrowing from a Christian is better than borrowing from a non-Christian. ☐ ☐

4. Borrowing is acceptable only if you are sure that you can repay the loan. ☐ ☐

5. Borrowing is good because it allows you the freedom to do things that you would otherwise not be able to afford to do. ☐ ☐

6. Borrowing is wise because, with the inevitability of inflation, you are able to pay back a debt with cheaper dollars. ☐ ☐

7. Borrowing is simply a form of corporate partnership. ☐ ☐

8. Borrowing demonstrates faith that God will provide the funds so that you will be able to repay the loan. ☐ ☐

9. Borrowing only becomes a debt when you cannot repay the loan. ☐ ☐

10. Borrowing for a college education is normal and proper. ☐ ☐

11. Borrowing is actually an indication that God's judgment is upon the borrower. ☐ ☐

12. Borrowing is making assumptions about the future that God does not want you to make. ☐ ☐

13. Borrowing and repaying the debt is necessary for you to be able to establish a line of credit. ☐ ☐

14. Borrowing is acceptable because of the way the present economy is structured. ☐ ☐

15. Borrowing is wrong because it encourages an independent spirit. ☐ ☐

16. Borrowing encourages impulse buying and leads to technical or actual bankruptcy. ☐ ☐

17. Borrowing is actually a form of slavery. ☐ ☐

18. Borrowing has benefits, because it encourages a person to be resourceful. ☐ ☐

19. Borrowing is safe today because those who lend must disclose the percentage of interest they charge. ☐ ☐

20. Borrowing limits the power of God in your life. ☐ ☐

TOTAL CORRECT ☐

EVALUATION SCORE:

20 correct	=	Freedom
19–15 correct	=	Deception
14–10 correct	=	Entrapment
9–6 correct	=	Bondage
5–0 correct	=	Slavery

Answers:

1. False 2. False 3. False 4. False 5. False 6. False 7. False 8. False 9. False 10. False 11. True 12. True 13. False 14. False 15. True 16. True 17. True 18. False 19. False 20. True

76

DEFINITIONS RELATED TO BORROWING

1. *What is debt?*

BORROW:
Old. Eng.: "Pledge"
MORTGAGE:
French: "Dead pledge"
(Payment on death)
AMORTIZE:
French: "To deaden"

Debt is the condition of being in bondage to another person. It is to be obligated to pay back what is owed. It is allowing another person to have a claim against you.

A debt creates a relationship of servitude to a creditor.

A debt can involve money, promises, possessions, meals, time, or favors.

In the Old Testament, loans in Israel were charitable, not commercial. The charging of any kind of interest to fellow Israelites was forbidden. However, interest could be charged to foreigners. (See Deuteronomy 23:20.)

2. *What is bankruptcy?*

BROKEN BENCH:
Babylonian, Egyptian,
Old Italian

Bankruptcy is the condition of having loans come due which cannot be repaid in acceptable currency.

A bankrupt person may have valuable assets; however, if they cannot be quickly sold and thereby turned into legal tender, a creditor may initiate foreclosure.

The word *bankrupt* is derived from the words for "broken bench." In the earliest records of Egypt, moneychangers would conduct their business while sitting on a bench that was usually located in the courtyard of a temple. When a banker went "bankrupt" his bench was broken. It was from such a temple bank that Christ drove out the moneychangers.

3. *What are depreciating items?*

EVIDENCES:
Moth holes
Rust
Thieves

A depreciating item is one which has a value that decreases the longer that it is used or owned.

The market value of an item may be reduced by wear, style, changing needs, or the inability of others to purchase it or use it.

When Christ compared temporal and eternal values, He warned of those things that are consumed by moths, rust, and thieves. *"Lay not up for yourselves treasures upon earth, where moth and rust doth corrupt, and where thieves break through and steal"* (Matthew 6:19).

God further warns about the vain practice of storing up depreciating items in James 5:1–2: *"Go to now, ye rich men, weep and howl for your miseries that shall come upon you. Your riches are corrupted, and your garments are motheaten."*

4. *What are appreciating items?*

An appreciating item is one that tends to increase in value the longer that it is used.

The ability of an item to appreciate in value is most clearly tied to its durability, usefulness, and scarcity. Thus, Paul compares durable works to gold, silver, and precious stones. (See I Corinthians 3:12.)

The most durable riches of all are those which are invested in God's kingdom, "*. . . where neither moth nor rust doth corrupt, and where thieves do not break through nor steal*" (Matthew 6:20).

If a man is not using his wealth for God's kingdom, even his gold and silver becomes a depreciating item. "*Your gold and silver is cankered; and the rust of them shall be a witness against you, and shall eat your flesh as it were fire . . .*" (James 5:3).

5. *What is credit buying?*

CHARGE:
Latin carrus:
"Baggage wagon"

Credit card buying is operating on another person's money. It is using an item before it is paid for.

To buy on credit is to charge an item to an approved account.

The word *charge* comes from *carrus*, the Latin term for a four-wheeled Roman baggage wagon. It denotes a "load"; and a person who makes purchases with a charge account puts himself under a burden.

6. *What is accumulating interest?*

CUMULUS:
Latin: "To heap"
"To pile up"

Compounding interest has many of the characteristics of cumulus clouds. In their early stages, cumulus clouds are just "puffs of cotton." They are signs of fair weather.

The "puffs of cotton" begin to rise into rounded, bulging summits. Even when they are large, though, they rarely bring a storm; but when cumulus clouds turn into cumulonimbus, a violent storm is underway. The great vertical development, with a flattened, anvil-shaped peak, contains strong vertical wind currents, violent thunderstorms, and, very often, hailstones.

At first, interest payments seem like typical signs of good times. As interest rates are compounded, they are still able to be managed while the cash flow from employment continues. However, unexpected troubles and bills are a part of life; and the loss of a job can bring financial disaster to one who is deeply in debt.

CONSEQUENCES OF BORROWING

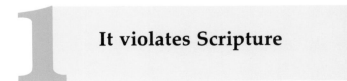

1   It violates Scripture

The message of Scripture on borrowing is quite clear: *Do not do it.* God commands Christians to keep out of debt altogether. "*Owe no man any thing, but to love one another . . .*" (Romans 13:8).

Strong's Exhaustive Concordance amplifies the message behind these words: "Owe to no one, no not anything, nothing at all."

2 It constitutes a judgment of God

God clearly relates borrowing to His judgment upon His people for failing to follow His ways.

"But it shall come to pass, if thou wilt not hearken unto the voice of the Lord thy God, to observe to do all his commandments and his statutes which I command thee this day; that all these curses shall come upon thee, and overtake thee. . . . He shall lend to thee, and thou shalt not lend to him: he shall be the head, and thou shalt be the tail" (Deuteronomy 28:15, 44).

3 It produces bondage to creditors

". . . The borrower is servant to the lender" (Proverbs 22:7). God intends for Christians to be free from earthly entanglements in order to serve Him.

"No man that warreth entangleth himself with the affairs of this life; that he may please him who hath chosen him to be a soldier" (II Timothy 2:4).

The very nature of borrowing is entanglement. The Hebrew words for borrowing are *'âbaṭ*, to entangle, and *lâvâh*, to twine, to take an obligation, to unite with.

4 It presumes upon the future

Borrowing is based on the assumption that future conditions will allow us to repay the debt. God warns against such presumption.

"Go to now, ye that say, To day or to morrow we will go into such a city, and continue there a year, and buy and sell, and get gain: Whereas ye know not what shall be on the morrow . . ." (James 4:13–14).

"Boast not thyself of to morrow; for thou knowest not what a day may bring forth" (Proverbs 27:1).

5 It gives the illusion of independence

Borrowing gives the temporary illusion of independence from authority. It allows final decisions to be made apart from God's provision of funds.

It causes an individual to feel that he is his own authority and that he does not need to wait for wise counsel or sufficient funds. Such an attitude is condemned by God.

"Who is he that saith, and it cometh to pass, when the Lord commandeth it not" (Lamentations 3:37).

". . . For what is your life? It is even a vapour, that appeareth for a little time, and then vanisheth away. For that ye ought to say, If the Lord will, we shall live, and do this, or that. But now ye rejoice in your boastings: all such rejoicing is evil. Therefore to him that knoweth to do good, and doeth it not, to him it is sin" (James 4:14–17).

6 It evades self-examination

When God withholds funds, there is a good reason. It is His signal for us to re-evaluate our lives, our plans for the money, and our faith in Him. Borrowing evades these purposes and allows the Christian to continue on in his own wisdom and efforts.

Borrowing causes pressure upon those who are depending on your leadership and provision, especially those who are in your family. They are aware that unexpected events can transfer the burden of debt directly upon them. The anguish of this consequence is illustrated by God in the plight of a widow in Elisha's day.

Her husband was in training for serving the Lord. However, he borrowed money while he was in training. When he died, his creditors demanded their money from his wife. She lost everything she had. Since she still could not pay off the debts, her creditors demanded that she turn over her sons to be their bondservants.

Not only did this woman lose her husband and her possessions, but she would have lost her sons also if she had not followed the counsel of Elisha. (See II Kings 4:1–7.)

7 It interferes with God's provision

God wants to demonstrate His supernatural power through the lives of men and women of faith. Only in this way can He contrast the false confidence which people have placed in their own wisdom, abilities, and riches.

"For the eyes of the Lord run to and fro throughout the whole earth, to shew himself strong in the behalf of them whose heart is perfect toward him . . ." (II Chronicles 16:9).

8 It removes barriers to harmful items

There are many things which we think will be beneficial to our lives, but God knows that they will be harmful to us. In His mercy and wisdom He may limit our funds so that we cannot afford them.

This is explained in James 4:3, *"Ye ask, and receive not, because ye ask amiss, that ye may consume it upon your lusts."*

When God does not provide the money, Satan tempts us to get the money in other ways. In so doing, we *". . . fall into temptation and a snare, and into many foolish and hurtful lusts, which drown men in destruction and perdition" (I Timothy 6:9).*

9 It demonstrates discontent with basics

God has promised to provide food and clothing. He wants us to be content with these things. (See I Timothy 6:8.)

Borrowing is usually done for items other than these basic necessities. If money is borrowed for basic needs, it usually indicates that money which God provided for food and clothing was used for non-essentials.

God warns about the consequences of coveting the power to buy whatever our heart desires. *"For the love of money is the root of all evil: which while some coveted after, they have erred from the faith, and pierced themselves through with many sorrows" (I Timothy 6:10).*

10 It devours resources through high interest payments

Most people who borrow money do not comprehend the final price tag of using someone else's money. They are taught to think only in terms of monthly payments.

Those who borrow money usually look upon the interest as a small amount, but in the final analysis interest payments constitute a very large part of the total cost of the loan.

In any case, God expects Christians to be good stewards of His money. To do so requires faithfulness in small amounts as well as large amounts.

"He that is faithful in that which is least is faithful also in much: and he that is unjust in the least is unjust also in much. If therefore ye have not been faithful in the unrighteous mammon, who will commit to your trust the true riches?" (Luke 16:10–11).

Interest payments constitute a deadly trap for every borrower. Each time a loan is repaid, the borrower tends to be reassured that borrowing is the way to meet the next financial urgency.

God has given us ample warning, however, that unexpected troubles and needs are a part of life. When they come, and when they cut off or use up the expected income, the real damage of past, present, and future interest on a loan is painfully clear.

11 It stifles resourcefulness

Christ gave two significant illustrations of men who wanted to buy expensive items. Although neither man had the money for the purchases, neither man borrowed any money. Instead, they sold what they had; and with the money from the sale they bought what they wanted.

"Again, the kingdom of heaven is like unto treasure hid in a field; the which when a man hath found, he hideth, and for joy thereof goeth and selleth all that he hath, and buyeth that field.

"Again, the kingdom of heaven is like unto a merchant man, seeking goodly pearls: Who, when he had found one pearl of great price, went and sold all that he had, and bought it" (Matthew 13:44–46).

Only when a man makes a firm and final decision that he will not borrow money, can he be mentally, emotionally, and spiritually free to be creatively resourceful.

"Easy" money is a deadening influence on creative solutions to financial needs.

12 It promotes impulse buying

God expects Christians to prayerfully consider their decisions regarding the management of the funds which He provides.

In contrast to this, the world encourages buyers to make impulsive decisions based on the desires of the moment. Easy access to money lends itself to impulsive purchases which by-pass prayerful thought and wise counsel.

"Also, that the soul be without knowledge, it is not good; and he that hasteth with his feet sinneth" (Proverbs 19:2).

13 It damages God's reputation

God has promised to provide for the needs of His children. *"But my God shall supply all your need according to his riches in glory by Christ Jesus" (Philippians 4:19).*

When Christians borrow, they are saying to the world, "God is not taking care of my needs, so I have to make up for the difference with a loan."

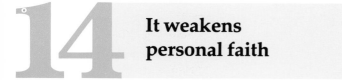

14 It weakens personal faith

In reality, a Christian who relies on credit does not feel that he needs to trust God during the most critical time of decision making.

He is convinced that, if he can afford the monthly payments, he can buy the item. However, God wants him to discern whether it is His will to buy it.

A clear evidence of God's will can be obtained by trusting God to provide the funds ahead of time. This is the kind of faith that pleases God. *"... Without faith it is impossible to please him ..." (Hebrews 11:6).*

15 It excludes help from others

God uses the needs in the life of one Christian and the abundance in the life of another Christian to bring them together in Christian fellowship.

The one with abundance is given grace to distribute to the necessity of the saints, and the one who receives is filled with joy and gratefulness because of God's grace through the giver.

The principle of interdependence is clearly explained in Scripture. *"But by an equality, that now at this time your abundance may be a supply for their want, that their abundance also may be a supply for your want: that there may be equality: As it is written, He that had gathered much had nothing over; and he that had gathered little had no lack" (II Corinthians 8:14–15).*

16 It causes overspending

The credit card system is a major way of borrowing for depreciating items. Credit card users tend to buy more than those who pay cash, and they tend to pay more for the items that they do buy.

There is a clear Scriptural explanation of this. Since the credit card represents additional money, the desires of the user increase accordingly. *"He that loveth silver shall not be satisfied with silver; nor he that loveth abundance with increase ..." (Ecclesiastes 5:10).*

Overspending is destructive in itself. However, when the overspending produces pressures and conflicts which damage family relationships, it is especially destructive.

Money problems are listed as a major cause of alienation in a large percentage of the divorces in the United States. Most studies show that the majority of arguments in the home center on money.

Behind overspending is a basic lack of self-control. When this is conquered by the power of the Holy Spirit, the habit of borrowing money can also be overcome.

THE DOUBLE BITE OF
THE DEBT TRAP

If you increase your indebtedness by only $1,000 a year at 12% interest, compounded annually, the interest after 15 years will be $26,754, and your total indebtedness will be $41,754!

Borrowing Years	Debt Addition	Interest	Total Debt
1	$1,000	$ 120	$ 1,120
2	1,000	254	2,374
3	1,000	405	3,779
4	1,000	574	5,353
5	1,000	762	7,115
6	1,000	974	9,089
7	1,000	1,211	11,300
8	1,000	1,476	13,776
9	1,000	1,773	16,549
10	1,000	2,106	19,655
11	1,000	2,479	23,134
12	1,000	2,896	27,030
13	1,000	3,363	31,393
14	1,000	3,887	36,280
15	1,000	4,474	41,754
		$26,754	

If you should then attempt to get out of debt by repaying the loan at $6,000 per year, it will take you almost 16 more years and cost an additional $53,696 in interest.

Your debt accumulation of $1,000 per year for 15 years has cost you a total of $80,450 in interest. This averages out to be $2,595 per year for the 31-year period.

Repaying Years	Repayment	Interest	Balance Due
16	$6,000	$5,010	$40,764
17	6,000	4,892	39,656
18	6,000	4,759	38,415
19	6,000	4,610	37,025
20	6,000	4,443	35,468
21	6,000	4,256	33,724
22	6,000	4,047	31,771
23	6,000	3,813	29,584
24	6,000	3,550	27,134
25	6,000	3,256	24,390
26	6,000	2,927	21,317
27	6,000	2,558	17,875
28	6,000	2,145	14,020
29	6,000	1,682	9,702
30	6,000	1,164	4,866
31	5,450	584	—
		$53,696	

TOTAL INTEREST $80,450

MEN OF GOD WHO REFUSED TO BORROW

NOAH

He could have borrowed money to build the ark. In fact, it would have been a shrewd move for him to have "floated" a loan; but it would have damaged his faith and his message. (See Genesis 6–7.)

JOASH

He could have borrowed money to pay the workmen who refurbished the temple. Instead, he collected the money ahead of time and gave it to the workmen as they had need of it. This caused joy among the people. (See II Chronicles 24:4–14.)

MOSES

He could have borrowed material to construct the tabernacle; but that would have made God the servant of the people, rather than teaching the people how to serve the true and living God. (See Exodus 25–27.)

EZRA

He could have borrowed money to rebuild the temple, but it would have been a poor testimony to the king and the heathen. God provided the funds through the king whom Ezra served. (See Ezra 7:11–28.)

DAVID

He could have borrowed money to build the temple. Instead, he spent his lifetime gathering the materials, and his son was then able to build a far more glorious structure—debt free. (See I Chronicles 17, 22.)

NEHEMIAH

He could have borrowed money to rebuild the walls of Jerusalem; but because of his obedience to the king, the king provided all that he needed for the building. (See Nehemiah 2:3–8.)

ABRAHAM

He could have borrowed money to buy the tomb for his wife, but it would have been a point of contention for many generations. Instead, he secured the land and the trees with a public contract. (See Genesis 23.)

PAUL

He could have borrowed money for his missionary journeys. He could have even asked people to support him. Instead, he earned his support by laboring night and day. He became an example to every Christian after him. (See Acts 18:3; 20:33–35.)

REJECT ARGUMENTS FAVORING DEBT

> *God's work done in God's way will not lack God's support. He is just as able to supply funds ahead of time as afterward and He much prefers doing so.*
>
> *J. Hudson Taylor*

ARGUMENTS FOR BORROWING	ANSWERS
1. Borrowing is necessary to prove your financial responsibility and establish good credit.	Credit is not necessary if you are not going to borrow. A letter of reference from your bank will certify your financial responsibility.
2. Credit cards are helpful for keeping records.	Paying by check and keeping sales receipts and a daily ledger are just as effective, and you avoid the traps of credit buying.
3. Borrowing for new equipment is wise, because you get special tax advantages.	The cost of depreciation, high interest rates, loss of capital availability, missing used equipment bargains, and violation of Scripture outweigh any tax benefits.
4. Borrowing money for school is all right, because education is not a depreciating item.	Borrowing limits God from either providing the money supernaturally or directing you to earn school money through practical work experience. It also presumes upon the future.

Personal Commitment to Keep Out of Debt

From this day forward, my wife and I purpose not to accumulate any further debt. Our goal is to keep out of debt altogether.

To help accomplish this, we are not using credit cards, we have returned any borrowed books, tools, or other items, and we purpose to establish spending disciplines which will remove all past debts.

Date _____

HOW DOES GOD ILLUSTRATE THE PAINFUL TRAPS OF BORROWING?

1. We have borrowed for food and taxes. We have mortgaged our houses and lands, and now our children are being sold as bondservants and we cannot redeem them.

2. I am in deep trouble. The creditors have come, and I have nothing in the house with which to pay them. They want to take my sons to be bondsmen.

Match each borrower with the statement that best expresses his or her cry for help.

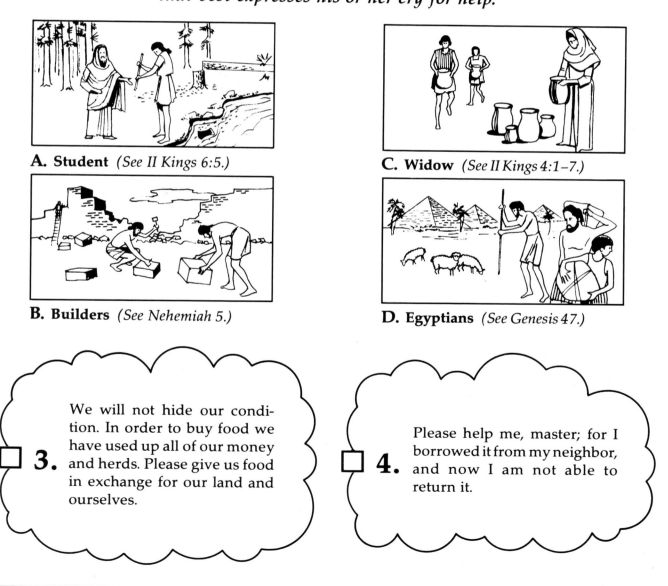

A. Student *(See II Kings 6:5.)*

C. Widow *(See II Kings 4:1–7.)*

B. Builders *(See Nehemiah 5.)*

D. Egyptians *(See Genesis 47.)*

3. We will not hide our condition. In order to buy food we have used up all of our money and herds. Please give us food in exchange for our land and ourselves.

4. Please help me, master; for I borrowed it from my neighbor, and now I am not able to return it.

Answers: 1.B 2.C 3.D 4.A

HOW MUCH DO YOU KNOW ABOUT BORROWING?

Choose the best answer for each question.

1. If you borrow $1,000 a year at 12% interest, compounded annually, how much will you owe in interest after fifteen years?

☐ **A.** $1,500
☐ **B.** $5,281
☐ **C.** $26,754

2. If you wanted to pay back a loan of $41,754 with $6,000 a year, how much would you pay in interest before the loan was repaid at 12% interest?

☐ **A.** $3,500
☐ **B.** $16,500
☐ **C.** $53,696

3. God told His own people that if they borrowed money they were:

☐ **A.** Endangering their future.
☐ **B.** Being cursed by God.
☐ **C.** Not using their resources.

4. The Hebrew word for borrowing is *'âbaṭ.* It means:

☐ **A.** To entangle.
☐ **B.** To use.
☐ **C.** To obligate.

5. God warned His own people not to lend money with interest to:

☐ **A.** Foreign nations.
☐ **B.** Widows.
☐ **C.** Their own people.

6. The anguish of indebtedness was illustrated in the Scriptural account of:

☐ **A.** Esther
☐ **B.** Ezra
☐ **C.** Nehemiah

7. If you have gotten into debt by borrowing for a car, you should:

☐ **A.** Pay it off and learn a lesson.
☐ **B.** Sell the car and buy a cheaper one.
☐ **C.** Ask your employer for a raise.

8. If you are heavily in debt and purpose not to borrow anymore, you can expect God to:

☐ **A.** Get you out of debt quickly.
☐ **B.** Get you out of debt slowly.
☐ **C.** Build disciplines while removing debt.

Answers: 1.C 2.C 3.B 4.A 5.C 6.C 7.B 8.C

WHAT REASONS WOULD YOU GIVE FOR NOT BORROWING?

Select the most appropriate answers for each case.
(Answers may be used more than once.)

CASE **A** BORROWING FOR EDUCATION

A friend has just been accepted to a Christian liberal arts college and has been offered a low interest loan. He asks for your opinion about the loan.

Answers _____

CASE **B** BORROWING FOR NEW EQUIPMENT

A neighbor has been given a contract for a large construction job, but in order to do it he must borrow money for some new equipment. When the job is finished he could pay off the loan.

Answers _____

CASE **C** BORROWING FOR A CAR

An older brother has found an exceptionally good buy on a new car. The payments are well within his monthly income, and after a year he could sell it for more than he paid for it.

Answers _____

CASE **D** BORROWING FOR MEDICAL BILLS

A missionary family has experienced serious illness. The medical bills are beyond their ability to pay. One of your friends offers to lend them the money for the medical bills. Should they accept the loan?

Answers _____

ANSWERS

1. It violates Scriptural injunctions against borrowing.

2. It constitutes a judgment of God.

3. It produces bondage to creditors.

4. It presumes upon the future.

5. It reveals prideful independence.

6. It evades self-examination.

7. It interferes with God's provision.

8. It removes barriers to harmful items.

9. It demonstrates discontent with basics.

10. It devours resources by interest.

11. It stifles resourcefulness.

12. It promotes impulse buying.

13. It damages God's reputation.

14. It weakens personal faith.

15. It excludes help from others.

16. It causes overspending.

Review pages 82–85 for answers.

PAUL
A man who forsook all for great eternal riches

SUFFERING NEED

"Thrice was I beaten with rods, once was I stoned, thrice I suffered shipwreck. . . . In weariness and painfulness, in watchings often . . . in cold and nakedness" (II Corinthians 11:25–27).

8 LEARN TO LIVE WITHIN YOUR INCOME

"I know both how to be abased, and I know how to abound:
every where and in all things I am instructed both to be full and to
be hungry, both to abound and to suffer need" (Philippians 4:12).

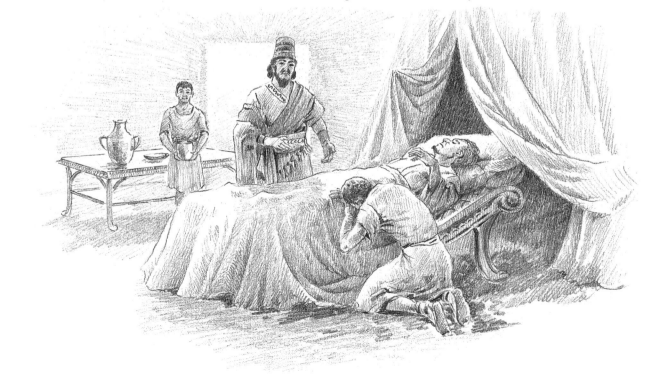

ABOUNDING

After being shipwrecked, Paul healed a chief man's father. "Who
also honoured us with many honours; and when we departed, they
laded us with such things as were necessary" (Acts 28:10).

DO YOU
UNDERSTAND
POVERTY
AND
WEALTH?

PERSONAL EVALUATION:

TRUE FALSE

1. A man is poor when he does not have enough money to pay his bills. ☐ ☐

2. If a man really sets his mind to making money, he can become wealthy. ☐ ☐

3. One of God's ways of punishing those who violate His Word is to cause them to lose money. ☐ ☐

4. God chooses to make some people rich and other people poor. ☐ ☐

5. Some people are destined to remain poor, while others are destined to remain rich. ☐ ☐

6. With the proper social programs, poverty can be eliminated. ☐ ☐

7. God has a cycle which takes people from riches to poverty to riches. ☐ ☐

8. God's only remedy for slothful people is to not give them food. ☐ ☐

9. God has special punishments for those who take advantage of the poor. ☐ ☐

10. God has ordained the government to provide jobs for the poor. ☐ ☐

11. A guaranteed income would violate the principles of God's Word. ☐ ☐

12. God compensates the poor by giving them things the rich do not have. ☐ ☐

13. God allows wicked people to prosper financially. ☐ ☐

14. It is possible for a truly dedicated Christian to be financially poor. ☐ ☐

15. It is Scripturally right for our government to take from the rich and give to the poor. ☐ ☐

16. Wealth is measured by how much money or possessions a person has. ☐ ☐

17. Poverty is more a state of mind than a condition of the pocketbook. ☐ ☐

18. The riches of the wicked are valuable because they provide security. ☐ ☐

19. We should adjust our standard of living to the income that God allows us to receive. ☐ ☐

20. It is unscriptural for a dedicated Christian to have an abundance of riches. ☐ ☐

TOTAL CORRECT ☐

EVALUATION SCORE:

20 correct = Excellent understanding
19–15 correct = Good understanding
14–10 correct = Incomplete understanding
9–6 correct = Poor understanding
5–0 correct = Dangerous lack of understanding

Answers:
1. False 2. False 3. False 4. True 5. False 6. False 7. True 8. True 9. False 10. False 11. True 12. True 13. True 14. True 15. False 16. False 17. True 18. False 19. True 20. False

BASIC INSIGHTS ON POVERTY AND WEALTH

1. Is a man poor when he does not have enough money to pay his bills?

No. A man is poor when he is not able to secure sufficient food, clothing, or shelter. God confirms this by His instructions on how to respond to the needs of the poor. *"Is it not to deal thy bread to the hungry, and that thou bring the poor that are cast out to thy house? when thou seest the naked, that thou cover him . . ."* (Isaiah 58:7).

Many people who have large incomes are not able to pay their bills. They spend the money which should have been used for food and clothing on other items. They are not poor in terms of money. They are poor in terms of managing their money.

2. If a man really sets his mind to making money, can he become wealthy?

No. There are many more factors to making and keeping money than just putting one's mind to it. God asks: *"Who is he that saith, and it cometh to pass, when the Lord commandeth it not?"* (Lamentations 3:37). Throughout Scripture God reminds us that He has the final word concerning a man's wealth: *"Ye looked for much, and, lo, it came to little; and when ye brought it home, I did blow upon it . . ."* (Haggai 1:9).

Furthermore, when a man sets his mind on making money, he violates the warnings of God not to seek after riches, and he will experience the consequences of doing so.

3. Is the loss of money one of God's punishments for those who violate His Word?

Yes. The Scriptures clearly establish a cause-and-effect sequence between violating God's laws and losing money.

VIOLATIONS OF GOD'S WORD THAT BRING FINANCIAL LOSS	
VIOLATION	**FINANCIAL CONSEQUENCES**
• Being immoral with a woman	*". . . Strangers [shall] be filled with thy wealth . . ."* (Proverbs 5:10).
• Spending too much time sleeping	*"So shall thy poverty come . . ."* (Proverbs 6:11).
• Getting money by doing evil	*"The Lord . . . casteth away the substance of the wicked"* (Proverbs 10:3).
• Failing to be diligent	*"He becometh poor that dealeth with a slack hand . . ."* (Proverbs 10:4).
• Co-signing a note	*"He that is surety for a stranger shall smart for it . . ."* (Proverbs 11:15).
• Having a stingy attitude	*". . . It tendeth to poverty"* (Proverbs 11:24).
• Provoking your family to anger	You *". . . shall inherit the wind . . ."* (Proverbs 11:29).
• Getting money without labor	It *". . . shall be diminished . . ."* (Proverbs 13:11).
• Refusing to listen to reproofs	*"Poverty and shame shall be to [you] . . ."* (Proverbs 13:18).
• Talking too much	It *". . . tendeth only to penury"* (Proverbs 14:23).
• Being slothful	You *". . . shall suffer hunger"* (Proverbs 19:15).
• Rejecting the cry of the poor	You *". . . shall cry . . . but shall not be heard"* (Proverbs 21:13).
• Loving pleasure	You *". . . shall be a poor man . . ."* (Proverbs 21:17).
• Loving wine	You *". . . shall not be rich"* (Proverbs 21:17).
• Giving to rich people	You *". . . shall surely come to want"* (Proverbs 22:16).
• Overeating	You *". . . shall come to poverty . . ."* (Proverbs 23:21).
• Charging usury on loans	You *". . . shall gather . . . [your money] for him that will pity the poor"* (Proverbs 28:8).
• Following vain persons	You *". . . shall have poverty enough"* (Proverbs 28:19).
• Trying to get rich quickly	*". . . Poverty shall come upon [you] . . ."* (Proverbs 28:22).

4. Does God choose to make some people rich and other people poor?

Yes. God chooses different means to accomplish different purposes for His glory.

TESTING: God chose to allow Job to become poor in order to test his faith. (See Job 1–2.) Later He chose to restore to Job twice the wealth that he had before. (See Job 42.)

CHASTENING: God chose to make King Zedekiah and the nation of Judah poor because they rebelled against God's ways and the warnings of all His prophets. (See II Chronicles 36:11–21.)

REDEEMING: God chose for His Son to be born in poverty and to be reared in a despised community, because He was to demonstrate the marvelous grace of redemption. *"For ye know the grace of our Lord Jesus Christ, that, though he was rich, yet for your sakes he became poor, that ye through his poverty might be rich"* (II Corinthians 8:9).

God's decision to make some people poor and other people rich is further emphasized in the following verses.

"For promotion cometh neither from the east, nor from the west, nor from the south. But God is the judge: he putteth down one, and setteth up another" (Psalm 75:6–7).

". . . It is he that giveth thee power to get wealth . . ." (Deuteronomy 8:18).

5. Are some people destined to remain poor, while others are destined to remain rich?

No. God's destiny for people is not centered around their earthly riches but around His eternal riches.

In the process of teaching men how to compare temporary riches with lasting riches, God may allow them to experience both riches and poverty.

He allows some wicked people to prosper, then to have trouble with their riches, and in many cases to lose their riches. He also allows righteous people to lose their money, so that they might discover more of God's riches and then experience God's financial provision.

"Thou hast caused men to ride over our heads; we went through fire and through water: but thou broughtest us out into a wealthy place" (Psalm 66:12).

6. Can government programs eliminate poverty?

No. Poverty will never be eliminated through social programs, because the real cause of poverty is not social but spiritual. Social programs may provide jobs, education, or money; but these alone do not conquer many of the forces which create poverty, such as drunkenness, drug addiction, laziness, and unwise investments.

Social programs which are designed to end poverty also overlook those benefits that God wants to be achieved through poverty, such as self-examination, seeking the Lord, and creative resourcefulness.

A further problem with social programs is the inherent corruption which tends to come with them because of greed.

Chastening poverty will only be eliminated when individuals and nations return to God's universal, Scriptural principles.

Starvation in India is not caused by a food shortage or overpopulation. It is the result of religious beliefs which are contrary to God's Word.

The Hindu religion teaches that people who die are reincarnated in the form of animals; thus it is against their laws and religion to kill rats, mice, cows, or other animals.

Every cow eats enough food to feed seven people, and there are two hundred million "sacred cows" in India.

If the people of India would just stop feeding these cows, they would have enough food to feed one billion, four hundred million people. That is one fourth of the entire world's population! [1]

1. Robert L. Sassone, *Handbook on Population*, 3rd ed., formerly published as "Report to California Legislature on Population at the Request of the Office of the Senate Majority Leader," 1973, pp. 53–54.

7. Does God have a cycle which takes people from riches to poverty to riches?

Yes. God illustrates this cycle in the life of our Lord Jesus Christ, as well as in the lives of many others in Scripture.

Christ went from the riches of heaven to the poverty of Nazareth, and then back to the riches of heaven.

Job went from being the wealthiest man in his day, to losing all of his money, to getting twice as much wealth back again.

Christ calls upon all those who want to be His disciples to voluntarily allow Him to take them through this cycle. *". . . If any man will come after me, let him deny himself, and take up his cross, and follow me. For whosoever will save his life shall lose it: and whosoever will lose his life for my sake shall find it"* (Matthew 16:24–25).

8. Is God's only remedy for slothful people not to give them food?

Yes. This is clearly taught in Scripture: *"For even when we were with you, this we commanded you, that if any would not work, neither should he eat"* (II Thessalonians 3:10).

A slothful person is not one who rejects work; he simply makes little daily surrenders to postpone it. *". . . A little sleep, a little slumber, a little folding of the hands to sleep: So shall thy poverty come as one that travelleth, and thy want as an armed man"* (Proverbs 6:10–11).

A slothful person justifies his soft choices by an endless number of reasons why he cannot perform a task. Giving him food will only reinforce his inertia. *"The sluggard will not plow by reason of the cold; therefore shall he beg in harvest, and have nothing"* (Proverbs 20:4).

9. Does God have special punishments for those who take advantage of the poor?

Yes. God sides with the poor against any who would mistreat them: *"He that oppresseth the poor reproacheth his Maker . . ."* (Proverbs 14:31). *"He that hath pity upon the poor lendeth unto the Lord . . ."* (Proverbs 19:17). *"Whoso stoppeth his ears at the cry of the poor, he also shall cry himself, but shall not be heard"* (Proverbs 21:13). *"He that oppresseth the poor to increase his riches . . . shall surely come to want"* (Proverbs 22:16).

God will hold responsible every individual who oppresses the poor. He will also condemn those in leadership positions who profit at the expense of the poor. *"The Lord will enter into judgment with the ancients of his people, and the princes thereof: for ye have eaten up the vineyard; the spoil of the poor is in your houses"* (Isaiah 3:14).

"Ye shall not afflict any widow, or fatherless child. If thou afflict them in any wise, and they cry at all unto me, I will surely hear their cry; And my wrath shall wax hot, and I will kill you with the sword; and your wives shall be widows, and your children fatherless" (Exodus 22:22–24).

10. Has God ordained the government to provide jobs for the poor?

No. It is not the function of a just government to provide jobs for its citizens.

God's primary function for government is to maintain a system of justice based upon His laws. Government officials *". . . are sent by him for the punishment of evildoers, and for the praise of them that do well"* (I Peter 2:14).

Under the protection of a Godly government, businesses are then free to fulfill their function of providing jobs for employees and work for the poor.

The gleaning laws were God's provision for the poor of the land. They provided income with the dignity of labor. *"And when ye reap the harvest of your land, thou shalt not wholly reap the corners of thy field, neither shalt thou gather the gleanings of thy harvest . . . thou shalt leave them for the poor . . ."* (Leviticus 19:9–10).

11. Would a guaranteed income violate the principles of God's Word?

Yes. A guaranteed annual income violates many Scriptural principles. It destroys personal responsibility and personal initiative. (See I Thessalonians 4:10–11; II Thessalonians 3:10). It shields a slothful man from God's discipline. (See Proverbs 20:4.) It weakens the family, which is the foundation of a strong nation, by taking working capital from it and giving it to the state. (See Proverbs 19:14).

12. Does God compensate the poor by giving them things that the rich do not have?

Yes. In the final analysis, faith is more important and more valuable than riches. *"But without faith it is impossible to please him [God] . . ."* (Hebrews 11:6).

Based on this, God's compensation to the poor is significant: *"Hearken, my beloved brethren, Hath not God chosen the poor of this world rich in faith, and heirs of the kingdom which he hath promised to them that love him?"* (James 2:5).

God also gives to the poor a freedom from certain fears and worries which plague the rich. The reward of this freedom is the greater potential for a good night's sleep. *"The sleep of a labouring man is sweet, whether he eat little or much: but the abundance of the rich will not suffer him to sleep"* (Ecclesiastes 5:12).

13. Does God allow wicked people to prosper financially?

Yes. God allows some evil men to prosper for a time. God's purpose is to let them see the emptiness and futility of their riches and then to bring them to repentance.

". . . For he maketh his sun to rise on the evil and on the good, and sendeth rain on the just and on the unjust" (Matthew 5:45).

The tragedy is that some of these very men misinterpret God's goodness. *". . . Despisest thou the riches of his goodness and forbearance and longsuffering; not knowing that the goodness of God leadeth thee to repentance?"* (Romans 2:4).

However, the riches of the wicked have built-in problems. *". . . In the revenues of the wicked is trouble"* (Proverbs 15:6). Even before financial ruin, there is trouble and sorrow in their riches. *"I have seen the wicked in great power, and spreading himself like a green bay tree. Yet he passed away, and, lo, he was not . . ."* (Psalm 37:35–36).

14. Is it possible for a truly dedicated Christian to be financially poor?

Yes. Paul affirmed that he and his fellow workers had no money for themselves. Yet they made others spiritually rich. *"But in all things approving ourselves as the ministers of God. . . . As poor, yet making many rich; as having nothing, and yet possessing all things"* (II Corinthians 6:4, 10). Elijah, Job, and others also had no money for a time.

Even though a Christian may experience poverty, God never forsakes him, and He gives a heritage of rich faith to his children. Thus, David was able to write: *"I have been young, and now am old; yet have I not seen the righteous forsaken, nor his seed begging bread"* (Psalm 37:25).

A Christian in a poverty-stricken country asked why his people were so poor. A visiting pastor replied, "I have been in churches throughout America, but I have never seen or experienced the spiritual power, love, and faith that you and your people have for the Lord. You have something more precious than money."

15. Is it Scripturally right for our government to take from the rich and give to the poor?

No. Forced redistribution of wealth is the program of a socialistic state, not a free nation as was founded by our forefathers.

Our government was based on God's laws which establish and protect private ownership and limited authority of government.

Our government also differs from a monarchy, which existed in Israel. When Israel wanted a king to rule over them, God warned them of what it would mean: *". . . This will be the manner of the king that shall reign over you . . . he will take your fields, and your vineyards, and your oliveyards, even the best of them, and give them to his servants. . . . And ye shall cry out in that day because of your king . . . and the Lord will not hear you in that day"* (I Samuel 8:11, 14, 18).

16. Is wealth measured by how much money or how many possessions a person has?

No. True wealth is measured by the value and lasting benefit which it brings to the life of its possessor.

The Christians in Laodicea thought that they were rich, but God said, ". . . *Thou sayest, I am rich, and increased with goods, and have need of nothing; and knowest not that thou art wretched, and miserable, and poor, and blind, and naked*" (Revelation 3:17).

The contrast between true wealth and temporal riches is further stated in Proverbs 11:24: "*There is that scattereth, and yet increaseth; and there is that withholdeth more than is meet, but it tendeth to poverty.*"

Jesus said of measuring riches, "*. . . Take heed, and beware of covetousness: for a man's life consisteth not in the abundance of the things which he possesseth*" (Luke 12:15).

17. Is poverty more a state of mind than a condition of the pocketbook?

There is no question that poverty is very real for those who experience it.

If it was not real, God would not command Christians to help the poor, nor would He judge those who take advantage of the poor.

The plea of Agur was, "*. . . Give me neither poverty nor riches . . . Lest I be full, and deny thee . . . or lest I be poor, and steal, and take the name of my God in vain*" (Proverbs 30:8–9).

Many of the difficulties which are associated with poverty, however, are the results of comparison and discontent rather than lack of funds.

A person can be poor by the world's standards, but very content because he has adequate food, clothing, and shelter. On the other hand, a person can have an abundance of money and still be discontent and unhappy.

CONTENTMENT
Realizing that God has given to me everything that I need for my present happiness.

---

18. Are the riches of the wicked valuable because they provide personal security?

No. Actually, the riches of the wicked are worse than useless. They are a dangerous liability and they breed insecurity. "*. . . In the revenues of the wicked is trouble*" (Proverbs 15:6). "*Better is little with the fear of the Lord than great treasure and trouble therewith*" (Proverbs 15:16).

The problems of the riches of the wicked are further described in Ecclesiastes 5:10, 12–13: "*He that loveth silver shall not be satisfied with silver; nor he that loveth abundance with increase . . . but the abundance of the rich will not suffer him to sleep. There is a sore evil which I have seen under the sun, namely, riches kept for the owners thereof to their hurt.*"

19. Should we adjust our standard of living to the income that God allows us to receive?

No. Our standard of living should be built around contentment with basics. If our income decreases, we should learn how to decrease our expenses or pray for God's provisions. If our income increases, we should determine how we can use this increase to advance God's kingdom, not our own pleasures. "*. . . If riches increase, set not your heart upon them*" (Psalm 62:10).

20. Is it unscriptural for a dedicated Christian to have an abundance of riches?

No. God does not condemn a Christian for possessing riches. He rebukes those who heap up riches for themselves (see Psalm 39:6), trust in their riches (see I Timothy 6:17), gain riches unjustly (see James 5:4), or put their love in riches (see Psalm 62:10).

God clearly teaches that the riches of a dedicated Christian are the result of God's grace and the basis for giving. "*And God is able to make all grace abound toward you; that ye, always having all sufficiency in all things, may abound to every good work*" (II Corinthians 9:8).

GOD'S CYCLE OF RICHES AND POVERTY

God does not view riches or poverty as permanent conditions in the life of an individual, family, or nation. They are variable, and they are related to higher purposes which God achieves through them.

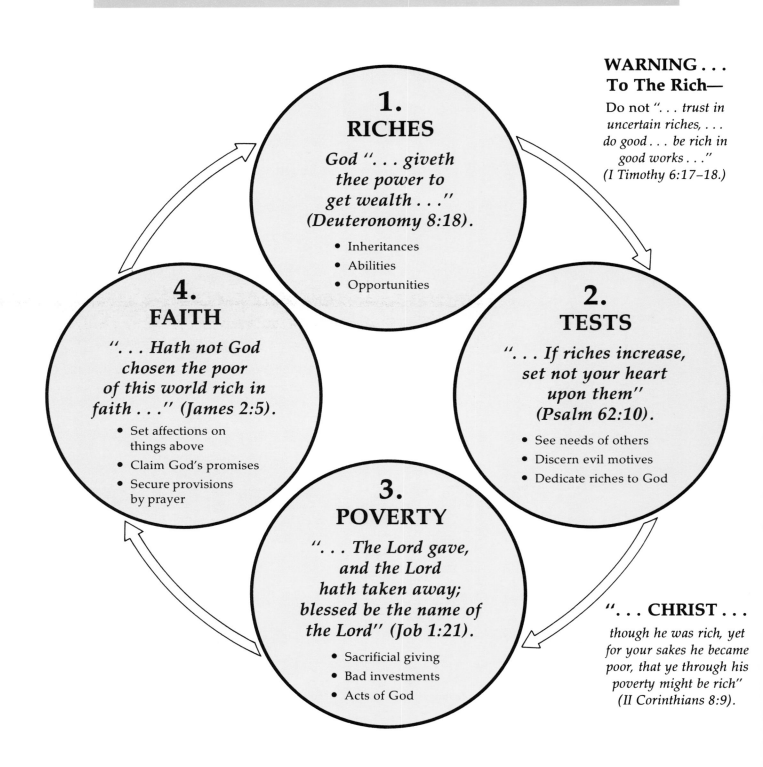

1. RICHES

God "... giveth thee power to get wealth ..." (Deuteronomy 8:18).

- Inheritances
- Abilities
- Opportunities

WARNING ...
To The Rich—

Do not "... trust in uncertain riches, ... do good ... be rich in good works ..." (I Timothy 6:17–18.)

2. TESTS

"... If riches increase, set not your heart upon them" (Psalm 62:10).

- See needs of others
- Discern evil motives
- Dedicate riches to God

"... CHRIST ... though he was rich, yet for your sakes he became poor, that ye through his poverty might be rich" (II Corinthians 8:9).

3. POVERTY

"... The Lord gave, and the Lord hath taken away; blessed be the name of the Lord" (Job 1:21).

- Sacrificial giving
- Bad investments
- Acts of God

4. FAITH

"... Hath not God chosen the poor of this world rich in faith ..." (James 2:5).

- Set affections on things above
- Claim God's promises
- Secure provisions by prayer

THE PURPOSE OF CYCLES—
TO TEACH CONTENTMENT WITH BASICS

Paul discovered the secret of living triumphantly above changing circumstances.

What Paul wrote:

"... I have learned ... to be content. I know both how to be abased, and I know how to abound: every where and in all things I am instructed both to be full and to be hungry, both to abound and to suffer need" (Philippians 4:11–12).

What he was teaching: The key to contentment.

The word which Paul used for *content* was *autarkēs*. It described the self-sufficient outlook of the Stoic philosophers of his day. The ultimate achievement of their teachings was to be independent of all external circumstances. They renounced all desire or want.

Paul gave their word a Christian meaning. Their ability to live without want was self-pride. Paul's ability was Christ's power flowing in and through him.

HE KNEW HOW TO ABOUND	HE KNEW HOW TO SUFFER NEED
• To be grateful for provisions that were given to him by the Philippian Christians	• To be silent about his needs when there was no provision for them.
• To enjoy an abundance of food	• To endure hunger when there was insufficient food
• To appreciate honor and recognition when it came	• To accept rejection, neglect, and abasement when it came
• To make use of material things when they were there	• To get along without material things when they were not there
• To appreciate physical comforts if they were available	• To do without physical comforts if they were not available
• To accept the help that came from others	• To draw upon the inner resources of Christ's strength
• To be pleased when outward circumstances worked out according to his plans	• To be cheerful when outward circumstances did not work out according to his plans
• To feel at home in friendly surroundings	• To be homeless and to face death

REDUCE YOUR BILLS AND IMPROVE
THE QUALITY OF YOUR LIFE

☐ Are there services that you are paying others to do that you could do, such as laundry and grass cutting?

☐ Do you subscribe to newspapers or magazines that you could do without?

☐ Can you cut down on long distance phone calls and write letters instead?

☐ Can you reduce the number of times that you eat out?

☐ Can you reduce the number of meals you have each week and spend that time in fasting and prayer?

☐ Are there possessions that you are not using that you could sell?

☐ Do you have high-depreciating items that you should sell?

☐ Are there credit cards that you should destroy?

☐ Can you reduce your heating bill or electric bill?

☐ Does your family pet require excessive time or money?

☐ Do you belong to clubs which require high fees or dues?

☐ Can you reduce your medical and dental bills by practicing preventive medicine?

☐ Can you cut down on your driving and do more walking?

☐ Do you spend an excessive amount of time or money on your hobbies?

☐ Do you spend money on entertainment or on habits which you should conquer?

Personal Commitment to Live Within My Income

In order to learn the qualities of contentment which God desires for my family and me to have, we will reduce our expenditures to well within our income.

Income last six months _____

Expenses last six months _____

Expense reduction next six months _____

Date _____

HOW DOES GOD ILLUSTRATE THE CYCLE OF RICHES AND POVERTY?

Match the symbols in each column with the following three people who went from riches to poverty to riches.

A. MOSES   B. JOSEPH   C. CHRIST

	☐ 1	☐ 2	☐ 3
RICHES GOD GAVE			
	☐ 4	☐ 5	☐ 6
RESPONSE TO RICHES			
	☐ 7	☐ 8	☐ 9
RESULTING POVERTY			
	☐ 10	☐ 11	☐ 12
ENTERING INTO NEW RICHES			

WHO FOLLOWED GOD'S CYCLE OF RICHES AND POVERTY?

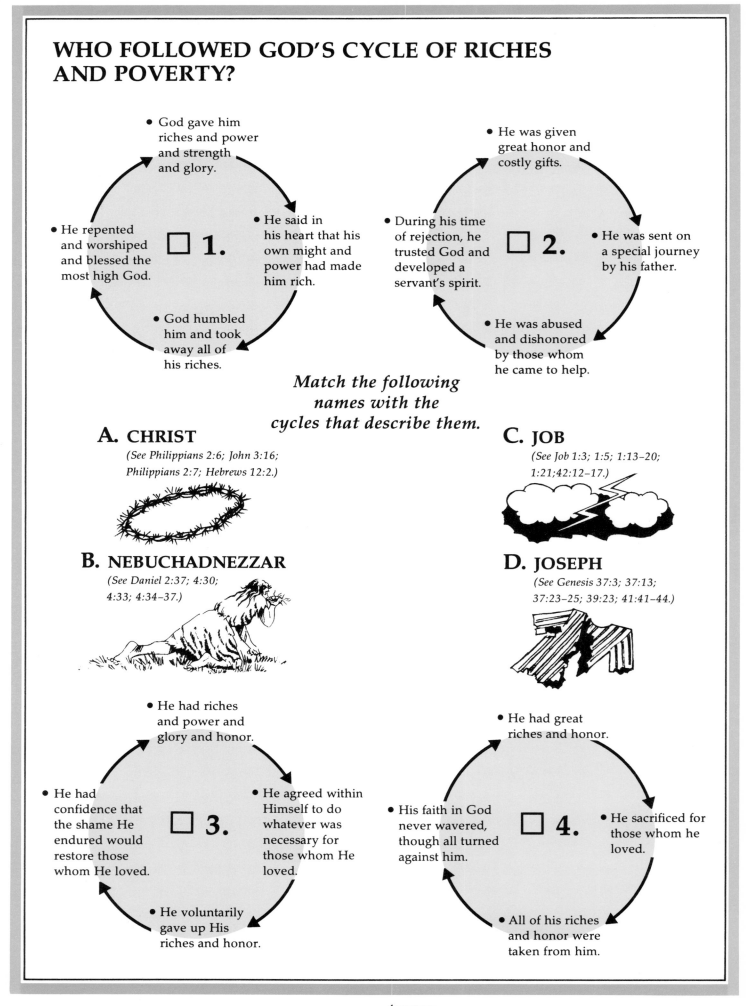

1.
- God gave him riches and power and strength and glory.
- He said in his heart that his own might and power had made him rich.
- God humbled him and took away all of his riches.
- He repented and worshiped and blessed the most high God.

2.
- He was given great honor and costly gifts.
- He was sent on a special journey by his father.
- He was abused and dishonored by those whom he came to help.
- During his time of rejection, he trusted God and developed a servant's spirit.

Match the following names with the cycles that describe them.

A. CHRIST
(See Philippians 2:6; John 3:16; Philippians 2:7; Hebrews 12:2.)

B. NEBUCHADNEZZAR
(See Daniel 2:37; 4:30; 4:33; 4:34–37.)

C. JOB
(See Job 1:3; 1:5; 1:13–20; 1:21;42:12–17.)

D. JOSEPH
(See Genesis 37:3; 37:13; 37:23–25; 39:23; 41:41–44.)

3.
- He had riches and power and glory and honor.
- He agreed within Himself to do whatever was necessary for those whom He loved.
- He voluntarily gave up His riches and honor.
- He had confidence that the shame He endured would restore those whom He loved.

4.
- He had great riches and honor.
- He sacrificed for those whom he loved.
- All of his riches and honor were taken from him.
- His faith in God never wavered, though all turned against him.

Answers: 1.B 2.D 3.A 4.C

100

APPLYING THE CYCLE OF RICHES AND POVERTY

Match each question with the best answer.

☐ **1.** Why does God allow the wicked to prosper?

A. Ill-gotten gain carries with it trouble and sorrow which do not let its possessor enjoy it; but *"the blessing of the Lord, it maketh rich, and he addeth no sorrow with it"* *(Proverbs 10:22).* (See also Proverbs 15:6, 27.)

☐ **2.** Why are some dedicated Christians poor?

B. The primary function of government is protection for the rich and poor and prosecution of any unjust gain. (See Proverbs 29:14; Romans 13:1–7.)

☐ **3.** Should the government take from the rich to give to the poor?

C. Poverty can be more imagined than real, since true riches are intangible. Thus, a family with love and only bread to eat is richer than a house of strife with steak dinners. (See Proverbs 17:1; 13:7; 15:17.)

☐ **4.** Is a "war on poverty" a good idea?

D. The goodness of God leads a man to repentance. The blessing of Godly parents is passed on to their children and God's principles of finance will work for whoever uses them. (See Romans 2:4; Matthew 5:45.)

☐ **5.** How does a totalitarian government counterfeit God's cycle of riches and poverty?

E. An unscrupulous government will build hatred toward the rich. It will then take control of large corporations. With these funds, it will give to the poor, but with the gifts come controls and the right to take from the poor at will. (See Proverbs 22:16, 22.)

☐ **6.** How do the riches of the wicked and the Godly differ?

F. God intends for the church to take care of the social welfare of its members. Christians are also to reach out to the lost, primarily with the Gospel and secondarily with food and clothing. (See I Timothy 5:1–16; Galatians 6:10.)

☐ **7.** Does God expect Christians to feed the poor?

G. God takes every Christian through a time of chastening and pruning to increase spiritual fruitfulness and to become more like Christ, Who focused on eternal riches. (See Hebrews 12:6–11; John 15; Colossians 3:1.)

☐ **8.** Can a person be poor and not know it?

H. To assume that poverty can be conquered is to overlook the basic purposes that God has for poverty. For this reason, Christ affirmed that there would always be some who are poor. (See I Samuel 2:7; Matthew 26:11.)

Answers: 1.D 2.G 3.B 4.H 5.E 6.A 7.F 8.C

MOSES
A man who rejected false treasures

DECEPTIVE RICHES

"Choosing rather to suffer affliction...than to enjoy the pleasures of sin for a season" (Hebrews 11:25).

9 DEVELOP SALES RESISTANCE

"It is naught, it is naught, saith the buyer: but when he is gone his way, then he boasteth" (Proverbs 20:14).

UNSEEN RICHES

"Esteeming the reproach of Christ greater riches than the treasures in Egypt: for he had respect unto the recompence of the reward" (Hebrews 11:26).

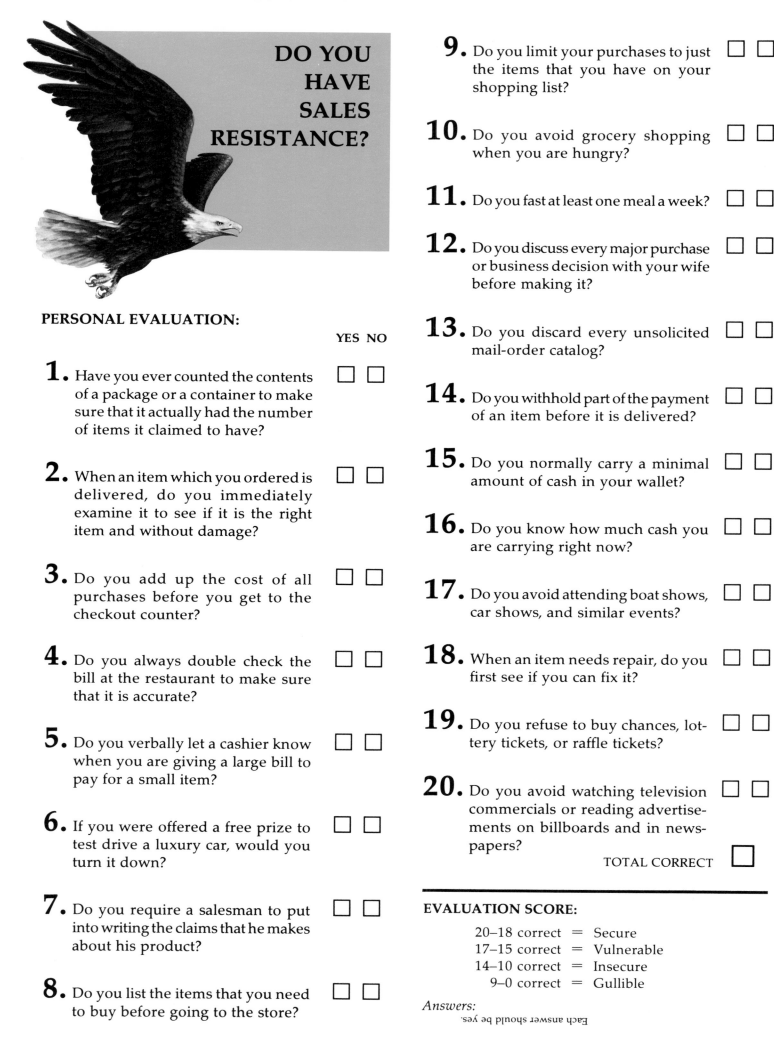

DO YOU HAVE SALES RESISTANCE?

PERSONAL EVALUATION:

YES NO

1. Have you ever counted the contents of a package or a container to make sure that it actually had the number of items it claimed to have?

2. When an item which you ordered is delivered, do you immediately examine it to see if it is the right item and without damage?

3. Do you add up the cost of all purchases before you get to the checkout counter?

4. Do you always double check the bill at the restaurant to make sure that it is accurate?

5. Do you verbally let a cashier know when you are giving a large bill to pay for a small item?

6. If you were offered a free prize to test drive a luxury car, would you turn it down?

7. Do you require a salesman to put into writing the claims that he makes about his product?

8. Do you list the items that you need to buy before going to the store?

9. Do you limit your purchases to just the items that you have on your shopping list?

10. Do you avoid grocery shopping when you are hungry?

11. Do you fast at least one meal a week?

12. Do you discuss every major purchase or business decision with your wife before making it?

13. Do you discard every unsolicited mail-order catalog?

14. Do you withhold part of the payment of an item before it is delivered?

15. Do you normally carry a minimal amount of cash in your wallet?

16. Do you know how much cash you are carrying right now?

17. Do you avoid attending boat shows, car shows, and similar events?

18. When an item needs repair, do you first see if you can fix it?

19. Do you refuse to buy chances, lottery tickets, or raffle tickets?

20. Do you avoid watching television commercials or reading advertisements on billboards and in newspapers?

TOTAL CORRECT

EVALUATION SCORE:

20–18 correct = Secure
17–15 correct = Vulnerable
14–10 correct = Insecure
9–0 correct = Gullible

Answers:
Each answer should be yes.

THE POWERFUL INFLUENCE OF ALLURING ADVERTISING

A study of Satan's conversation with Eve in the Garden of Eden reveals the subtle tactics and enormous influence of alluring advertising.

Consider how difficult it was for Satan to enter the perfect environment of the Garden of Eden and to cause Eve to be discontent.

1. Eve was the crowning achievement of God's creative power.

2. Eve had no sinful nature.

3. Eve lived in a perfect environment.

4. Eve had an abundance and variety of food.

5. Eve had no fear of poverty, sickness, old age, or death.

6. Eve had the perfect husband.

7. Eve's husband had daily fellowship with the Lord.

8. Eve and her husband walked with God in the cool of each day.

9. Eve had no tensions or pressures with in-laws, neighbors, or relatives.

10. Eve had a fulfilling role as helpmeet to her husband.

If Eve could become discontent with all of this, there is little hope for us unless we identify and reject the subtle tactics of alluring advertising.

THE SUBTLE TACTICS OF ADVERTISING

HEY KIDS!

GET THIS DREAM HOUSE FOR YOUR DOLL.

When advertisers appeal directly to children, by-passing the parents, they promote the very attitudes of discontent and rebellion that parents are responsible to correct.

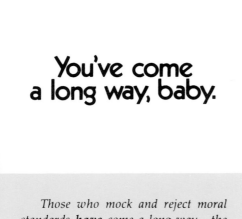

You've come a long way, baby.

*Those who mock and reject moral standards **have** come a long way—the wrong way.*

1. USING BEAUTIFUL AND SUCCESSFUL-APPEARING MODELS

"Now the serpent was more subtil than any beast of the field ..." (Genesis 3:1).

Before the serpent was cursed by God for its part in beguiling Eve, it must have been a very beautiful creature, possessing qualities of subtlety and charm.

When advertisers use attractive and successful-looking people as models, they are communicating the message that if you buy their product you will also become attractive and successful.

2. APPEALING DIRECTLY TO THOSE WHO ARE UNDER AUTHORITY

"... And he said unto the woman..." (Genesis 3:1).

It is significant to note that Satan did not approach Adam first. He did not even get to Eve through Adam. He went directly to Eve. Once she was mentally and emotionally ready to follow his instructions, he used her to influence her authority.

When an advertiser aims his campaign at those who are under authority, he is by-passing their God-given protection. The result is often improper pressure on the authority, which can cause him to override God-given cautions.

3. CREATING DOUBTS ABOUT ESTABLISHED RULES

"... Hath God said, Ye shall not eat of every tree of the garden?" (Genesis 3:1).

There was only one limitation which God placed on Adam and Eve in the garden. They were not to eat of the fruit of one particular tree. Satan caused Eve to focus on that one restriction and convinced her that she would be happier and more successful if it was removed. In reality, the opposite was true.

Alluring advertising encourages one generation to ignore, question, or ridicule those standards of their parents which are based on God's Word.

4. REJECTING WARNINGS

". . . Ye shall not surely die" (Genesis 3:4).

Even though God clearly warned Eve that she would experience death by eating the forbidden fruit, she allowed Satan to convince her that the warning did not apply to her.

Most people tend to believe that what happens to others will not happen to them. Those who promote products which are damaging to health or morals count on this tendency. By focusing on the assumed benefits of a product, they effectively deny or disregard the warnings of danger.

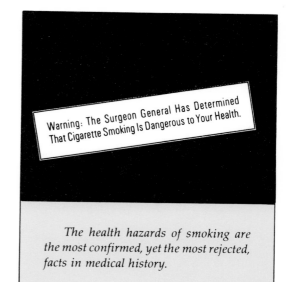

Warning: The Surgeon General Has Determined That Cigarette Smoking Is Dangerous to Your Health.

The health hazards of smoking are the most confirmed, yet the most rejected, facts in medical history.

5. CREATING DISCONTENTMENT

"For God doth know that in the day ye eat thereof, then your eyes shall be opened . . ." (Genesis 3:5).

Satan convinced Eve that she was missing a vital ingredient to a happy and successful life. In reality, God had already given her everything that she needed for her happiness, security, and fulfillment.

Alluring advertising promotes attitudes of self-rejection and discontentment. It focuses on what we do not have, and it encourages instant gratification.

Along with the "you owe it to yourself" philosophy, there is the encouragement to gratify your wants now and make payments in the future.

Why not change your life for something better?

Self-rejection is a basic problem with many people. Advertisers know this, and instead of curing the problem, they only treat the symptoms.

6. PROMOTING AN INDEPENDENT SPIRIT

". . . Ye shall be as gods . . ." (Genesis 3:5).

Satan's basic temptation to Eve was to be her own boss, and to have equal rights with her husband and with God. Eve assumed that, if she were to eat the forbidden fruit, she would have all that she needed to become independent.

Alluring advertising promotes the delusive idea of being equal with authority. It fosters divisive independence by encouraging each person to do what is right in his own eyes. It promotes the idea that we can isolate ourselves from any restrictions or hindrances to living out our dreams and fantasies.

Get out of the rat race with your own business.

Those who have started their own businesses will usually tell you that the "rat race" really began when they became self-employed.

7. DEPENDING ON HUMAN REASONING

". . . Knowing good and evil" (Genesis 3:5).

Satan wants us to choose between good and evil with our minds. God wants us to discern between good and evil through His Spirit. (See I John 4:1.)

The very temptation of Satan illustrated the consequence of relying on human understanding rather than trusting in divine discernment.

Advertisers are very aware that people flatter themselves into thinking that they can make wise choices by the limited information and evidences which are presented to them.

8. OVERRIDING CAUTIONS TO MEET BASIC NEEDS

"And when the woman saw that the tree was good for food . . ." (Genesis 3:6).

Satan effectively planted doubts in Eve's mind about God's motives and about the benefits of the forbidden fruit. Then Eve used rationalization to remove God's warnings.

Advertisers understand basic human needs and wants such as food, clothing, shelter, recognition, and companionship.

Products that do not fulfill basic needs are often associated with those which do. This allows the buyer to easily justify unwise or harmful purchases.

9. APPEALING TO THE LUST OF THE EYE

". . . And that it was pleasant to the eyes . . ." (Genesis 3:6).

Eve had never tasted the forbidden fruit. She had tasted other fruit which was very delicious and enjoyable. When she considered violating God's limitations, she allowed her eye to associate the forbidden fruit with previous pleasurable experiences. The fruit itself was appealing to the eye.

Alluring advertising uses pictures of elegant living, beautiful women, and "rugged" men to imply that these things come with buying the product.

10. OFFERING FULFILLMENT APART FROM GOD

"*. . . A tree to be desired to make one wise . . .*" (Genesis 3:6).

Eve had daily contact with the God of all wisdom! She also had continuous contact with her husband, and he had been personally trained by God. What need would she have for a new and different source of wisdom?

The essence of idolatry is looking to something else for that which only God can provide.

Deceptive advertising leads people to believe that they can find security, love, and happiness, and meet their needs through people or things rather than through God.

> ## Pleasure is where you find it.
>
> *God warns that there will be many who will be ". . . lovers of pleasures more than lovers of God . . . from such turn away" (II Timothy 3:4–5).*

11. DESIGNING MISLEADING PHRASES

Only three sentences beguiled Eve.

Satan is a master at conveying false conclusions with partial truth and incomplete ideas. He used one question and two short statements with Eve. The question involved only fourteen words, and the two statements included only thirty-two words.

Alluring advertising uses nebulous "weasel" words or incomplete phrases to prompt the buyer to fill in the blanks and arrive at false conclusions.

Few people stop to analyze the accuracy of their conclusions when they read short advertising words or phrases such as: "This product offers more" (More of what?); "Tests prove this product is better" (What was tested? Better than what?).

> ## When you know what counts.
>
> *The cigarette company which uses this statement pictures a runner smoking while sitting down. When a runner knows what counts, he does not smoke.*

12. DENYING THE PRODUCT'S WEAKEST POINT

"*. . . Ye shall not surely die . . . ye shall be as gods . . .*" (Genesis 3:4–5).

Satan did not discuss the quality of the forbidden fruit, its taste, or its appearance. He focused on the false idea that Eve would not die by eating it but instead would experience a new dimension of life as a god.

Alluring advertising takes the weakest point of a product and tries to turn it into a positive quality. The liquor industry focuses on life; in reality its product produces death. A cigarette company advertises satisfaction. That is one thing the buyer does not get. If cigarettes satisfied, one pack would do it for life.

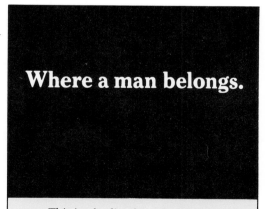

> ### Where a man belongs.
>
> *This is a by-line for a cigarette advertisement. It implies that to be a real man you must smoke this brand. A real man can break wrong habits. A wise man does not begin them.*

THE CONSEQUENCES OF ALLURING ADVERTISING

1. THE LIVES OF OTHERS ARE DAMAGED

"... She took of the fruit ... and gave also unto her husband ..." (Genesis 3:6).

The decisions that we make not only affect our lives, but the lives of those whom we influence. Adam followed Eve's example and became even more of a transgressor than she.

It was through Adam's transgression that sin entered the world and death passed upon everyone.

It is through the smoking and "social drinking" of parents that many teenagers have justified drugs and alcohol.

What parents allow in moderation, their children will often do in excess.

2. THE LOSS IS USUALLY IRREVOCABLE

"And the eyes of them both were opened, and they knew that they were naked ..." (Genesis 3:7).

Rather than gaining what she expected, Eve lost what she had. She lost her relationship with the Lord, her sinless state, her ideal environment, her perfect husband, her good health, and a host of other benefits that God had provided for her.

When we fall victim to alluring advertising, we soon realize our mistake. By that time, however, it is usually too late.

3. THERE IS BLAME AND JUSTIFICATION

"And the man said, The woman whom thou gavest to be with me, she gave me of the tree. . . . And the woman said, The serpent beguiled me . . ." (Genesis 3:12–13).

When mistakes are made, someone must take the blame. The natural inclination of the one who made the mistake is to justify himself and to blame others. This results in resentment and bitterness.

4. THE DIFFICULTY OF LIFE INCREASES

"... I will greatly multiply thy sorrow. . . . In the sweat of thy face shalt thou eat bread ..." (Genesis 3:16, 19).

Wrong decisions bring new limitations. God designs these limitations as reminders and motivations not to make the same mistake again.

Those who fall prey to habit-forming products must establish daily disciplines to overcome new appetites.

Those who get deeply into debt become servant to those who have lent them the money.

Those who become victims of one financial scheme often have their names given to similar promoters who will also prey upon them.

5. THE FRUIT OF DESTRUCTION BEGINS

"Therefore the Lord God sent him forth from the garden of Eden . . ." (Genesis 3:23).

A Christian who becomes involved in the philosophy of alluring advertising will become carnal in his thinking and actions.

The spiritual consequence of a carnal mind is defined in Romans 8:6–7: *"For to be carnally minded is death; but to be spiritually minded is life and peace. Because the carnal mind is enmity against God. . . ."*

HOW TO BUILD SALES RESISTANCE

1 EXPECT SALESMEN TO OVERRATE THEIR PRODUCTS

"The simple believeth every word: but the prudent man looketh well to his going" *(Proverbs 14:15).*

A salesman is trained to make sales. To be successful, he will point out the positive features of a product. You must search out the negative ones. He will make sweeping claims. You must establish their accuracy. He will put pressure on you to buy immediately. You must wait until you have all of the facts.

2 LEARN TO ENJOY THE POSSESSIONS YOU HAVE

"The slothful man roasteth not that which he took in hunting: but the substance of a diligent man is precious" *(Proverbs 12:27).*

The goal of most advertising is to make us discontent with what we already have. What we have is labeled as outdated and inadequate. What we do not have is promoted as the missing ingredient to our happiness or success.

We can enjoy our possessions by remembering that they are entrusted to us in order to fulfill God-given responsibilities. We should, therefore, give them the care which demonstrates that they really belong to God.

3 MAKE USE OF THE THINGS IN LIFE THAT ARE FREE

". . . A man's life consisteth not in the abundance of the things which he possesseth" *(Luke 12:15).*

The Apostle Paul realized that material possessions hindered his ability to grasp the riches of Christ. Therefore, he was willing to experience the loss of all things and even count them as worthless in order to gain a greater understanding of Christ.

Through the riches that we have in Christ, we are able to enjoy the splendor of His creation, fellowship with other people, and the depths of His Word.

4 BUILD PERSONAL DISCIPLINES

"A gracious woman retaineth honour: and strong men retain riches" *(Proverbs 11:16).*

God expects us to develop disciplines in food, drink, sleep, friends, thoughts, words, tithing, and other areas of our Christian life. God gives us, as Christians, the desire and power to develop this discipline by engrafting Scripture into our lives and claiming our victory in Christ. By using this power, we will also have the wisdom and strength to exercise proper sales resistance.

BUILD SALES RESISTANCE

PERSONAL DISCIPLINES	HOW THEY BUILD SALES RESISTANCE
1. Schedule times of fasting (after checking with your physician).	Possessions lose their appeal.
2. Read Proverbs each day.	Wrong types of people will be identified and their motives exposed.
3. Give God weekly tithes.	Treasures and affections are transferred to heaven.
4. Find out the full price before evaluating a product.	Emotions are not allowed to overrule sound reason.
5. Maintain a pure thought life.	Alluring advertising, which uses sensuality, will be avoided.
6. Seek out counsel before buying.	Impulse buying will be eliminated.
7. Pray for and about needed items.	Supernatural provisions and direction will be experienced.
8. Avoid "sales" on items that you were not intending to buy.	Items that you do not need will not be purchased.
9. Check with your wife before buying.	Her cautions can help you to avoid unwise financial decisions.

Personal Commitment to Building Sales Resistance

From this day forward my expenditures will be guarded and guided by the disciplines required for wise sales resistance.

I will analyze advertising and require documentation for advertising claims.

Date _____

CAN YOU DETECT SUBTLE MESSAGES IN THESE SLOGANS?

Match the subtle advertising techniques with the clearest example.

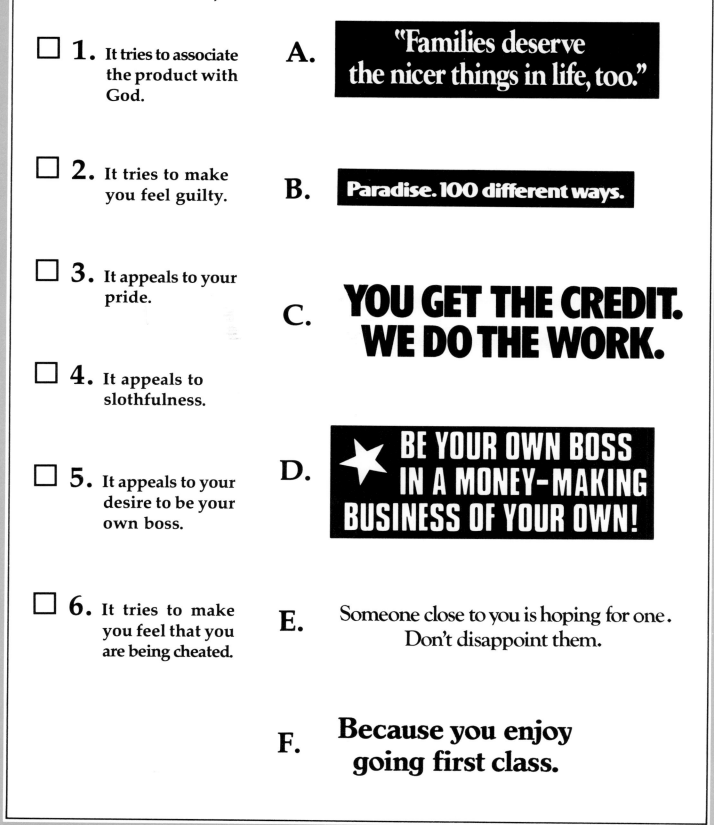

☐ **1.** It tries to associate the product with God.

A. "Families deserve the nicer things in life, too."

☐ **2.** It tries to make you feel guilty.

B. Paradise. 100 different ways.

☐ **3.** It appeals to your pride.

C. YOU GET THE CREDIT. WE DO THE WORK.

☐ **4.** It appeals to slothfulness.

☐ **5.** It appeals to your desire to be your own boss.

D. ★ BE YOUR OWN BOSS IN A MONEY-MAKING BUSINESS OF YOUR OWN!

☐ **6.** It tries to make you feel that you are being cheated.

E. Someone close to you is hoping for one. Don't disappoint them.

F. Because you enjoy going first class.

Answers: 1.B 2.E 3.F 4.C 5.D 6.A

113

CAN YOU RELATE SATAN'S TEMPTATIONS TO ALLURING ADVERTISING?

Match the tactics of alluring advertising with Satan's temptation of Eve. (See Genesis 3:1–6.)

SATAN'S TEMPTATION OF EVE

☐ **1.** *"Now the serpent was more subtil than any beast of the field. . . ."*

☐ **2.** *". . . And he said unto the woman. . . ."*

☐ **3.** *". . . Hath God said. . . ."*

☐ **4.** *". . . Ye shall not surely die."*

☐ **5.** *". . . In the day ye eat thereof, then your eyes shall be opened. . . ."*

☐ **6.** *". . . Ye shall be as gods. . . ."*

☐ **7.** *". . . The tree was good for food. . . ."*

☐ **8.** *". . . It was pleasant to the eyes. . . ."*

☐ **9.** *". . . A tree to be desired to make one wise. . . ."*

ALLURING TACTICS

A. Creating discontentment

B. Appealing to the lust of the eye

C. Rejecting harmful consequences

D. Using successful-appearing models

E. Promoting independence from authority

F. Justifying unwise purchases in meeting basic needs

G. Creating doubts about established limitations

H. Appealing to pride

I. Appealing directly to those under authority

Answers: 1.D 2.I 3.G 4.C 5.A 6.E 7.F 8.B 9.H

WHAT TACTICS DO YOU SEE IN THESE SLOGANS?

Choose the slogan that best illustrates each tactic.

☐ **1.** Appealing to those who are under authority.

☐ **2.** Creating doubts about established moral standards.

☐ **3.** Rejecting warnings.

☐ **4.** Encouraging an independent spirit.

☐ **5.** Trusting human reasoning.

☐ **6.** Using basic human needs as a motivation to buy.

☐ **7.** Offering fulfillment that only God can give.

☐ **8.** Using misleading phrases.

☐ **9.** Making positive statements about the product's most negative aspect.

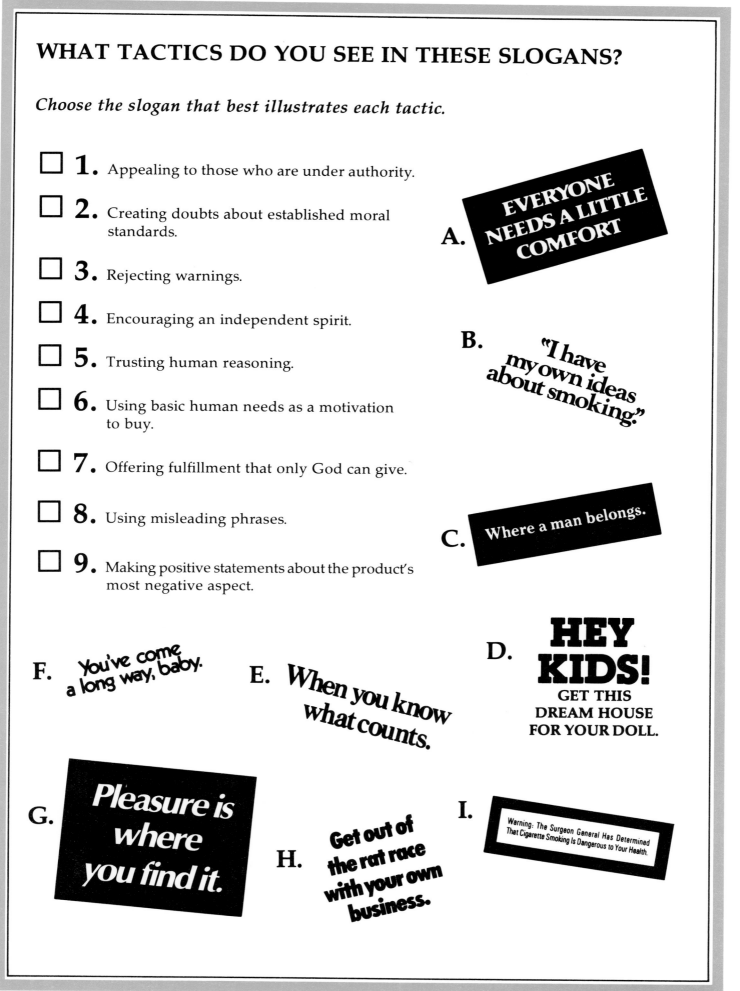

A. **EVERYONE NEEDS A LITTLE COMFORT**

B. "I have my own ideas about smoking."

C. Where a man belongs.

D. **HEY KIDS!** GET THIS DREAM HOUSE FOR YOUR DOLL.

F. You've come a long way, baby.

E. When you know what counts.

G. **Pleasure is where you find it.**

H. Get out of the rat race with your own business.

I. Warning: The Surgeon General Has Determined That Cigarette Smoking Is Dangerous to Your Health.

Answers: 1.D 2.F 3.I 4.H 5.B 6.A 7.G 8.E 9.C

PETER
A great exposer of evil motives

HIS WORKS WERE CONVINCING

"... Pray ye to the Lord for me, that none of these things which ye have spoken come upon me" (Acts 8:24).

10 FLEE FROM THE HIDDEN TRAPS OF SWINDLERS

"A prudent man forseeth the evil, and hideth himself; but the simple pass on, and are punished" (Proverbs 27:12).

MOTIVES PERCEIVED

When Simon offered Peter money to buy the power of the Holy Spirit, Peter said, "Thy money perish with thee.... For I perceive that thou art in the gall of bitterness, and in the bond of iniquity" (Acts 8:20, 23).

HOW WELL DO YOU UNDERSTAND FRAUDS?

PERSONAL EVALUATION:

TRUE FALSE

1. Frauds are difficult to detect because they appeal to human strength. ☐ ☐

2. Swindlers find most of their victims among the elderly. ☐ ☐

3. People who have been swindled once usually have learned their lesson. ☐ ☐

4. There are only a few basic types of frauds, but they are used with repeated success. ☐ ☐

5. An effective swindle has four parts: the bait, the hook, the plant, and the bite. ☐ ☐

6. Swindlers usually work alone. ☐ ☐

7. Frauds are hard to pass up, because they promise to fulfill our secret dreams. ☐ ☐

8. A person who is informed about frauds can usually avoid them. ☐ ☐

9. One of the most lucrative types of swindles involves promises of medical cures. ☐ ☐

10. The invitation to "be your own boss" is an effective come-on for a fraud. ☐ ☐

11. Swindlers often use sensual pleasure to lure their victims. ☐ ☐

12. Once you discover that you have been swindled, there is very little that you can do about it. ☐ ☐

13. A sales program that involves a pyramid profit structure is illegal. ☐ ☐

14. The language of the swindler is deceptive, because it avoids flowery adjectives and focuses on facts. ☐ ☐

15. A person who refuses to profit from someone else's loss will avoid many frauds. ☐ ☐

TOTAL CORRECT ☐

EVALUATION SCORE:

15–14 correct = Clear understanding
13–12 correct = Fair understanding
11–9 correct = Poor understanding
8–0 correct = Don't talk to strangers

HOW PETER RECOGNIZED A FRAUD
Acts 8:9–25

- He saw that the fraud was a new and immature Christian (vs. 13).

- He realized that the fraud had been involved in sorcery and deception (vs. 9).

- He knew that the fraud enjoyed popularity and admiration (vs. 10).

- He detected wrong motives when the fraud offered him money to buy the power of the Holy Spirit (vss. 18–20).

- He discerned the root problems of bitterness and impurity (vs. 23).

Answers:

1. False 2. False 3. False 4. False 5. True 6. False 7. True 8. False 9. True 10. True 11. True 12. True 13. True 14. False 15. True

LEARN HOW TO DETECT FRAUDS AND SWINDLERS

THE PROBLEM

Every year millions of people fall victim to clever schemes which are designed to take their money in exchange for worthless ideas or products.

Swindlers are experts in their trade. Once given a hearing, few swindlers miss their mark. They use their intended victims' feelings of inferiority, guilt, greed, and other human weaknesses to their fullest advantage.

THE TARGETS

Swindlers prey upon the self-confident. They look for those who are their own authority and who make their own decisions. The young and the elderly feel their sting most painfully.

The middle-aged victims are often too embarrassed to admit that they were cheated. Both the educated and the uneducated, the rich and the poor, the religious and the atheist, and men and women are all easy marks for frauds and swindlers.

THE TRAPS

Frauds and schemes are so numerous and varied that it would be difficult to protect the public by trying to list all of them.

To make matters worse, even people who have been trained to detect swindles have been cheated. In fact, many who were swindled once fall victim again, in the same or a different scheme!

DETECT THE  TRAP OF THE SWINDLER

3 THE PLANT—*Documentation*

Swindlers often work in teams. They place people around you who will get excited about the scheme. Swindlers will give you testimonials as though they were satisfied customers.

The "plants" will show you phony tests and demonstrations. The group pressure of the swindler and his accomplices will reinforce and justify your unscriptural motives, while at the same time keeping your focus on the bait.

The "plant" is there to reassure you. He and the swindler may even let you win the first time around in order to set you up for a much bigger loss.

1 THE BAIT—*Secret desires*

The swindler takes your secret dreams and assures you that you can have them fulfilled. His bait involves your human "needs" and desires.

"How would you like to double your money in only three weeks?"

"Are you interested in a guaranteed program to lose weight?"

"Would you like to be the boss of your own prosperous company?"

4 THE BITE—*Pressure to act*

In order to get you to "bite," pressure is put upon you. You are told that time is running out. If you do not act now, you will lose the opportunity of a lifetime.

The swindler and his "plants" will assure you that someone else is waiting in line if you do not accept their offer, or that the price will go up tomorrow.

A further reason for this pressure is to stop you from getting counsel from those who would know better or could see through the fraud.

Protection from swindlers is lost when you get out from under God-ordained authority and choose to ignore Scriptural principles or inward cautions.

2 THE HOOK—*True statements*

The incredible success of a swindler is achieved by the hook which he puts with his bait.

The hook involves true statements which penetrate the hidden motives of our fallen human nature—the desire to get something for nothing, the eagerness to gain at someone else's expense, impatience with unchangeable defects, and the rejection of growing old.

> *The only protection against the swindler is a commitment to follow Scriptural principles without compromise.*

LEARN HOW TO ESCAPE FRAUDS BY APPLYING SCRIPTURAL PRINCIPLES

TYPE OF FRAUDS	PRINCIPLES OF ESCAPE *

1. QUACK "CURES"

Medical quackery thrives because people want to believe that there is a quick cure for any illness and an easy way to correct any physical imperfection.

God's Word gives basic guidelines on different types of illnesses and proper steps to respond to them. However, the swindler exploits his victims by advertisements which combine mysticism, pseudoscience, and sensationalism.

STOP AND THINK . . .

If the claims of a swindler were really true, he would not have to depend on advertising. Word-of-mouth recommendations would bring more business than he could handle.

---

2. "BE YOUR OWN BOSS" FRAUDS

The swindler will create an unrealistic picture of how you can avoid the pressures of working for someone else.

He explains how easy it is to make all of the profit that your boss is making. All that you have to do, he claims, is to form your own company. To help you get started, the swindler has just the right opportunity; and for several thousand dollars it can be yours.

1. APPLY SCRIPTURAL PRINCIPLES OF SELF-ACCEPTANCE

When we view ourselves from God's perspective and accept His design and purpose for unchangeable physical features, we remove the problem of inferiority and resolve the pressure of trying to change what cannot be changed.

When we are obedient to basic Scriptural principles and through them remove such destructive pressures as guilt, bitterness, greed, worry, insecurity, fear, envy, and jealousy, we avoid unnecessary illnesses and diseases.

By developing inward character, we are able to see how God is using defects and infirmities to conform us to the image of Christ.

This mature outlook frees us from the desperation which drives many people to the medical quack.

2. RESPOND PROPERLY TO AUTHORITY

God warns that any person who gets out from under the protection of authority is exposed to destructive temptations.

People who have evil motives are usually able to detect a rebellious spirit. Rebels become easy prey. *"The eye that mocketh at his father, and despiseth to obey his mother, the ravens of the valley shall pick it out, and the young eagles shall eat it"* (Proverbs 30:17).

---

* These principles are taught in detail during the Institute in Basic Youth Conflicts' *Basic Seminar.*

TYPE OF FRAUDS	PRINCIPLES OF ESCAPE

What the "be your own boss" swindler does not explain to you is that:

- The expensive franchise which you must buy from him is with a little-known or nonexistent parent company.

- The overpriced starter kit or training program does not guarantee any success in your business.

- The exorbitant price of your supplies, if you can get them, greatly decreases any profits you might make.

- The success you may have will soon be copied or tapped into by unscrupulous competitors or partners.

- In order for you to make any money, you will usually involve your friends in the same scheme and expose them to the same dangers.

3. "PROFIT FROM MISFORTUNE" SCHEMES

The famous expression "you can't cheat an honest man" may apply to this group of fraudulent traps. The swindler will tell you how you can gain by someone else's loss or misfortune.

One example of this group of fraudulent schemes is the "pigeon drop."

A stranger engages you in conversation at some public location. Soon another stranger approaches. Suddenly the three of you discover an envelope full of money.

One of the strangers just happens to work for a banker or lawyer. He proceeds to call the boss for counsel on what to do with the money.

The boss says that it is appropriate to divide the money three ways, since it was probably gained illegally. However, each of you should put up a good faith deposit to prove that you could repay the money if the owner were to claim it later.

The strangers put up their money and accompany you to the bank to withdraw your money. They tell you to wait while they deposit the good faith money in a separate account.

One of the primary purposes for God's structure of authority is to protect us from unscrupulous people and unwise decisions. God will usually give our authorities cautions when we are about to make a wrong decision.

Christ's parable of the prodigal son provides a vivid picture of the financial calamity which comes to those who reject authority.

GAIN PROTECTION BY . . .

1. *Asking your authorities to explain their experiences with frauds and swindlers.*
2. *Refusing to make business decisions without first obtaining counsel from your authorities.*

---

3. OBTAIN A CLEAR CONSCIENCE

A clear conscience not only involves removing the guilt of past failures; it also involves establishing a set of Scriptural standards for any present or future business dealings.

The foundation of a clear conscience is contained in the two greatest commandments, ". . . *Thou shalt love the Lord thy God with all thy heart, and with all thy soul, and with all thy mind,*" and ". . . *Thou shalt love thy neighbour as thyself*" (Matthew 22:37, 39).

In order to love the Lord, we must have Godly motives; and we must delight in the things of eternal value, rather than secretly coveting riches and temporal possessions.

To love our neighbor as ourselves requires protecting him from loss and watching out for his welfare.

Based on these goals, the following guidelines must be used:

- Never engage in a business deal that requires you to compromise your standards even slightly.

THE "QUACK" LANGUAGE OF SWINDLERS

A. Amazing	**N.** Natural
B. Breakthrough	**O.** Original
C. Clinical	**P.** Proven
D. Discovery	**Q.** Quick
E. Exciting	**R.** Revolutionary
F. Fast-working	**S.** Satisfactory
G. Guaranteed	**T.** Technology
H. Home-cure	**U.** Unsolicited
I. Instant	**V.** Vanish
J. Just	**W.** Wonder
K. Know-how	**X.** X-ray
L. Laboratory	**Y.** Youthful
M. Miraculous	**Z.** Zero-in

TYPE OF FRAUDS	PRINCIPLES OF ESCAPE

That is the last you see of them or your money.

Other schemes are built on your investing money in a slightly illegal venture and receiving big returns. The swindler then uses your guilt to force you to invest in an even bigger venture, only to lose it all.

4. "NEW INVENTION" SHAM

Inventors are, by their very nature, incurable optimists. They do not look at failure as an end, but rather as being one step closer to achievement.

Nor is time a problem for an inventor. Weeks, months, and even years can slip by while the inventor's mind is absorbed in working out solutions and beginning new inventions.

The claims which an inventor makes for his invention may sound impossible, but the technological advances of our day have made ready believers of the most skeptical minds.

Swindlers can gain control of you by encouraging you to violate the law. They will assure you that no one will ever find out or that everyone is doing it, but they will return to blackmail you.

- Reject business ventures which require others to lose so that you will win.

A classic and now illegal example of this is the "Pyramid Club." Another illustration is an offer of a free car if you can get ten of your friends to buy an overpriced car.

4. YIELD YOUR PERSONAL RIGHTS TO GOD

Once we dedicate our money to the Lord, we give Him the right to direct its expenditure. This means that we must not violate any Scriptural principles in the course of managing money.

The following questions are based upon Scriptural directives:

- Is the inventor someone whom you know personally, and is he living by God's principles?

TYPE OF FRAUDS	PRINCIPLES OF ESCAPE

Swindlers take all of these factors into account as they dazzle the imaginations of investors with the potential of a fortune when a certain invention hits the market.

False claims for new inventions give the swindler a built-in advantage—the factor of secrecy. He is easily able to convince his victims that they should not tell others about the invention lest it be copied and they lose their big opportunity.

This secrecy effectively hinders the victim from getting proper counsel until it is too late.

Once a swindler has your money on an investment scheme, he is always able to return to get more money in order to protect your original investment.

"... If thou hast stricken thy hand with a stranger, Thou are snared with the words of thy mouth, thou art taken with the words of thy mouth. Do this now, my son, and deliver thyself..." (Proverbs 6:1–3).

- Has the inventor demonstrated his ability in other inventions, and has he wisely managed the money from them?

   "But let every man prove his own work, and then shall he have rejoicing in himself alone, and not in another" (Galatians 6:4).

- Are you looking at an invention as a source of income that is needed for your financial responsibilities?

   "He that tilleth his land shall have plenty of bread: but he that followeth after vain persons shall have poverty enough" (Proverbs 28:19).

5. "EQUIPMENT REPAIR" CLAIMS

Perhaps the most common and prevalent of all frauds is in the repair and replacement of equipment.

Every day, legions of "experts" fan out into neighborhoods and offer to give you a free examination of your chimney, roof, furnace, car, or anything else that is vital to you.

During the free inspection, a major problem is "discovered." This requires an expensive new replacement which they just happen to be selling.

The swindlers in this vast field thrive because of the frustration, impatience, and ignorance of their victims.

Swindlers know that most people do not really understand the facts about the products which they own and which need fixing. They also realize that most people refuse to live with an irritation and will pay extra money to remove it.

5. RESPOND CORRECTLY TO IRRITATIONS

A source of irritation is a frustration-producing agent over which we have little or no control.

Irritations in the home certainly include faulty appliances, a leaky roof, broken plumbing, a car that does not start, and maintenance on the things that do work.

Responding properly to irritations means that we welcome them as friends rather than resenting them as intruders. (See James 1:2–5.)

When an irritation occurs, God wants us to turn to Him first rather than to repairmen. Here are the responses that He is looking for:

- Thank God for the purposes that He has for this irritation, and realize that He can remove it any time that He wishes. (See I Thessalonians 5:18.)

- Recognize that God's primary purpose in allowing irritations is to teach you patience. (See Romans 5:1–5.)

TYPE OF FRAUDS	PRINCIPLES OF ESCAPE

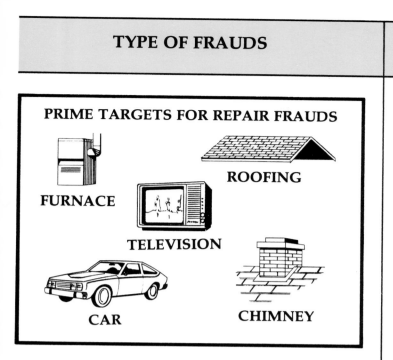

PRIME TARGETS FOR REPAIR FRAUDS

FURNACE

ROOFING

TELEVISION

CAR

CHIMNEY

- Accept the irritation as an opportunity to learn as much as you can about the item needing repair. Seek as much counsel and do as much research on your own as you can.

- After taking the above steps, you should be ready to call a reputable repairman if you cannot make the repairs yourself.

6. SENSUAL PLEASURE TRAP

The most painful and destructive kinds of swindlers are those who lure people to moral impurity. They offer their victims the most fulfillment and render them the most helpless.

The charms of a sensual woman or an evil man are highly trained to get rather than to give. The tragedy is that they get more than a man's treasure. They also ruin his body, soul, and reputation.

So dangerous is the bait of this fraud that God fills the first part of Proverbs with urgent warnings to young men. Scripture gives tragic testimonials of broken heroes who fall prey to sensual frauds, and young men like Timothy are urged to flee youthful lusts. (See II Timothy 2:22.)

Both Solomon, the wisest man who ever lived, and Samson, the strongest man who ever lived, fell to Satan's trap of sensual pleasure.

The sensual trap encourages men to enjoy pleasure for the moment and then forces them to pay money to protect the future. The hopelessness of escaping such a trap, once it is sprung, is explained in Proverbs 6:27–35.

6. GAIN MORAL FREEDOM

Moral freedom is not a license to fulfill sensual pleasure. It is the power to reject sensual temptations.

God promises victory over sensual habits when we engraft Scripture into our soul and quote it whenever we are tempted. He also expects us to detect sensual women and to flee from them.

SIGNS OF A SENSUAL WOMAN *

- Saucy and pert
- Seductively dressed
- Unpredictable responses
- Solicitous eyes
- Flattering tongue
- Impudent attitudes
- Independent spirit
- Sensually perfumed
- Persuasive

STEPS OF ACTION
- Avoid her. (See Proverbs 5:8.)
- Flee from her. (See II Timothy 2:22.)
- Do not look at her. (See Proverbs 4:25.)
- Do not think about her. (See Job 31:1.)

* Based on Proverbs 7:10–22.

STEPS TO TAKE IF YOU ARE SWINDLED

1. Quickly pursue any possibility of escape

". . . Go, humble thyself . . . Give not sleep to thine eyes, nor slumber to thine eyelids. Deliver thyself as a roe from the hand of the hunter, and as a bird from the hand of the fowler" (Proverbs 6:3–5).

2. Get under the protection of God-given authority

Explain what has happened to the proper government officials and to the Better Business Bureau. Seek their counsel for any steps that can be taken.

"For rulers are not a terror to good works, but to the evil . . ." (Romans 13:3).

3. Cry out to God

Very often God allows financial tragedies in order to direct our attention back to Him. He also instructs the widow to cry out to Him if she is the victim of a swindle.

"Ye shall not afflict any widow, or fatherless child. If thou afflict them in any wise, and they cry at all unto me, I will surely hear their cry" (Exodus 22:22–23).

4. Determine what caused your susceptibility to fraud, and take steps to correct it

☐ Were you out from under God-given authority?

☐ Were you the victim of a guilty conscience?

☐ Did you have greed and attempt to get rich quickly?

☐ Because you were lazy, did you attempt to make money without work?

☐ Did you reject yourself and try to change unchangeable features?

Personal Commitment to Detect and Avoid Swindles

I hereby reject the philosophy which holds that money may be earned without corresponding labor. I will refuse all get-rich-quick schemes including gambling, bingo, futures trading, speculative investments, and gaining at another's expense.

I will not listen to proposals by those whose lives violate God's moral standards, and I will get counsel prior to major financial decisions.

My financial advisor is _____

CAN YOU DETECT THE "QUACK" LANGUAGE OF SWINDLERS?

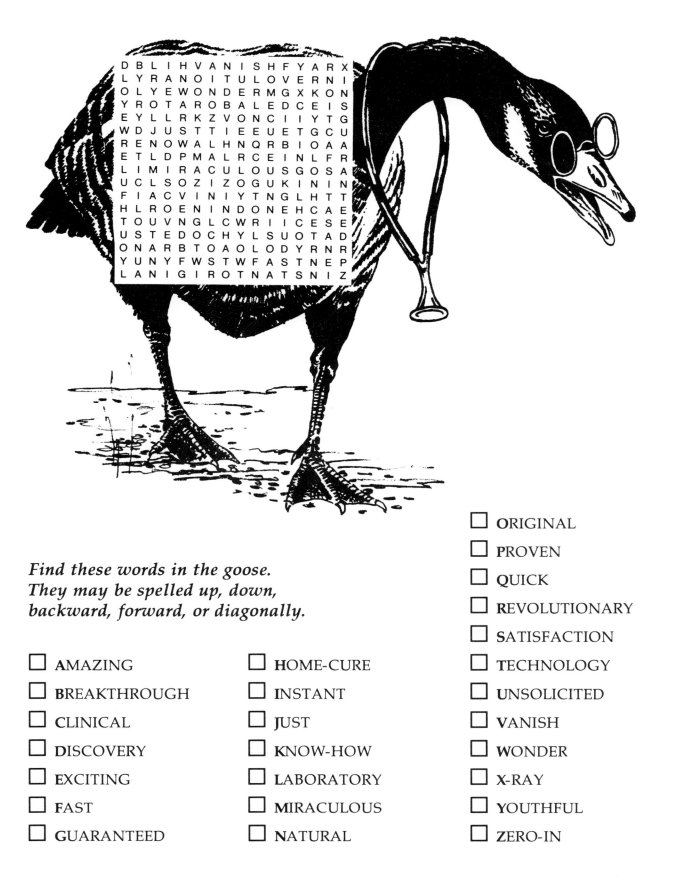

```
D B L I H V A N I S H F Y A R X
L Y R A N O I T U L O V E R N I
O L Y E W O N D E R M G X K O N
Y R O T A R O B A L E D C E I S
E Y L L R K Z V O N C I I Y T G
W D J U S T T I E E U E T G C U
R E N O W A L H N Q R B I O A A
E T L D P M A L R C E I N L F R
L I M I R A C U L O U S G O S A
U C L S O Z I Z O G U K I N I N
F I A C V I N I Y T N G L H T T
H L R O E N I N D O N E H C A E
T O U V N G L C W R I I C E S E
U S T E D O C H Y L S U O T A D
O N A R B T O A O L O D Y R N R
Y U N Y F W S T W F A S T N E P
L A N I G I R O T N A T S N I Z
```

*Find these words in the goose.
They may be spelled up, down,
backward, forward, or diagonally.*

- [ ] **A**MAZING
- [ ] **B**REAKTHROUGH
- [ ] **C**LINICAL
- [ ] **D**ISCOVERY
- [ ] **E**XCITING
- [ ] **F**AST
- [ ] **G**UARANTEED
- [ ] **H**OME-CURE
- [ ] **I**NSTANT
- [ ] **J**UST
- [ ] **K**NOW-HOW
- [ ] **L**ABORATORY
- [ ] **M**IRACULOUS
- [ ] **N**ATURAL
- [ ] **O**RIGINAL
- [ ] **P**ROVEN
- [ ] **Q**UICK
- [ ] **R**EVOLUTIONARY
- [ ] **S**ATISFACTION
- [ ] **T**ECHNOLOGY
- [ ] **U**NSOLICITED
- [ ] **V**ANISH
- [ ] **W**ONDER
- [ ] **X**-RAY
- [ ] **Y**OUTHFUL
- [ ] **Z**ERO-IN

CAN YOU SPOT A SWINDLE IN THE MAKING?

Match each approach with the swindle that would most likely occur.

APPROACHES	SWINDLES

1. A man rings your doorbell and offers to give you a free inspection of your furnace.

A. You are counseled to put up your own money as a good faith deposit. When this is done, your money and unexpected riches vanish.

2. A stranger engages you in conversation at a shopping center, and together you find an envelope filled with money.

B. A defect is "discovered." You are warned of its danger and urged to buy a new, overpriced replacement.

3. A man introduces himself as an inventor. He demonstrates his invention and offers to cut you in on the profits if you invest in it.

C. A close friendship develops and leads to intimacy. The husband suddenly shows up and threatens to expose you unless you pay money to him.

4. All of your life you have resented a certain physical affliction. One day you see an advertisement stating that a medical breakthrough has found a cure for it.

MIRACLE TREATMENT

DR. PHOOLS

D. First you are required to buy an expensive starter kit; and then you find that your money comes by getting others to buy starter kits, too.

5. An advertisement promises $50,000 a year if you form your own company and follow their easy instructions.

MAKE $50,000. THE FIRST YEAR IN YOUR OWN COMPANY

E. After cautiously investing your money, you find that the claims are false. You contact the company for your money-back guarantee and find that the "company" has moved and left no forwarding address.

6. You are doing some work in a customer's home. His attractive wife tells you that her husband is away on a business trip, and she comments on how lonely she gets.

F. Unexpected problems and delays occur; and then more money is required in order to protect the money you have already invested.

Answers: 1B. 2A. 3F. 4E. 5D. 6C.

WHO SWINDLED IN THE BIBLE AND WHAT WERE THE CONSEQUENCES?

Match the swindlers in column one with their characteristics (column two) and then with the consequences they received (column three).

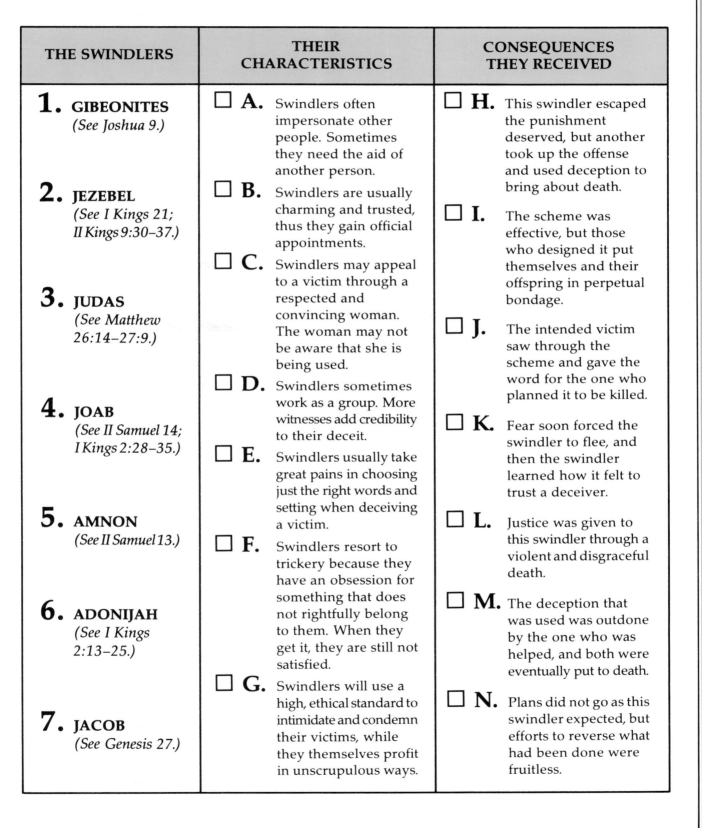

THE SWINDLERS	THEIR CHARACTERISTICS	CONSEQUENCES THEY RECEIVED
1. **GIBEONITES** *(See Joshua 9.)*	☐ **A.** Swindlers often impersonate other people. Sometimes they need the aid of another person.	☐ **H.** This swindler escaped the punishment deserved, but another took up the offense and used deception to bring about death.
2. **JEZEBEL** *(See I Kings 21; II Kings 9:30–37.)*	☐ **B.** Swindlers are usually charming and trusted, thus they gain official appointments.	☐ **I.** The scheme was effective, but those who designed it put themselves and their offspring in perpetual bondage.
3. **JUDAS** *(See Matthew 26:14–27:9.)*	☐ **C.** Swindlers may appeal to a victim through a respected and convincing woman. The woman may not be aware that she is being used.	☐ **J.** The intended victim saw through the scheme and gave the word for the one who planned it to be killed.
4. **JOAB** *(See II Samuel 14; I Kings 2:28–35.)*	☐ **D.** Swindlers sometimes work as a group. More witnesses add credibility to their deceit.	☐ **K.** Fear soon forced the swindler to flee, and then the swindler learned how it felt to trust a deceiver.
5. **AMNON** *(See II Samuel 13.)*	☐ **E.** Swindlers usually take great pains in choosing just the right words and setting when deceiving a victim.	☐ **L.** Justice was given to this swindler through a violent and disgraceful death.
6. **ADONIJAH** *(See I Kings 2:13–25.)*	☐ **F.** Swindlers resort to trickery because they have an obsession for something that does not rightfully belong to them. When they get it, they are still not satisfied.	☐ **M.** The deception that was used was outdone by the one who was helped, and both were eventually put to death.
7. **JACOB** *(See Genesis 27.)*	☐ **G.** Swindlers will use a high, ethical standard to intimidate and condemn their victims, while they themselves profit in unscrupulous ways.	☐ **N.** Plans did not go as this swindler expected, but efforts to reverse what had been done were fruitless.

Answers: 1.D,I 2.G,L 3.B,N 4.E,M 5.F,H 6.C,J 7.A,K

SOLOMON
A man who obtained great riches through wisdom

HE MADE A WISE OFFER

"And the house which I build is great: for great is our God above all gods. . . . Send me now therefore a man cunning to work . . . also cedar trees . . . for I know that thy servants can skill to cut timber in Lebanon; and, behold, my servants shall be with thy servants . . . And, behold, I will give to thy servants . . ." (II Chronicles 2:5, 7–8, 10).

11 LEARN HOW TO GET THE BEST BUY

"A false balance is abomination to the Lord: but a just weight is his delight" (Proverbs 11:1).

HIS CONTRACTOR WAS DRAWN TO GOD

"Then Huram the King of Tyre answered in writing . . . Blessed be the Lord . . . who hath given to David the king a wise son . . ." (II Chronicles 2:11–12).

CAN YOU DETECT THE BEST BUY?

PERSONAL EVALUATION:

        A   **B**

1. Car A is new and costs $8,000. Car B is the same make and model, one year old, with 12,000 miles and costs $6,000. Both cars are in excellent condition. Which car would you buy? ☐ ☐

2. Car A and B are the same make and model and year. Car A was driven 20,000 miles in Arizona. Car B was driven 20,000 miles in Illinois. Which car would you buy? ☐ ☐

3. Power drill A is heavy duty metal and costs $300. Power drill B is plastic and costs $29.95. If you used a drill on an occasional basis, which drill would you buy? ☐ ☐

4. Houses A and B are identical in cost, construction, and condition. House A is within walking distance of a shopping center but three miles from a school. House B is within walking distance of a school and three miles from a shopping center. Which house would you buy? ☐ ☐

5. Water heaters A and B are of the same quality and made by the same company. A department store sells water heater A with a ten-year guarantee. Heater B costs $50 less, but only has a two-year guarantee. Which would you buy? ☐ ☐

6. Canned vegetables A and B are both the same quality and quantity. Can A is a name brand and costs 10¢. Can B is a house brand and costs 8¢. Which can would you buy? ☐ ☐

7. An electrical line needs to be put underground to connect two of your buildings. Company A will do the job for $1,000. Company B will do the job for $700 if you dig the two-foot wide, 100-foot long ditch. Which company would you hire? ☐ ☐

8. Washing machines A and B cost the same. Washing machine A has eight different cycles. Washing machine B has only the three basic cycles, but a larger capacity. Which washing machine would you buy? ☐ ☐

9. Dresser A is solid wood and costs $200. Dresser B is made of wood veneer and costs $100. Which dresser would you buy? ☐ ☐

10. Car battery A costs $70 and has a five-year guarantee. Car battery B costs $30 and has only a three-year guarantee. Which battery would you buy? ☐ ☐

11. Man's suit A is made by a well-known manufacturer and costs $300. The identical suit B, made by the same manufacturer, is sold in a discount store with a different label for $160. Which suit would you buy? ☐ ☐

TOTAL CORRECT ☐

EVALUATION SCORE:

11–10 correct = You are a wise buyer
9–5 correct = You need some counsel
4–0 correct = You need much counsel

Answers:

1. B (Avoid depreciation) 2. A (Avoid rust) 3. B (Low usage and easy handling) 4. B (More stable location) 5. A (Need for guarantee) 6. B (20% savings) 7. B ($300 for a day's labor) 8. B (More washing, less repair) 9. A (Investment for generations) 10. A (Longer guarantee means more powerful battery) 11. B (Label does not affect suit).

132

15 BASIC STEPS TO GETTING THE BEST BUY

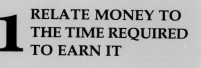

1 RELATE MONEY TO THE TIME REQUIRED TO EARN IT

The first step in getting the best buy is to learn the value of money. Value is understood by comparison, and time is an important basis of comparison.

If you and your family decide to eat out at a restaurant and the bill comes to $30, how long would it take you to earn the money if you made $10 an hour?

The answer is not three hours. You must figure in your direct costs in making the money, such as transportation and taxes. Your net hourly wage may only be $7 per hour.

Thus, it would require over four working hours, or half a day's wages, to pay for that meal, not counting transportation to the restaurant and tips.

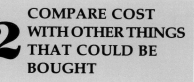

2 COMPARE COST WITH OTHER THINGS THAT COULD BE BOUGHT

Consumer tunnel vision destroys the potential of good buys. Tunnel vision involves evaluating a product without any reference to what that same money could buy in other areas.

By comparing items with other items, we not only have a further basis of value; we also have signals to either make a purchase or to continue shopping.

Christ's parables of the treasure in the field and the pearl of great price illustrate this step in action. The buyers decided that the field and the pearl were of greater value than the things that they owned. Thus, they sold what they had and purchased the items of greater value. (See Matthew 13:44–46.)

If, for example, you are planning to buy a car for $20,000, realize that you can buy a new car of another make for half that amount and earn interest on the remaining $10,000.

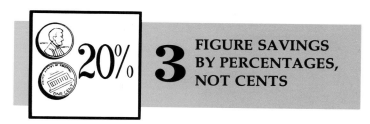

3 FIGURE SAVINGS BY PERCENTAGES, NOT CENTS

A wise and wealthy businessman explained why it was important to save two cents on a can of soup.

"If one can costs ten cents and another can of equal quality and quantity costs eight cents, you should buy the eight-cent can."

Those who listened to this counsel could not understand why a multi-millionaire would talk about saving two cents, until he explained its significance.

"You are not just saving two cents; you are saving twenty per cent. Just think of how much you could reduce your whole food bill if you reduced it by twenty per cent. Furthermore, you cannot get that great a return on interest from a bank.

This kind of thinking helps to show why this man is a multi-millionaire; and his counsel is confirmed by the teaching of Christ.

"He that is faithful in that which is least is faithful also in much . . ." (Luke 16:10).

> **A good buy is not paying more than is necessary for a product or a service.**

4 PUT ALL EARNINGS DIRECTLY INTO THE BANK

Getting the best buy requires that you carefully guard and account for every dollar.

When your paycheck is not immediately deposited in the bank but instead is cashed and used for personal expeditures, unwise decisions are usually made and record keeping is much more difficult.

The account into which you deposit your money should be interest bearing.

5 CARRY AS LITTLE CASH AS NECESSARY

One day a young man complained to his employer that his $250-a-week paycheck was not sufficient to meet his expenses.

His employer asked if he was buying a home. He said, "No." His rental payments were very small. His employer asked if he owned his own car. He replied that he was still making payments on his car.

The employer then shocked him by asking, "You have been working here for ten years. What do you have to show for the $150,000 that we have already paid you?"

At first the young man could not believe that he had actually made that much money. It was equally hard for him to realize that he had gone through that much money with nothing to show for it.

This young man had made it a practice to carry large amounts of money with him and to freely spend it on things that had little or no lasting value.

6 KNOW WHAT YOU WANT BEFORE SHOPPING

A wise buyer will make a list of the items he needs to buy before he goes shopping. There are several important purposes in doing this.

Displays in stores are designed to promote impulse buying. Without a prearranged list, you are very likely to buy more than you need.

By listing what you need beforehand, you can contact the stores to make sure they have what you are looking for. This will save travel time, let you know the cost of the item, and indicate whether you need to do further shopping in order to get the best buy.

For regular purchases, the following inventory list has many advantages:

No.	ITEMS	CHECK WHEN USED				COST
3	Tooth paste	✓				.89
4	Bars bath soap	✓	✓	✓		.60
2	Boxes laundry soap	✓				$3.00
1	Gallon bleach	✓				.50
2	Cans black shoe polish					

By listing all of the items on sheets such as the above, you have the basis for inventories, usages, cost analyses, and ready re-order forms.

7 FOCUS ON THE BUY, NOT YOUR BANK BALANCE

Extravagance begins by thinking about how much money you will have left in your bank account rather than thinking, "Am I getting the most value for each dollar spent?"

A wise buyer may have $10,000 in savings. If he considers buying an item for $100, he will not say to himself, "I will have $9,900 left in my account." Such thinking leads to slothfulness in investigating products, and it encourages others to take advantage of the slothful buyer.

Only after deciding that he is getting the best buy will a wise buyer look at his resulting bank balance.

8 LOOK AT THE PRICE BEFORE YOU LOOK AT THE PRODUCT

Always find out the full price before setting your heart on buying a product.

One of the greatest enemies to securing the best buy is becoming emotionally attached to an item before you can determine whether you can afford it.

The whole thrust of advertising is to influence people to want something so strongly that they will rationalize paying an exorbitant price or living beyond their means. This is the basis of credit buying.

When you see that the price of a car is beyond your spending range, it is wise discipline not to look at the car. When you get a menu at a restaurant, it is wise training to begin with the price and read backward to the entree.

9 MAKE SURE YOU REALLY KNOW THE FULL PRICE

The price you actually pay is usually much higher than the retail price of the product. For example, if you buy a car with a base price of $7,900, you must also pay the following:

- Initial cost $7,900
- Tax @ 5%   395
- Freight   150
- Dealer preparation   150
- License plates   40
- Village sticker   10
- Title fee   12
- Insurance   400
- Extra needed equipment   300
- Required maintenance package   60
- Gas for one year (10,000 miles)   575
- Lost interest on money @ 10%   790

ACTUAL COST $10,782

If you were barely able to justify the car at $7,900, you would certainly have financial pressures with the final cost.

Knowing the full price before you buy has an important spiritual application. Satan's program of temptation is based on letting you see only a part of the cost of sin. If Adam and Eve would have comprehended the compounding cost of their sin, they would have had powerful motivation not to enter into it.

Advertisements which offer so much down and so much per month are in reality saying, "If you knew the full price, you probably would not buy it, so we won't tell you the full price."

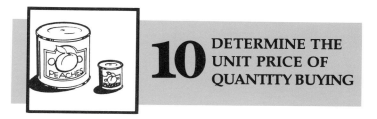

10 DETERMINE THE UNIT PRICE OF QUANTITY BUYING

It would seem obvious that a large economy size is less expensive per ounce than smaller containers of the same product. However, a wise buyer will investigate this.

Many items are actually more expensive per ounce in the large "economy size" than they are in the smaller size.

In order to figure the unit price, divide the cost by the number of ounces. A 32-ounce jar of mustard at 96¢ is 3¢ per ounce. If a 12-ounce jar sold for 24¢, the unit price would be 2¢ per ounce. Thus, three 12-ounce jars would be a 25% savings over the one "economy" jar.

A very successful purchasing agent repeatedly got outstanding buys by working with the unit price.

If he needed to buy a quantity of blankets, he would first contact the factory to see if he could purchase them direct. If not, he would ask a merchant how much of a discount he would get if he bought ten blankets. He would then ask if he could receive a greater discount if he bought fifty blankets or even better if he bought 100 blankets.

 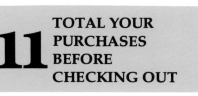

11 TOTAL YOUR PURCHASES BEFORE CHECKING OUT

You may think that you have acquired the best buys in shopping. However, if you are over-charged, then you lose the benefit of all of your work.

To avoid being overcharged, it is wise to calculate the costs of your purchases before you reach the checkout counter. This is a double check to the accuracy of the cashier or the waitress in a restaurant or the salesman who writes out your bill.

A pocket calculator is an excellent means of adding up the grocery bill before reaching the checkout counter.

By using your calculator to check the total cost of your groceries, and by shopping for desserts and less nutritious foods last, you gain the added benefit of keeping within your budget.

12 CHECK PRODUCTS IN A CONSUMER GUIDE

One of the most helpful aids in getting the best buy is a consumer guide or *Consumer Reports*. These publications evaluate the strengths and weaknesses of products and point out features and limitations which must be understood in making wise decisions.

A trip to the local library is all that is necessary to gather this valuable counsel. Often the librarian will assist you in finding exactly what you are looking for.

The time to check the consumer guide is before you start shopping for a product. What you learn from this research will give you the basis for asking the right questions, letting the salesman know that you understand what you are buying, and obtaining the best price.

13 WRITE OUT QUESTIONS AND ANSWERS

When making a major purchase, it is important to write out the questions which determine the value, function, care, and special features of a product.

The source of your questions will come from your research in the consumer guide, as well as information that you have gathered from other users.

These questions not only form the basis of your discussion with the salesman, but they allow you to write down his answers and then make sure that they are more than "sales puff."

Wherever possible, get documentation for the claims that are made. If such claims are not written out, you cannot prove that they were stated.

14 GET COUNSEL FROM OWNERS AND REPAIRMEN

Some of the wisest counsel that you can get before buying an appliance, car, machine, or home is from present and former owners, and especially from repairmen.

Most people get sufficient counsel on a major expenditure. The problem is that most of the counsel comes after a product has been purchased or a contract has been signed.

Those who have had experience with a product are usually more than willing to tell you about it.

> *The key to wise buying is getting the experiences of others as cheaply as you can. They paid a high price for it, and they usually enjoy sharing it without charge.*

BASIC QUESTIONS BEFORE BUYING

- *Do I really need it?*
- *Am I buying more quality than I need?*
- *Does it do what it claims to do?*
- *Does the company stand behind it?*
- *Will it soon be outdated?*
- *Does my use justify its purchase?*
- *Is the upkeep economical?*
- *Would rental be cheaper?*
- *Can I avoid unnecessary middlemen?*
- *Will it unite or divide my family?*

15 CHECK WITH YOUR WIFE BEFORE BUYING

God designed the woman as a "help meet" to her husband. One of her valuable helps is an ability to sense when her husband is about to make an unwise purchase.

She may not be able to explain why a decision is wrong, but if she has a hesitation, her husband would be wise to do further investigation about the intended purchase.

KNOW WHEN AND HOW TO MAKE A JUST OFFER

Sometimes it is not possible or appropriate to make an offer lower than the listed price of an item. However, many times it is; in fact, the higher the cost of an item, the more appropriate it is for you to make your own offer.

If you have done proper research, you should have a reasonable basis for making a just offer.

You may base your offer on the fact that a competitor is selling the identical item at a lower price, or that the product is damaged, or that you could reduce the seller's cost in providing the item or service.

Solomon illustrated the wisdom and benefits of making an offer for goods and services.

When he needed lumber to build the temple, he realized that he could reduce the cost by providing his laborers to work with King Hiram's skilled craftsmen.

When making an offer, it is vital that you do not downgrade the product or the seller. Instead, praise where you can and point out facts that clearly establish your offer. Solomon illustrated this in his offer. *". . . My servants shall be with thy servants . . . for thou knowest that there is not among us any that can skill to hew timber like unto the Sidonians"* (I Kings 5:6).

A homeowner applied this principle of making an offer in replacing the eaves and gutters on his home. The lowest of three bids was $2,500. He believed that this was too much, so he did the research that he should have done at the start.

He checked the price of materials in a lumber yard and a gutter company. He determined how much paint it would require and how many hours of labor would be involved. The cost came to less than $1,000. Another company accepted his offer and did an excellent job for $1,150.

GET THE BEST BUY BY ASKING PRECISE QUESTIONS

What questions would you ask a company that offered to paint your house?

- ☐ **1.** How long have you been in the painting business?
- ☐ **2.** How experienced are your painters?
- ☐ **3.** Are you bonded or licensed?
- ☐ **4.** What other jobs have you done in this area?
- ☐ **5.** Will you clean and scrape before painting?
- ☐ **6.** What kind of paint would you use—water or oil base?
- ☐ **7.** What is the quality of the paint that you will use?
- ☐ **8.** Can you guarantee that the paint is fresh?
- ☐ **9.** Will you use drop cloths and remove any spilled paint?
- ☐ **10.** Will you brush, spray, or roll the paint on?
- ☐ **11.** Will you paint all of the trim?
- ☐ **12.** How long will it take you to paint the house?
- ☐ **13.** When can you guarantee that the job will be finished?
- ☐ **14.** Will you give a signed guarantee for the job?
- ☐ **15.** Can I pay when the job is completed to my satisfaction?
- ☐ **16.** Will you give me a "waiver of lien" agreement?

Personal Commitment to Get the Best Buy

As a steward of God's funds, I purpose to be faithful in getting the best buy. This means that I will do thorough research, get wise counsel, offer a just price, and be willing to walk away from purchases that do not meet the factors of a best buy.

Date _____

CAN YOU DETERMINE THE VALUE OF PURCHASES?

Check the correct answer for each question.

1. After working all day, you stop at an ice cream parlor. A snack and sundae cost $6. How many hours would it take you to pay for it if you earned $2 an hour on the job?

    A. ☐ 3 hours

    B. ☐ 4½ hours

    C. ☐ More than 6 hours

2. If each of the following items costs $10, which would be the best buy?

    A. ☐ A two-pound box of chocolates

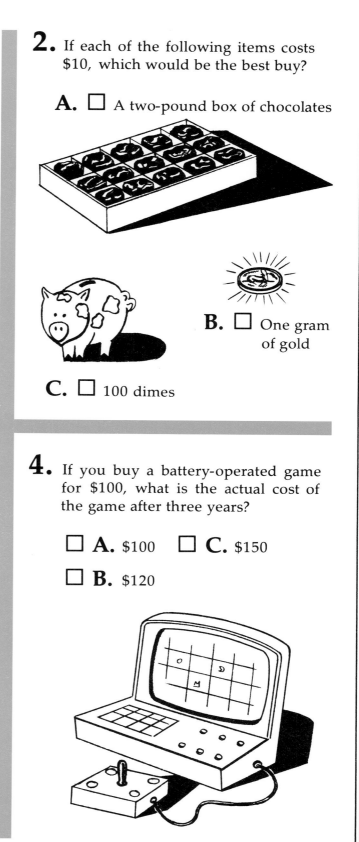

    B. ☐ One gram of gold

    C. ☐ 100 dimes

3. If you wanted to get the best buy on a used stove, which of the following steps would you take? (Number in order of importance.)

☐ **A.** Give an offer to the seller.

☐ **B.** Inspect the stove.

☐ **C.** Get counsel from others who own the same type of stove.

☐ **D.** Check a consumer guide on that year and make of stove.

4. If you buy a battery-operated game for $100, what is the actual cost of the game after three years?

☐ **A.** $100   ☐ **C.** $150

☐ **B.** $120

HOW DOES GOD ILLUSTRATE OUR RESPONSIBILITY TO SELLERS?

Match each responsibility with each Scriptural example.

☐ **1.** Treat him as an equal, not a servant.

☐ **2.** Know exactly what you want in quality, style, and price range before you talk to him.

☐ **3.** Get him excited about the importance of your project and his part in it.

☐ **4.** Make sure that your seller is satisfied with your payment.

☐ **5.** Pay your bills promptly.

☐ **6.** Praise the quality of his work where you can, and recommend him to others.

☐ **7.** Do not use your influence or position to get what you want.

☐ **8.** Be aware of the pressures he faces from family, health, and business, and help him whenever possible.

A. King Hiram and King Solomon
"... The cities which Solomon had given him ... pleased him not" (I Kings 9:12).

B. Solomon and the Sidonians
"... There is not among us any that can skill to hew timber like unto the Sidonians" (I Kings 5:6).

C. Ahab and Naboth
"And Jezebel ... said ... I will give thee the vineyard ..." (I Kings 21:7).

D. Boaz and the kinsman
"... If thou wilt redeem it, redeem it ..." (Ruth 4:4).

E. Solomon and the Queen of Sheba
"... Solomon told her all her questions ..." (I Kings 10:3).

F. Abraham and Ephron
"... And Abraham weighed to Ephron the silver ..." (Genesis 23:16).

G. King David and King Hiram
"... For Hiram was ever a lover of David" (I Kings 5:1).

H. King Solomon and King Hiram
"... When Hiram heard the words [proposal] ... he rejoiced greatly ..." (I Kings 5:7).

Answers: 1.G 2.D 3.H 4.A 5.F 6.B 7.C 8.E

CAN YOU IDENTIFY SCRIPTURAL EXAMPLES OF GETTING THE BEST BUY?

Match the basic principles of getting the best buy with the most precise Scriptural illustration.

PRINCIPLES OF BUYING	SCRIPTURAL ILLUSTRATIONS
☐ **1.** Learn to appreciate the value of money.	**A. Parable of the pearl** *(See Matthew 13:45–46.)*
☐ **2.** Do not display wealth. It encourages carelessness and invites others to take advantage of you.	**B. Parable of the tower** *(See Luke 14:28–30.)*
☐ **3.** Pay on the basis of what an item is worth, not on how much money you will have remaining after the purchase.	**C. Solomon and King Hiram** *(See I Kings 5.)*
☐ **4.** Find out the full price of an item before you set your emotions on it or begin to buy it.	**D. Parable of the lost coin** *(See Luke 15:8–10.)*
☐ **5.** Accept the way God has made you. Self-rejection leads to wrong companions and unwise decisions.	**E. Parable of the vineyard owner** *(See Matthew 20:1–16.)*
☐ **6.** Inspect an item before you buy it to make sure it is worth what you are going to pay for it.	**F. Boaz redeeming the land** *(See Ruth 4:1–17.)*
☐ **7.** Learn how to make a wise and equitable offer.	**G. Abraham buying Machpelah** *(See Genesis 23:3–20.)*
☐ **8.** Listen to the cautions of your wife regarding an important decision.	**H. Jepthah's responses** *(See Judges 11:1–40.)*
☐ **9.** Get the seller personally excited about the project you are working on.	**I. Ahasuerus and Esther** *(See Esther 3–7.)*
☐ **10.** Pay your bills promptly when the work is done or when the goods are delivered.	**J. Hezekiah with the Babylonians** *(See II Kings 20:12–19.)*

Answers: 1.D 2.J 3.G 4.B 5.H 6.A 7.F 8.I 9.C 10.E

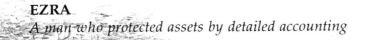

EZRA
A man who protected assets by detailed accounting

GOD ENTRUSTS WEALTH

"And I [Ezra] weighed unto them the silver,
the gold, and the vessels, even the offering of the h
of our God. . . . And I said unto them, Ye are holy unt
Lord; the vessels are holy also; and the silver an
gold. . . . Watch ye, and keep them, until ye weigh the
(Ezra 8:25, 28–29).

12 BECOME ACCOUNTABLE TO A WISE RECORD SYSTEM

"Moreover it is required in stewards, that a man be found faithful" (I Corinthians 4:2).

DETAILED ACCOUNTING IS REQUIRED

When Ezra and his companions safely reached their destination, they weighed all the silver and the gold and the vessels in front of trusted witnesses, "by number and by weight of every one: and all the weight was written at that time" (Ezra 8:34).

WHO SHOULD PAY THE BILLS?

PERSONAL EVALUATION:

Both you and your wife should complete this quiz. It will help both of you to identify needs and direction for record keeping in your home.

If your wife wrote out the checks to pay the bills:

YES NO

1. Would she have a greater sense of security? ☐ ☐

2. Would she have a better picture of needs for which to pray? ☐ ☐

3. Would she feel that she has a more vital role in the home? ☐ ☐

4. Would she have more time to do it than you do? ☐ ☐

5. Would there be more openness and unity in your marriage? ☐ ☐

6. Would she be more understanding when money is tight? ☐ ☐

7. Would she be under extra pressure? ☐ ☐

8. Would she be able to eliminate unrealistic expectations? ☐ ☐

9. Would you be more able to work together on financial goals? ☐ ☐

10. Would she no longer fear the lack of provision? ☐ ☐

11. Would she then have the basis for appealing for family needs? ☐ ☐

12. Would she refrain from pressuring for money? ☐ ☐

13. Would her opinions and counsel have more value? ☐ ☐

14. Would there be more trust and interdependence? ☐ ☐

15. Would she have a greater sense of dignity and worth? ☐ ☐

16. Would there be a basis for discussing expenditures together? ☐ ☐

17. Would difficult financial decisions be more easily made? ☐ ☐

18. Would there be more of a check and balance? ☐ ☐

19. Would she be able to more wisely respond to unusual circumstances? ☐ ☐

20. Would she be more prepared to handle financial needs if you were to die? ☐ ☐

TOTAL YOU ACCURATELY PREDICTED ☐

EVALUATION NOTES

- The needs of record keeping often change during the course of a marriage.
- Your wife may sense a need to keep the checkbook now, but later she may find that it has become a burden.
- It may be necessary to delegate a portion of bill paying to your wife.
- It is important to discuss which bills she needs to pay.
- Often a wife will feel insecure if her husband loses total interest in, or supervision of, the checkbook.
- Conversely, a wife may feel insecure if her husband refuses to allow her to participate in financial matters.

TEN REASONS WHY WE MUST HAVE AN EFFECTIVE ACCOUNTING SYSTEM

1 IT LETS US SEE WHAT GOD HAS ENTRUSTED TO US

• Value

Esau knew that the birthright belonged to him because he was the firstborn son. However, it did not have any value to him. It did not fit into his program of achievement; thus he was willing to sell it to his brother for one bowl of soup. *". . . Who for one morsel of meat sold his birthright"* (Hebrews 12:16).

Years after he sold it, he recognized its value and tried to reclaim it, but it was too late. *"For ye know how that afterward, when he would have inherited the blessing, he was rejected: for he found no place of repentance, though he sought it carefully with tears"* (Hebrews 12:17).

• Scope

An effective accounting system goes much further than totaling our financial assets. It allows us to see and appreciate the larger scope of what God has entrusted to us.

- Spiritual riches
- Health
- Family/Friends
- Opportunities
- Skills
- Time
- Possessions
- Money

An accounting system is the basis for personal inventory and self-examination. If our accounting system only involves material posses-

sions, we will be like the Christians in the Laodicean church. *". . . I will spue thee out of my mouth. Because thou sayest, I am rich, and increased with goods, and have need of nothing; and knowest not that thou art wretched, and miserable, and poor, and blind, and naked"* (Revelation 3:16–17).

2 IT MOTIVATES US TO USE WHAT GOD HAS GIVEN TO US

• Motives

Two men in Christ's parables used the riches that they had. Although they both multiplied their assets, Jesus called one faithful and the other foolish.

Christ's evaluation could not be seen on a ledger sheet. It was revealed in the hidden motives of each man's heart. The faithful steward's motive was to multiply what he had for the purposes of his master. (See Matthew 25:20–21.)

The foolish rich man's motive was to heap up riches for a life of ease in his later years. *". . . God said unto him, Thou fool . . ."* (Luke 12:20).

• Wise Investments

Using what God has entrusted to us involves making wise investments. Our investments will witness for us or against us.

Investing even a cup of cold water in the name of Christ will bring a witness of eternal reward; but investing in unnecessary perishable things will bring a witness of God's reproof. *"Your gold and silver is cankered; and the rust of them shall be a witness against you . . ."* (James 5:3).

 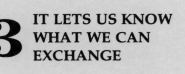 **3** **IT LETS US KNOW WHAT WE CAN EXCHANGE**

 **4** **IT FORCES US TO LIVE WITHIN OUR MEANS**

• *Real Wealth*

God intended for our wealth to increase by trading, buying, or selling—not by inflation. Inflation is actually a form of stealing.

When there is no inflation, people must increase their wealth by greater productivity, resourcefulness, and savings.

It is against this backdrop that Jesus gives the parables of the treasure in the field and the pearl of great price. He uses wise business principles to explain spiritual realities.

". . . The kingdom of heaven is like unto treasure hid in a field; the which when a man hath found, he hideth, and for joy thereof goeth and selleth all that he hath, and buyeth that field. Again, the kingdom of heaven is like unto a merchant man, seeking goodly pearls: Who, when he had found one pearl of great price, went and sold all that he had, and bought it" (Matthew 13:44–46).

• *Trading vs. Collecting*

Notice that in each parable the wise merchant sold what he had and purchased something of far greater value.

Without an effective accounting system, our collector's instinct takes over, stifling creativity, eliminating resourcefulness, and allowing greed to go unchecked. As a result, we heap up things that have little or no value either for the present or for the future.

The church of Laodicea was warned to trade temporal things for eternal riches. *"I counsel thee to buy of me gold tried in the fire, that thou mayest be rich . . ."* (Revelation 3:18).

Life itself requires trading things that we esteem to be of lesser value for things that we esteem to be of greater value. We trade time for money, and we trade money for food.

Paul took account of his spiritual life and saw the need to trade temporal things for eternal riches. (See Philippians 3:8.)

One of the principle functions of an effective accounting system is to make sure that we do not make expenditures beyond our income or resources. Christ emphasizes this point in His parable of the unfinished tower. (See Luke 14:28–30.)

• *Clear Plans*

"For which of you, intending to build a tower. . . ."

Each of us should visualize how we can use our assets to advance the kingdom of God. However, the ideas we get must be clearly thought out.

Noah was given plans to build an ark. Moses was instructed to make a tabernacle. David visualized a temple. Nehemiah purposed to build the walls of Jerusalem.

• *Accurate Estimates*

". . . Sitteth not down first, and counteth the cost. . . ."

Wise planning involves knowing costs. This requires the skill of working out your own estimate of what it will require to do a job.

• *Available Assets*

". . . Whether he have sufficient to finish it. . . ."

When God is behind a program, He provides sufficient funds beforehand to finish the job.

Moses collected sufficient funds before he began to construct the tabernacle. David gathered all that was needed in order to finish the temple.

• *Precise Timing*

"Lest haply, after he hath laid the foundation, and is not able to finish it. . . ."

If sufficient funds are not available for a project, it is a clear indication for us to stop and wait for God's timing.

Effective records will not only confirm the amount of funds needed, but will indicate God's timing.

• Public Reputation

"... All that behold it begin to mock him, Saying, This man began to build, and was not able to finish."

The ultimate result of an effective accounting system is that God's name is publicly praised, and the ridicule that comes from making unwise decisions is avoided.

5 IT PREPARES US TO GIVE AN ACCOUNT TO GOD

An accounting system is a daily reminder that we must someday give a full and detailed account to God for all that He has entrusted to us. *"So then every one of us shall give account of himself to God"* (Romans 14:12).

The need for clear records is well illustrated in Christ's parables of stewardship. *"... Lord, thou deliveredst unto me five talents: behold, I have gained beside them five talents more"* (Matthew 25:20).

God rewarded this steward by praise and increased responsibility. In contrast to this, the steward who failed to trade his talent was condemned. *"... Thou wicked and slothful servant, thou knewest that I reap where I sowed not, and gather where I have not strawed"* (Matthew 25:26).

Even the unjust steward was commended because he put his accounting system in order before he was fired, and in so doing he reaped personal gain. Accounting requires accuracy and faithfulness in little amounts as well as in large amounts. *"He that is faithful in that which is least is faithful also in much: and he that is unjust in the least is unjust also in much"* (Luke 16:10).

6 IT ESTABLISHES OUR CHARACTER BEFORE MEN

• Motives

One of the most revealing tests of a man's character is his attitude toward the use of money.

Men who are being considered for church leadership must pass the tests of wise and Godly money management: *"... Not greedy of filthy lucre..."* (I Timothy 3:3).

Character that is revealed by money management is so important that Christians are warned not even to eat a meal with a person who claims to be a Christian but is a swindler in business dealings. (See I Corinthians 5:11).

• Defense

Expect your financial dealings to be challenged. When you are accused, you must be able to defend yourself by proving that you have followed wise and accurate procedures in your finances.

For this purpose, detailed and complete record keeping is essential. Agreements must be clearly understood, fully written out, and safely kept in organized files.

The danger of being falsely accused in financial matters is extremely high, because those who judge you are usually guilty of the very thing which they condemn.

Thus, all of those with whom you have any business dealings and who have secret greed are potential accusers. For this reason God instructs us to *"... provide things honest in the sight of all men"* (Romans 12:17).

7 IT CONFIRMS LEADERSHIP IN THE FAMILY

A family can only function to its full potential if the father demonstrates the quality of leadership which Christ demonstrated to the Church.

"Husbands, love your wives, even as Christ also loved the church, and gave himself for it" (Ephesians 5:25).

• True Headship

The purpose of your head, including your brain, eyes, ears, and nose, is to be fully aware of the needs of your body and to give direction in meeting those needs.

If your hand is on a hot stove and the signals of pain do not reach your head, there will be severe damage. Similarly, if there is unseen damage occurring in your family, home, or business and you are not aware of it, your leadership will be challenged in your home, business, and church. *"For if a man know not how to rule his own house, how shall he take care of the church of God?"* *(I Timothy 3:5).*

• A Wife's Security

Many women whose husbands make large salaries are financially insecure. After carefully studying this paradox, the real cause becomes clear.

It is not the amount of money that a man makes which gives his wife and family security, but it is how carefully and wisely he manages whatever amount he makes. If a wife senses that her husband is careless in his handling of small amounts of money, she knows that he can also carelessly mismanage large amounts of money.

One of the most practical ways to give your wife a sense of security is to let her know where the following documents can be found and how they should be used:

1. Bankbooks, savings records
2. Birth certificates
3. Contracts, leases
4. Insurance policies
5. Licenses, permits
6. Marriage certificate
7. Medical records
8. Military records
9. Mortgage papers
10. Pension information
11. Real estate records
12. Social security information
13. Securities
14. Tax records
15. Vehicle titles
16. Will

The story of Joseph in Egypt is one of the classic illustrations of how an accounting system helped to save lives. Because he knew that the famine was coming, Joseph urged Pharaoh to keep accurate records on each person's harvest and to gather twenty per cent of it to sustain the people during the famine. (See Genesis 41:1–57.)

God also demonstrates that His work is accomplished by first acquiring the necessary provisions. David desired to build the temple, but God postponed the construction of the building until David had all the provisions ready. This preparation to build the temple continued for the rest of David's life; but his son Solomon was the one who actually built the temple. (See I Chronicles 22:1–5.)

Similarly, God instructs every Christian to set aside a portion of his resources so that he is able to accomplish God's program. *"Upon the first day of the week let every one of you lay by him in store, as God hath prospered him, that there be no gatherings when I come"* *(I Corinthians 16:2).*

Planning ahead for needs, both seen and unseen, is not possible without an effective accounting system. For this reason, God warns us to follow His commands and testimonies, and even to take a lesson from nature on this point.

"Go to the ant, thou sluggard; consider her ways, and be wise: Which having no guide, overseer, or ruler, Provideth [prepares] her meat in the summer, and gathereth her food in the harvest" *(Proverbs 6:6–8).*

 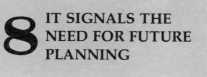

8 IT SIGNALS THE NEED FOR FUTURE PLANNING

9 IT DISCOURAGES THEFT OF WHAT WE HAVE

God's program of provision occurs in cycles of plenty and need, of harvest and winter. God wants us to learn how to adjust to these varying conditions with wise planning and preparation. *". . . In all things I am instructed both to be full and to be hungry, both to abound and to suffer need"* *(Philippians 4:12).*

God knows that the tendency to steal is a part of fallen human nature. God warns and illustrates that the ones whom you may least suspect can be guilty of thievery.

None of the disciples suspected that Judas was a thief. Also, one would think that the assistant to the Godly prophet Elisha would have been an honest man; but when Gehazi saw the riches that Elisha rejected, he wanted to appropriate them for himself. (See II Kings 5:20–27.)

• Responsible Stewardship

The resources and possessions of a Christian should receive the most careful accounting of all, since they actually belong to the Lord.

Furthermore, the Lord will hold us responsible for the money and goods which He has entrusted to our care. "... *For unto whomsoever much is given, of him shall be much required: and to whom men have committed much, of him they will ask the more"* (Luke 12:48).

God set forth clear guidelines of responsibility to those who held the property of another. *"If a man deliver unto his neighbour an ass, or an ox, or a sheep, or any beast, to keep.... And if it be stolen from him, he shall make restitution unto the owner thereof.... And if a man borrow ought of his neighbour, and it be hurt, or die, the owner thereof being not with it, he shall surely make it good" (Exodus 22:10, 12, 14).* Careless accounting invites loss by theft.

• Internal Controls

Accurate accounting is essential to expose a thief, while poor records tend to encourage thievery.

Ezra was very aware of the tendency of people to steal. Therefore, when he had the responsibility of transporting all the valuable gold and silver treasures of the temple, he carefully weighed each item and entrusted it to a specific individual.

When the caravan reached Jerusalem, each person had to weigh the piece that was given to him. All was accounted for, because the people knew that they would be answerable for any loss. (See Ezra 8:25–34.)

• Unexpected Danger

We tend to be too trusting of the people around us; and in so doing, we may be putting temptation in their way.

It is a loving father who keeps careful records in order to spare his children from the destruction that will come to them if they steal from him. *"Whoso robbeth his father or his mother, and saith, It is no transgression; the same is the companion of a destroyer" (Proverbs 28:24).*

10 IT QUALIFIES US FOR TRUE RICHES

The principles that we use for accurate accounting of our money are the very same principles that are used to gain Scriptural wisdom. It is for this reason that God was able to tell Solomon that, because he asked for wisdom and not money, he would get both. (See I Kings 3:12–13.)

It is also for this reason that God is able to state, *"If therefore ye have not been faithful in the unrighteous mammon [money], who will commit to your trust the true riches?" (Luke 16:11).*

• Financial Growth

The first step to increase wealth is to keep account of everything that we earn and to put our money in an insured investment.

The second step is to wisely manage our earnings by making wise purchases.

The third step is to be on guard against anyone who would take those earnings from us.

• Wisdom Growth

The first step to increase wisdom is to write out all of the insights and ideas which God gives to us, and keep them in a safe place—a life notebook.

The second step is to wisely invest these Scriptural truths in our lives and conversation with others. This encourages others to share with us their wisdom.

The third step is to be on guard against spiritual dangers that would rob us of Godly wisdom. God will reward practices of stewardship wherever and whenever they are used. *"Moreover it is required in stewards, that a man be found faithful" (I Corinthians 4:2).*

BE ACCOUNTABLE TO RECORD KEEPING

1. SPIRITUAL RICHES

☐ *Daily Bible Reading*

Do you have an effective system of Bible reading and someone to keep you accountable to it?

☐ *Effective Prayer*

Do you keep a list of prayer requests and the answers which God gives?

☐ *Records of Growth*

Do you maintain a life notebook of Scriptural insights?

☐ *Eternal Treasures*

Do you keep records of weekly tithes and offerings?

2. TIME

☐ *Annual Planning*

Do you have a calendar that lists your responsibilities?

☐ *Daily Schedule*

Do you plan each day around God-given priorities?

3. HEALTH

☐ *Physical Care*

Do you eat wholesome meals and get sufficient sleep, exercise, and medical and dental checkups?

4. SKILLS

☐ *Training and Practice*

Do you have a program to expand and improve your God-given abilities?

☐ *Tool Care*

Do you have a place for each one of your tools, and are they kept in good condition?

5. POSSESSIONS

☐ *Library*

Have you removed the wrong kinds of books? Are you bringing the right kinds of books into your home?

☐ *Kitchen*

Do you have food inventories clearly organized?

☐ *Storage*

Do you have uncluttered closets, drawers, and shelves in your basement, garage, and office?

6. MONEY

☐ *Checkbook and Records*

Do you keep accurate accounting of all expenditures through your checkbook, and do you file important documents?

Personal Commitment to Effective Record Keeping

I purpose to take whatever time and energy necessary to organize, inventory, and maintain the spiritual and physical assets which God has entrusted to me.

I will enlist aid and counsel where needed and become accountable for achieving these goals by given time periods.

Accountable to _____

Date _____

To be completed by _____

WHAT ITEMS ARE CONTAINED IN GOD'S RECORDS?

Match each item at right with the correct verse below.

☐ **1.** *"And whosoever was not found written in the book of life was cast into the lake of fire" (Revelation 20:15).*

☐ **2.** *"Thine eyes did see my substance, yet being unperfect; and in thy book all my members were written, which in continuance were fashioned, when as yet there was none of them" (Psalm 139:16).*

☐ **3.** *"For God is not unrighteous to forget your work and labour of love, which ye have shewed toward his name, in that ye have ministered to the saints, and do minister" (Hebrews 6:10).*

☐ **4.** *"But I say unto you, That every idle word that men shall speak, they shall give account thereof in the day of judgment" (Matthew 12:36).*

☐ **5.** *"But lay up for yourselves treasures in heaven, where neither moth nor rust doth corrupt, and where thieves do not break through nor steal" (Matthew 6:20).*

☐ **6.** *"... Put thou my tears into thy bottle: are they not in thy book" (Psalm 56:8).*

☐ **7.** *"But the very hairs of your head are all numbered" (Matthew 10:30).*

☐ **8.** *"He telleth the number of the stars; he calleth them all by their names" (Psalm 147:4).*

☐ **9.** *"Then they that feared the Lord spake often one to another: and the Lord hearkened, and heard it, and a book of remembrance was written before him for them that feared the Lord, and that thought upon his name" (Malachi 3:16).*

A. Names of Christians

B. Names of stars

C. Hairs of our head

D. All of our tears

E. Physical features

F. Every spoken word

G. Every Godly work

H. Money given to God

I. Those who fear God

Answers: 1.A 2.E 3.G 4.F 5.H 6.D 7.C 8.B 9.I

WHEN DID GOD REQUIRE ACCURATE ACCOUNTING?

Match each statement with the person to whom it best applies.

☐ **1.** My needs were great and my possessions were few. God required me to give an accurate accounting of everything I had in my house before He miraculously provided what I needed. Who am I?

☐ **2.** God required me to keep careful records so that I could remove that which would hinder His miracle-working power. Who am I?

☐ **3.** I prayed that God would work supernaturally among His people. But before I prayed, I determined God's timing from the books which I studied. Who am I?

☐ **4.** My very life depended upon my obedience in keeping an accurate count. Who am I?

☐ **5.** I tried to change God's plans by making a very careful inventory. Who am I?

A. DANIEL *(See Daniel 9:1–2.)*

B. NAAMAN *(See II Kings 5:1–19.)*

C. ABRAHAM *(See Genesis 18:22–33.)*

D. ANDREW *(See John 6:5–14.)*

E. WIDOW *(See II Kings 4:1–7.)*

F. PETER *(See John 21:1–14.)*

G. GIDEON *(See Judges 7:1–25.)*

H. NOAH *(See Genesis 6:14—7:16.)*

☐ **6.** God performed a mighty sign in my day; but before He did, I had to complete a major inventory. Who am I?

☐ **7.** God wanted to show me His power of provision, but first I had to evaluate my own efforts during a night of work. Who am I?

☐ **8.** I was asked to give an account of food on hand before a group could be fed by God's supernatural power. Who am I?

Answers: 1.E 2.G 3.A 4.B 5.C 6.H 7.F 8.D

152

HOW DOES GOD ILLUSTRATE THE IMPORTANCE OF ACCURATE RECORD KEEPING?

Match each statement with the best answer.

☐ **1.** God instructed me to number all the people and to carefully organize them for travel, worship, and battle.

☐ **2.** I asked My heavenly Father to provide for the needs of a large group of people, but before I prayed I organized them into groups of 50 and 100.

☐ **3.** After I gave God the results of my accounting, I was reproved because it was so inaccurate. I was 6,999 off.

☐ **4.** God requires accurate accounting, but my motives were wrong in the count I made. Because of this, God severely judged me with a plague.

☐ **5.** As a part of my God-given responsibility, I thoroughly cleaned the temple. As a result, scrolls of Scripture were discovered and a revival began.

☐ **6.** I challenged God's people to give to His work, and every day I made a careful accounting of the gifts which they brought.

☐ **7.** I kept careful records of the events which took place in my life. By reviewing them one night, I had an idea that ultimately saved my wife and many other people.

☐ **8.** I kept careful records of the resources which were being stored for the future. Because of this careful accounting, multitudes were saved from starvation.

☐ **9.** I wrote a book and recorded an important way that you can detect a false teacher: You do it by measuring and testing his "fruit."

☐ **10.** The task that I was given seemed impossible, but by breaking it down to achievable goals and organizing the workers, we accomplished it in 52 days.

A. ELIJAH
(See I Kings 19:9–18.)

B. JOSIAH
(See II Kings 22:1–14.)

C. JOSEPH
(See Genesis 41:37–57.)

D. AHASUERUS
(See Esther 6:1–14.)

E. NEHEMIAH
(See Nehemiah 2:12—3:32.)

F. MOSES
(See Numbers 2–3.)

G. MATTHEW
(See Matthew 7:15–20.)

H. JESUS
(See Mark 6:34–44.)

I. JOASH
(See II Chronicles 24:8–12.)

J. DAVID
(See II Samuel 24.)

Answers: 1.F 2.H 3.A 4.J 5.B 6.I 7.D 8.C 9.G 10.E.

NEHEMIAH
A great protector of God's people

PAINFUL LOANS

"And there was a great cry of the people and of their wives. . . . We have mortgaged our lands, vineyards, and houses. . . . We have borrowed money for the king's tribute . . . and, lo, we bring into bondage our sons and our daughters . . . neither is it in our power to redeem them . . ." (Nehemiah 5:1–5).

13 NEVER LEND TO FRIENDS OR CO-SIGN FOR A LOAN

"Be not thou one of them that strike hands, or of them that are sureties for debts" (Proverbs 22:26).

USURY REBUKED

". . . I rebuked the nobles, and the rulers, and said unto them, Ye exact usury, every one of his brother. And I set a great assembly against them. . . . Also I said, It is not good that ye do: ought ye not to walk in the fear of our God . . ." (Nehemiah 5:7, 9).

HOW MUCH DO YOU KNOW ABOUT CO-SIGNING AND LENDING?

PERSONAL EVALUATION:

TRUE FALSE

1. Since Jesus taught that you should not turn away a borrower, you should certainly make commercial loans to your friends. ☐ ☐

2. When the Bible speaks about usury, it is referring to exorbitantly high interest rates. ☐ ☐

3. Charging high interest rates is consistently condemned by God. ☐ ☐

4. By charging low interest rates to friends, you avoid the possibility of their becoming resentful towards you. ☐ ☐

5. Scripture teaches that you should lend money to the poor. ☐ ☐

6. If a friend wants to borrow money, you should actually give it to him as a gift and not expect it to be returned. ☐ ☐

7. If you are not able to lend to a friend, you could assist him financially by co-signing for him. ☐ ☐

8. Co-signing should only be done if you personally know and trust the one for whom you are signing. ☐ ☐

9. The Biblical phrase *becoming surety* means the same as the present-day phrase *charging usury*. ☐ ☐

10. Co-signing is the same as becoming a business partner with the one for whom you sign. ☐ ☐

11. By co-signing for a friend, you are able to help him live within his budget. ☐ ☐

12. When someone asks you for a loan, he is usually asking you to take risks which a lending institution would not be willing to take. ☐ ☐

13. The parable of the slothful servant who buried his talent teaches you that it is permissible for banks to lend your money, with interest, to strangers. ☐ ☐

14. When a friend asks you for a loan, he is secretly hoping that you will give it to him as a gift. ☐ ☐

15. If you have co-signed for a stranger, you should wait and see if he will pay you back. ☐ ☐

TOTAL CORRECT ☐

EVALUATION SCORE:

15–14 correct = Safe understanding
13–10 correct = Doubtful understanding
9–6 correct = Hazardous understanding
5–0 correct = You are likely to suffer loss.

Answers:

1. False 2. False 3. False 4. False 5. False 6. True 7. False 8. True 9. False 10. True 11. False 12. True 13. True 14. True 15. False.

WHY WE SHOULD NOT LEND TO FRIENDS OR CO-SIGN FOR A LOAN

When the finances of individuals or the economy of a nation are built upon borrowing, it is an evidence of God's judgment; and, if allowed to continue, it will result in the ever-increasing consequences of inflation, bankruptcy, and, ultimately, loss of freedom.

What about lending to, or co-signing for, a friend? Our natural inclination would tell us that we are demonstrating true friendship by lending money to a friend at a time of need. Just the opposite is true, however. Many a friendship has been destroyed over a well-intentioned loan.

When a friend or relative asks us to co-sign for their purchase or their loan, it seems even easier to do than giving a loan. However, it is far more dangerous and usually much more costly than even making a loan. By lending, we can only lose the money that we lend; but by co-signing, we can lose everything that we own.

Here are specific reasons why it is wrong to lend to friends or to co-sign for a loan.

1 LENDING TURNS A FRIEND INTO A SERVANT

Scripture is very clear on this point. *". . . The borrower is servant to the lender"* (Proverbs 22:7). Thus, if you desire to maintain a friendship, it would certainly be an unfortunate move to lend your friend money.

In addition to making your friend a servant, you cause him to put you in God's place when you lend. The need for a loan usually indicates that a person is experiencing serious financial pressure. God uses pressure to get our attention and to get us to seek Him. He promises: *". . . Call upon me in the day of trouble: I will deliver thee, and thou shalt glorify me"* (Psalm 50:15).

By lending to your friend, you take his focus off of God and put it on yourself.

157

2 BIBLICAL "LENDING" IS CHARITABLE, NOT COMMERCIAL

The guidelines which God gave to His people Israel for lending money were clearly based on the idea of helping a neighbor through a crisis, not to set up or expand a business. The loan was actually looked upon as a gift, and no interest was to be charged. *"Thou shalt not lend upon usury [interest] to thy brother; usury of money, usury of victuals, usury of any thing that is lent upon usury"* (Deuteronomy 23:19).

Not only does God prohibit the charging of interest to a "brother," He also says that a brother is not to be kept in financial bondage. Thus, He provided the releases of the seventh year and the year of jubilee.

"At the end of every seven years thou shalt make a release. And this is the manner of the release: Every creditor that lendeth ought unto his neighbour shall release it; he shall not exact it of his neighbour, or of his brother; because it is called the Lord's release" (Deuteronomy 15:1–2).

The exception to this release is to "foreigners." However, God continuously encourages giving to the poor rather than lending.

Notice how God emphasizes this point in Psalm 37:21 and again in Proverbs 19:17: *"The wicked borroweth, and payeth not again: but the righteous sheweth mercy, and giveth." "He that hath pity upon the poor lendeth unto the Lord; and that which he hath given will he pay him again."*

As we give to the poor, *in the name of the Lord,* we actually lend unto the Lord. By doing this, we cause the poor to glorify God; and we focus our expectations of return upon the Lord, not upon others.

This important truth is re-emphasized by the Lord when He discusses loans in Luke 6:30–36. *"... Lend, hoping for nothing again; and your reward shall be great, and ye shall be the children of the Highest. ..."*

3 USURY IS CONSISTENTLY CONDEMNED BY GOD

It is important to see the many Scriptural references which condemn interest loans to a brother. *"If thou lend money to any of my people that is poor by thee, thou shalt not be to him as an usurer, neither shalt thou lay upon him usury"* (Exodus 22:25).

The consequences of violating this instruction are explained in the following passages.

- **IT HINDERS GOD'S BLESSING ON YOU**

"... But unto thy brother thou shalt not lend upon usury: that the Lord thy God may bless thee in all that thou settest thine hand to ..." (Deuteronomy 23:20).

- **IT DESTROYS THE FEAR OF GOD**

"Take thou no usury of him, or increase: but fear thy God; that thy brother may live with thee. Thou shalt not give him thy money upon usury, nor lend him thy victuals for increase. I am the Lord your God..." (Leviticus 25:36–38).

- **IT LEADS TO FORGETTING GOD**

"... Thou hast taken usury and increase, and thou hast greedily gained of thy neighbours by extortion, and hast forgotten me, saith the Lord God. Behold, therefore I have smitten mine hand at thy dishonest gain which thou hast made ..." (Ezekiel 22:12–13).

- **IT RESULTS IN SPIRITUAL STUMBLING**

"Lord, who shall abide in thy tabernacle? who shall dwell in thy holy hill? ... He that putteth not out his money to usury, nor taketh reward against the innocent. He that doeth these thngs shall never be moved" (Psalm 15:1, 5).

- **IT CAUSES OTHERS TO GET OUR MONEY**

"He that by usury and unjust gain increaseth his substance, he shall gather it for him that will pity the poor" (Proverbs 28:8).

- **IT CALLS FOR GOD'S JUDGMENT**

"If he beget a son that is a robber, a shedder of blood, and that doeth the like to any one of these things. ... [If he] hath given forth upon usury, and hath taken increase: shall he then live? he shall not live: he hath done all these abominations; he shall surely die; his blood shall be upon him" (Ezekiel 18:10, 13).

If God equates usury with extortion, then usury is an offense which Paul instructs the New Testament Church to discipline. (See I Corinthians 5:8–13.)

INTEREST BITES YOUR FRIEND LIKE A SNAKE

The Biblical word for usury, *nâshak*, does not have the modern meaning of exorbitant interest. It simply means charging any interest at all. This has also been the primary dictionary definition, "the fact or practice of lending money at interest." (See the *Oxford Universal Dictionary*.)

The Hebrew meaning of usury is "to strike with a sting (as a serpent), to oppress, to bite." The implications of this definition are both significant and far-reaching. The "sting of interest" was heard in many a cry of those whose testimonies are recorded in Scripture.

Even in secular literature, there are abundant warnings to avoid all forms of borrowing and lending. This would clearly include co-signing. In Shakespeare's *Hamlet*, for example, Polonius gave his son the following advice as he went to a foreign country: "Neither a borrower, nor a lender be; for loan oft loses both itself and friend, and borrowing dulls the edge of husbandry."

How interest is similar to the bite of a snake

A SNAKE BITE	USURY (INTEREST)
1. The snake is a hidden danger to an unsuspecting passerby.	**1.** The final cost of interest is usually not comprehended by a borrower.
2. Getting close to a snake will usually result in being bitten.	**2.** Those who profit from interest make it easy for people to borrow money.
3. A snake usually strikes before its victim is aware of its presence.	**3.** Interest usually brings financial bondage before a borrower realizes what has taken place.
4. The realization of a snake bite results in anxiety and fear.	**4.** Compounded interest causes the borrower to develop anxiety and fearfulness.
5. The venom of the snake can produce alarming symptoms such as swelling, hemorrhaging, decreased circulation, lowered blood pressure, weakening pulse, nausea, and high temperature.	**5.** The result of interest can produce alarming physical, mental, emotional, and spiritual problems in the life of a borrower.
6. The ultimate result of a poisonous snake bite is the physical death of the victim.	**6.** The ultimate consequence for a borrower is the inability to repay the high interest loan and the loss of his property.

5 INTEREST CAUSES FRIENDS TO SECRETLY CURSE YOU

When friends come to you with financial pressures, they are often too embarrassed to ask you for charity. Instead, they will ask you for a loan, secretly hoping that you will insist on a gift or a loan without interest.

This secret desire may be based on their understanding of friendship or on the many Scriptural commands for Christians to help other Christians in times of need. *". . . At this time your abundance may be a supply for your want: that there may be equality"* (II Corinthians 8:14). (See also Romans 12:13; Galatians 6:10.)

The fact that loans with interest prompt cursing is emphasized in Jeremiah 15:10. *"Woe is me. . . . I have neither lent on usury, nor men have lent to me on usury; yet every one of them doth curse me."*

6 ONLY STRANGERS SHOULD BE CHARGED INTEREST

God makes a distinction between charitable loans and commercial loans. *"Unto a stranger thou mayest lend upon usury . . ."* (Deuteronomy 23:20).

This distinction also extended to the practice of releasing debts every seven years. *"Of a foreigner thou mayest exact it [the loan] again: but that which is thine with thy brother thine hand shall release; Save when there shall be no poor among you . . ."* (Deuteronomy 15:3–4). These loans may collect interest, but not exorbitant interest, since that would be unjust gain.

God promised His people that if they followed all of His laws that He would so richly bless them that they would never need to borrow. *". . . And thou shalt lend unto many nations, but thou shalt not borrow . . ."* (Deuteronomy 15:6).

It is against this backdrop that the parables of Jesus on lending and interest must be understood. *"Wherefore then gavest not thou my money into the bank, that at my coming I might have required mine own with usury?"* (Luke 19:23). (See also Matthew 25:27.)

Financial dealings with non-Christians are understood to be appropriate in light of I Corinthians 5:10.

7 CO-SIGNING IS A DANGEROUS FORM OF LENDING

If someone asks you to co-sign a note, it means that he is borrowing the money from someone else, but he is asking you to stand behind the loan.

When you co-sign, you are pledging whatever assets you have against the debt. Most people do not co-sign with the idea of having to assume the debt.

For this reason, the loss of money or assets usually comes as a shock and a financial setback to the one who co-signs.

8 GOD CONSISTENTLY CONDEMNS CO-SIGNING

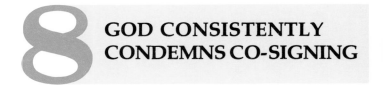

Scripture uses the word *surety* for the term *co-signing.* Six times God pleads with us to reject all co-signing.

- **CO-SIGNING IS A TRAP FOR YOU**

"My son, if thou be surety for thy friend, if thou hast stricken thy hand with a stranger, Thou art snared with the words of thy mouth, thou art taken with the words of thy mouth. Do this now, my son, and deliver thyself, when thou art come into the hand of thy friend; go, humble thyself, and make sure thy friend. Give not sleep to thine eyes, nor slumber to thine eyelids. Deliver thyself as a roe from the hand of the hunter, and as a bird from the hand of the fowler" (Proverbs 6:1–5).

- **CO-SIGNING WILL BRING YOU GRIEF**

"He that is surety for a stranger shall smart for it: and he that hateth suretiship is sure" (Proverbs 11:15).

- **CO-SIGNING REVEALS YOUR LACK OF UNDERSTANDING**

"A man void of understanding striketh hands, and becometh surety in the presence of his friend" (Proverbs 17:18).

- **CO-SIGNING CAN COST YOU EVERYTHING THAT YOU HAVE**

"Take his garment that is surety for a stranger . . ." (Proverbs 20:16). (See also Proverbs 27:13).

"Be not thou one of them that strike hands, or of

"Be not thou one of them that strike hands, or of them that are sureties for debts. If thou hast nothing to pay, why should he take away thy bed from under thee?" (Proverbs 22:26–27).

One day before Christmas, a woman asked one of the pastors of her church if he would co-sign for certain items that she wanted to buy for her family. She explained that since her husband filed for bankruptcy, the store would no longer let them buy on credit.

The pastor stated that God's Word prohibited him from co-signing but that he would like to give her some money toward the purchase. The woman refused, saying that she was not asking for charity.

A month later the woman was in the hospital with cancer. With tears running down her cheeks, she said to that pastor, "I can never thank you enough for refusing to co-sign for me. After I talked to you, I realized that the purchases I wanted to make really were not wise. I bought other gifts with the money that I had and we had our first debt-free Christmas. If you had co-signed, you would have had to pay for all the things that I was going to buy."

9 CO-SIGNING IS AN UNSCRIPTURAL PARTNERSHIP

According to *Strong's Exhaustive Concordance*, the root definition of the word translated *surety* is "to tie together, to braid, to mix together."

This is actually what is done when you vouch for the debt of another person—you become a partner with him and the errors of his way.

- Your partnership gives approval to the loan which he is securing.

- Your partnership encourages him to live beyond his income.

- Your partnership discourages him from waiting for God's timing on a business transaction.

- Your partnership hinders God's supernatural provision for the need which he has.

When you co-sign for a Christian in need, you violate Christ's commands to give; and when you co-sign for a non-Christian, you violate God's command not to be yoked together with an unbeliever. (See II Corinthians 6:14.)

10 CO-SIGNING EXPOSES YOU TO SWINDLERS

One of the methods which swindlers use to ply their evil trade is co-signing. They will offer rich rewards to you if you will stand behind their debt. They will convince you that they are against the wall and are willing to take a loss if you will help them out.

What you do not realize is that by listening to them and considering the possiblity of co-signing, you are the one who is against the wall, and you will take a loss.

For this reason, God wants all of us to hate co-signing.

By co-signing you are pledging your assets against three things—the borrower's ability to meet the loan payments, his intentions to pay you back if he defaults, and his ability to pay you back.

11 LENDING OR CO-SIGNING OVERRIDES DEEPER PROBLEMS

Financial pressures are usually symptoms of deeper problems. By removing the pressure, you only avoid or postpone dealing with the problems.

When someone comes with a request for a loan or for co-signing, you have the responsibility to ask enough questions to determine whether or not there is a deeper "root" problem of bitterness, greed, or moral impurity.

By helping him resolve any of these, you invest in his life that which is far greater than money. You give him true riches with freedom, and direction to seek God and experience riches without sorrow. (See Proverbs 10:22.)

> **When you co-sign for a person whom God is chastening, you will share the pain of his discipline.**

IF YOU HAVE LENT MONEY TO YOUR FRIEND . . .

1. Acknowledge to God that you have violated Scriptural principles by lending and have caused your friend to violate Scriptural principles by borrowing.

2. Ask your friend to forgive you for violating Scripture and for putting him under bondage by lending the money to him. Explain that you want to be a true friend by helping him to be financially free.

3. Gather facts from your friend to determine what his real financial needs are and what underlying spiritual problems may have caused them.

4. Determine what amount God would have you give to your friend, as well as what other counsel and direction you can give to him.

5. Expect that the financial bondage that your friend is in may take a long time to remove and that you will have to share the burden with him until he is financially free.

IF YOU HAVE CO-SIGNED . . .

"Deliver thyself as a roe from the hand of the hunter . . ." (Proverbs 6:5).

1. Realize that you are in trouble.

"Thou art snared with the words of thy mouth . . ." (Proverbs 6:2).

2. Before each step, cry out to God and seek wise counsel.

3. Seek release.

"Do this now, my son, and deliver thyself . . ." (Proverbs 6:3).

4. Take the initiative and plead.

". . . Go, humble thyself. . . . Give not sleep to thine eyes, nor slumber to thine eyelids" (Proverbs 6:3–4).

Personal Commitment to Reject Lending and Co-signing

In accordance with the clear teachings of Scripture, I will not lend money to friends or co-sign for anyone.

From this day forward, it will be my policy to explain to anyone who asks for financial assistance that my money belongs to God and that I would need at least 24 hours to prayerfully consider what He would have me do.

Signed _____ Date _____

CAN YOU IDENTIFY BASIC FINANCIAL TERMS?

Match the following Biblical terms with the best definition.

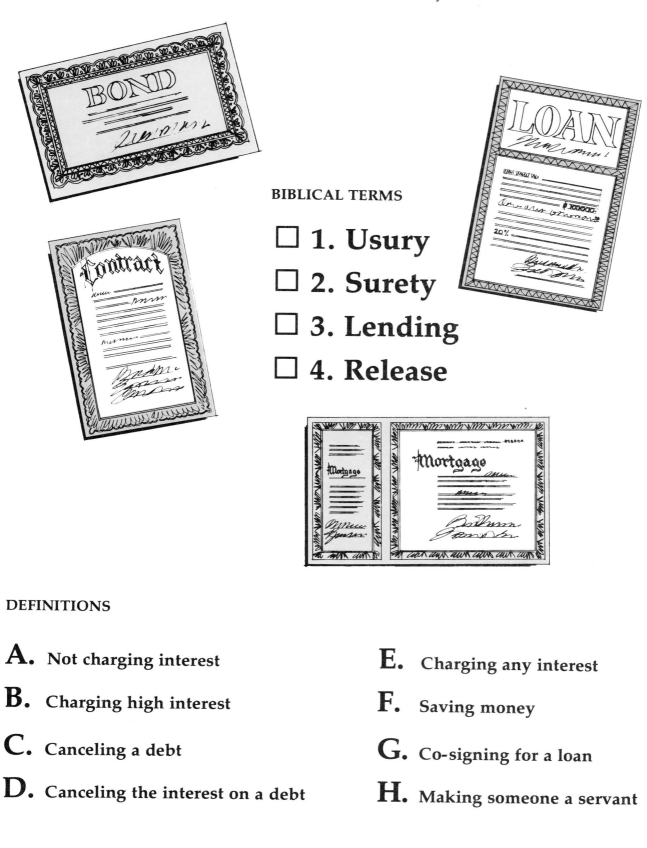

BIBLICAL TERMS

☐ **1. Usury**

☐ **2. Surety**

☐ **3. Lending**

☐ **4. Release**

DEFINITIONS

A. Not charging interest

B. Charging high interest

C. Canceling a debt

D. Canceling the interest on a debt

E. Charging any interest

F. Saving money

G. Co-signing for a loan

H. Making someone a servant

WHO FOLLOWED OR VIOLATED GOD'S PRINCIPLES OF LENDING AND CO-SIGNING?

Match each statement with the person who is most likely to have said it.

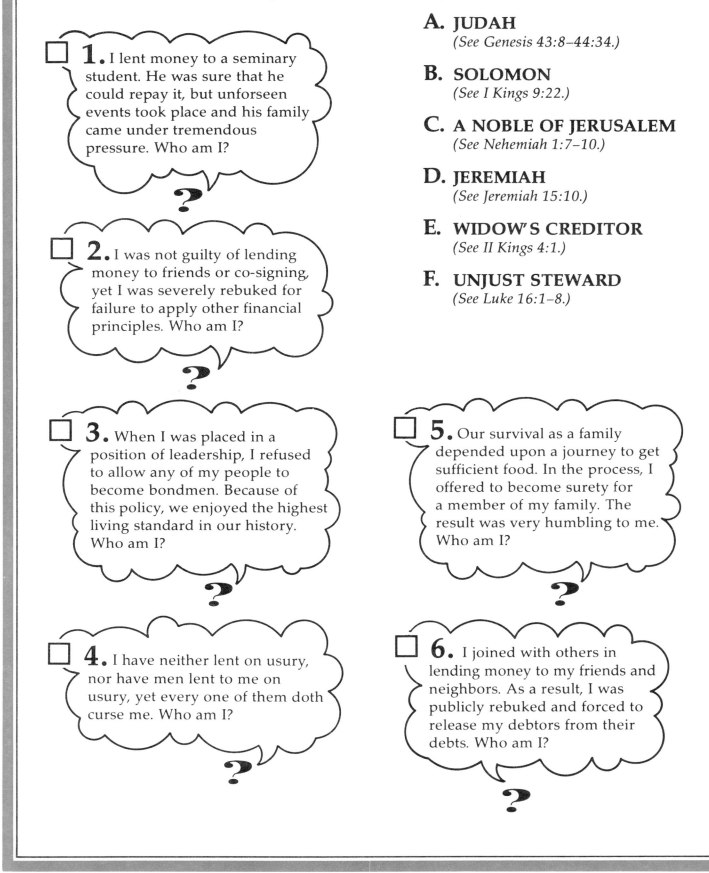

1. I lent money to a seminary student. He was sure that he could repay it, but unforseen events took place and his family came under tremendous pressure. Who am I?

2. I was not guilty of lending money to friends or co-signing, yet I was severely rebuked for failure to apply other financial principles. Who am I?

3. When I was placed in a position of leadership, I refused to allow any of my people to become bondmen. Because of this policy, we enjoyed the highest living standard in our history. Who am I?

4. I have neither lent on usury, nor have men lent to me on usury, yet every one of them doth curse me. Who am I?

5. Our survival as a family depended upon a journey to get sufficient food. In the process, I offered to become surety for a member of my family. The result was very humbling to me. Who am I?

6. I joined with others in lending money to my friends and neighbors. As a result, I was publicly rebuked and forced to release my debtors from their debts. Who am I?

A. JUDAH
(*See Genesis 43:8–44:34.*)

B. SOLOMON
(*See I Kings 9:22.*)

C. A NOBLE OF JERUSALEM
(*See Nehemiah 1:7–10.*)

D. JEREMIAH
(*See Jeremiah 15:10.*)

E. WIDOW'S CREDITOR
(*See II Kings 4:1.*)

F. UNJUST STEWARD
(*See Luke 16:1–8.*)

Answers: 1E 2F 3B 4D 5A 6C

DO YOU KNOW GOD'S PRINCIPLES OF LENDING AND CO-SIGNING?

Choose the best answer.

1. LENDING TO NEEDY FRIENDS:
- ☐ A. Makes you their servant
- ☐ B. Makes them your servant
- ☐ C. Makes their load lighter

2. LENDING IN THE OLD TESTAMENT:
- ☐ A. Was basically commercial
- ☐ B. Was basically charitable
- ☐ C. Was basically conditional

3. LOANS TO FELLOW ISRAELITES WERE:
- ☐ A. Low in interest
- ☐ B. High in interest
- ☐ C. With no interest

4. LOANS TO FELLOW ISRAELITES WERE:
- ☐ A. Forgiven after three years
- ☐ B. Forgiven after four years
- ☐ C. Forgiven after six years

5. LOANS WITH INTEREST ARE:
- ☐ A. Compared to traps
- ☐ B. Compared to snake bites
- ☐ C. Compared to wolves

6. FRIENDS WHO ASK FOR A LOAN:
- ☐ A. Expect a loan with interest
- ☐ B. Expect a loan with no interest
- ☐ C. Expect a gift from you

7. GOD EXPECTS US TO GIVE:
- ☐ A. Low interest loans to friends
- ☐ B. No interest loans to friends
- ☐ C. Outright gifts to friends

8. WHEN WE CO-SIGN FOR A LOAN:
- ☐ A. We make larger returns
- ☐ B. We make smaller returns
- ☐ C. We form a partnership

9. WE SHOULD ONLY CO-SIGN FOR:
- ☐ A. Christians
- ☐ B. No one
- ☐ C. Trustworthy people

10. GOD WANTS US TO:
- ☐ A. Be careful of co-signing
- ☐ B. Avoid co-signing
- ☐ C. Hate co-signing

11. CO-SIGNING INCREASES OUR:
- ☐ A. Potential to make money
- ☐ B. Potential to make friends
- ☐ C. Potential to be swindled

12. CO-SIGNING FOR A FRIEND:
- ☐ A. Helps solve his problem
- ☐ B. Avoids the real problem
- ☐ C. Helps identify the problem

13. CO-SIGNING FOR A FRIEND IS:
- ☐ A. Better than lending
- ☐ B. Worse than lending
- ☐ C. The same as lending

14. IF WE HAVE CO-SIGNED:
- ☐ A. We should follow through
- ☐ B. We should do nothing
- ☐ C. We should seek release

Answers: 1.B 2.B 3.C 4.C 5.B 6.C 7.C 8.C 9.B 10.C 11.C 12.B 13.B 14.C

A PRAISEWORTHY WIFE
A developer of God-given potential

NURTURING

"She looketh well to the ways of her household, and eateth not the bread of idleness" (Proverbs 31:27).

TEACHING

"She openeth her mouth with wisdom; and in her tongue is the law of kindness" (Proverbs 31:26).

14 DEVELOP THE FULL POTENTIAL OF YOUR HOME

"Who can find a virtuous woman? for her price is far above rubies. The heart of her husband doth safely trust in her . . . and let her own works praise her in the gates" (Proverbs 31:10–11, 31).

MINISTERING

"She stretcheth out her hand to the poor; yea, she reacheth forth her hands to the needy" (Proverbs 31:20).

HAVE YOU DEVELOPED THE GOD-GIVEN POTENTIAL OF YOUR HOME?

PERSONAL EVALUATION:

YES NO

1. Have you and your wife discussed the possibility of educating your children at home? ☐ ☐

2. Are you using home repairs as opportunities for teaching your children practical skills? ☐ ☐

3. Have you taken specific steps to free your children from the false pressures of advertising? ☐ ☐

4. Do you have a place where guests can stay in your home? ☐ ☐

5. Do you regularly invite guests for a meal or a visit in your home? ☐ ☐

6. Do you invite guests who are not able to repay you for your hospitality? ☐ ☐

7. Do you have a planned program to care for those who become sick or needy? ☐ ☐

8. Have you made adequate provision in your home for your wife to develop her skills and abilities? ☐ ☐

9. Have you provided the resources to allow your wife to use her skills in homemaking responsibilities? ☐ ☐

10. Can you list at least thirty character qualities with their operational definitions? ☐ ☐

11. Do you eat at least one meal each day with all of your family present? ☐ ☐

12. Are you sure that your family practices dental hygiene daily? ☐ ☐

13. Do you have first-aid training and equipment in your home? ☐ ☐

14. Do you have a Bible Study in your home? ☐ ☐

15. Have you been able to lead at least one neighbor to salvation? ☐ ☐

16. Do you plan to care for your parents when they are old? ☐ ☐

17. Have you determined that it is not wise for your wife to work outside the home? ☐ ☐

18. Have you instilled in your wife the real value of her working in the home? ☐ ☐

19. Have you avoided putting pressure on your wife to work outside the home? ☐ ☐

20. Does your wife reflect happiness and contentment in being a homemaker? ☐ ☐

TOTAL CORRECT ☐

EVALUATION SCORE:

20–19 yes = Full potential developed
18–16 yes = Good potential developed
15–12 yes = Potential being developed
11–8 yes = Potential to be developed
7–0 yes = Much to develop

168

TEACHING CENTER

When a family is functioning according to Scripture, the basic factors of learning are present. These include acceptance, security, example, reinforcement, motivation, discipline, consistency, and reward.

Learning in the home is related to life and is motivated by both planned and unplanned events. It is in this context that God commands parents to make use of the times during the day in which a child will have the greatest learning readiness. *"And thou shalt teach them [the commandments] diligently unto thy children, and shalt talk of them when thou sittest in thine house, and when thou walkest by the way, and when thou liest down, and when thou risest up"* *(Deuteronomy 6:7).*

If parents delegate the total teaching of their children to others, they not only lose vital links of communication with their children, but they also forfeit the special love and admiration which children naturally have for those who faithfully teach them.

No one knows the basic needs of the child better than the parents; and the greatest potential

KNOW WHAT FUNCTIONS GOD INTENDED TO BE IN YOUR HOME

Many families have lost interest in the home because it no longer has the vital functions which God intended for it. When these Scriptural functions are restored in the home, they will have a significant effect on reaching financial freedom. These functions are as follows:

influence on the child are the parents, as well as older brothers and sisters.

• *First objective—Character training*

God has given children a great potential of faith. *". . . Except ye be converted, and become as little children, ye shall not enter into the kingdom of heaven"* *(Matthew 18:3).*

From birth to six years of age, children should be taught Godly character qualities and their operational definitions. Effective resources for doing this include the Character Clues game, *Character Sketches* volumes, and *The Eagle Story.*

• *Second objective—Standing alone*

By the age of twelve a son or daughter must be able to effectively stand against evil, whatever the cost.

The ability to stand alone is the heritage of those who know that they have a "superior" way of life. Therefore, it is essential for parents to instill in their children basic Scriptural principles along with a wide knowledge of the Bible. Effective resources for doing this include the *Men's Manual* series, the Commands of Christ game, the *Life Notebook*, and *The Pineapple Story.*

• Third objective—Mighty in spirit

Between the ages of twelve and twenty, sons and daughters must understand basic life concepts. Wise concepts come by applying Scriptural principles to the functions and relationships of marriage, family, ministry, vocation, and government. Resources for reaching this goal include the Basic Seminar, Advanced Seminar, and *The Eagle Story.*

• Fourth objective—Basic skills

A by-product of the first three objectives should be the learning of practical life skills.

These skills, with the wisdom and character behind them, will become the basis for true success.

HOSPITALITY CENTER

The best financial investment that any Christian can make is in the lives of others. One of the most practical ways of doing this is to open your home to others.

God promises to reward the family who shows hospitality. In fact, He explains that this function should grow out of disciplines which the family learns together. *"Is not this the fast that I have chosen . . . to deal thy bread to the hungry, and that thou bring the poor that are cast out to thy house? . . . Then shall thy light break forth as the morning, and thine health shall spring forth speedily . . ."* (Isaiah 58:6–8).

This function is so important that God makes it one of the prerequisites for a woman to qualify for church support when she becomes a widow, *". . . If she have lodged strangers . . ."* (I Timothy 5:10).

Christ gave specific guidelines regarding the motives of such hospitality. We are not to look to guests to reward us financially, because God promises that He will. *". . . When thou makest a dinner or a supper, call . . . the poor, the maimed, the lame, the blind: And thou shalt be blessed; for they cannot recompense thee: for thou shalt be recompensed at the resurrection of the just"* (Luke 14:12–14).

The immediate benefits of home hospitality are as follows:

• Godly goals are reinforced

Guests provide a marvelous motivation for both parents and children to work toward the spiritual goals which they have set for themselves and their home. Parents are also able to give proper recognition of their children's achievements.

• Valuable insights are learned

Every guest will have a storehouse of valuable insights, ideas, and lessons learned.

By learning how to ask precise questions, rich counsel and information can be gained. Wise parents will invite guests who will reinforce the teachings that they are practicing in the home.

• Principles of sharing are learned

A family should look at their home as a channel of help and encouragement to others, not simply as a storehouse to gather for themselves. God promises to bless whatever a family gives in His name—even a cup of cold water.

• The home is cleansed

Guests notice things which Christians have in their homes. Making the house ready for guests, therefore, involves an evaluation of how the books, art, and other contents of the home will reflect the true message of Christian living.

A Christian home should have in it items which God has provided by answers to prayer. These items become dynamic reminders to the family and effective illustrations which can be shared with guests.

CRAFT CENTER

Many businesses were started as a result of people using their skills to meet needs in the home. Not only can home products become a means of income, but they can also be a source of fulfillment to the family and encouragement to others.

One mother had a special ability to grow plants. Soon she was providing plants for exclusive offices in her town. This ability not only provided additional income, but it also provided a significant opportunity to witness to her customers.

A mother who uses the home as a craft center, however, must be careful to keep her priorities in balance. She must be sensitive to her husband's cautions and counsel, and she must not allow her business to crowd out her family's needs.

God explains the qualities of a praiseworthy mother in Proverbs 31. A significant amount of space is devoted to her ability to use available resources in providing quality items for her family, as well as for others.

- *"She seeketh wool, and flax, and worketh willingly with her hands" (vs. 13).*
- *"She considereth a field, and buyeth it: with the fruit of her hands she planteth a vineyard" (vs. 16).*
- *"She perceiveth that her merchandise is good: her candle goeth not out by night" (vs. 18).*
- *"She layeth her hands to the spindle, and her hands hold the distaff" (vs. 19).*
- *"She maketh herself coverings of tapestry . . ." (vs. 22).*
- *"She maketh fine linen, and selleth it . . ." (vs. 24).*

"She riseth also while it is yet night, and giveth meat to her household, and a portion to her maidens. . . . Her children arise up, and call her blessed . . ." (vss. 15, 28).

The range of crafts is as wide as the imagination of the family and the needs of the family and others. The general categories could include food, clothing, merchandise, and services.

HOME POTENTIAL ILLUSTRATED

"What could I, as a housewife, do to make a little extra money? I want to send a gift to a Christian ministry."

That was the motivation that a mother had several years after becoming a Christian. Her husband was a supervisor in a bakery. She took care of their two young daughters at home.

One evening she made up ninety small cartons of salad. The next morning she asked her grocer and other store owners if they would stock them. They each said, "You've really got something here, but it's the wrong time of the year to sell salad."

Each store owner bought several samples and put them on the shelves. When she returned home, the phone was ringing. The salad was sold out and the store owners wanted more. She informed them that she could not return until the end of the week, because this was only to be a part-time project.

When her husband arrived home, phone calls were still coming in. He encouraged her to make up a new batch for the next day.

A year later, the manager of a national food chain that had stopped selling salads tasted hers and asked if she would prepare salads for their stores.

Soon the business outgrew the home. Today, her two sons-in-law and her grandson are directing the thriving interstate company.

Her desire to invest in God's work has resulted in more benefits than she ever imagined. Her family has been drawn closer together; her joy in giving continues; and her financial needs are being met, since her husband has gone to be with the Lord.

NURTURING CENTER

A harmonious home adds to the health of family members. A loving, caring family will speed recovery and ease the pain of illness.

The day of the doctor's house call seems to be over. It is being replaced with the emergency center of the hospital. As more and more medical care is taken out of the home, hospital and medical costs are becoming enormous.

Obviously, certain medical problems must be treated at the hospital. However, the home's place in God's program for health care is far greater than most of us realize.

• *Healthy attitudes*

The home must be the place of accountability for attitudes of forgiveness and clearing of conscience.

If this is not accomplished, bitterness and guilt will be like poisons in the system, producing innumerable medical, psychological, and spiritual problems.

• *Nutritious meals*

The praiseworthy woman described in Proverbs 31 took special care in planning and preparing nutritious meals. (See Proverbs 31:14–15.)

The obvious result of well-balanced meals will be the increased health of the family and decreased medical bills.

• *Regular fasting*

God designed fasting for specific spiritual objectives. Those who voluntarily set aside one or more meals in order to spend time in reading God's Word and in prayer will be drawn closer to the Lord. They will discern God's leading more clearly and receive His promised blessings. (See Matthew 6:16–18.)

Fasting is also being used by many people to achieve significant physical benefits. Carefully planned fasts will eliminate dangerous toxins in the body system and increase spiritual and physical alertness.

Before entering into a fast, it is wise to check with a physician who is knowledgeable about fasts as well as your medical history.

• *Dental care*

The cost of repairing tooth decay and treating gum disease is rapidly increasing; and, as most dentists will admit, there would be little or no need for their services if proper eating and cleaning practices were maintained.

• *Home safety*

Home accidents are both painful and costly. A parent's watchful eye and careful training of the children will avoid many accidents. However, if accidents do happen, first-aid procedures should be known and used.

• *Home treatment*

Many patients go into the hospital with one problem and come out with another.

The difficulty of maintaining sanitary conditions is a constant challenge to hospitals. Whenever possible, the home should be considered for the treatment of, and recovery from, medical problems.

• *Believing prayer*

When a family member has a serious illness, one of the steps which should be followed is to call for the elders of the church. Instructions for this procedure are given in James 5:14–16:

"Is any sick among you? let him call for the elders of the church; and let them pray over him, anointing him with oil in the name of the Lord: And the prayer of faith shall save the sick, and the Lord shall raise him up; and if he have committed sins, they shall be forgiven him. Confess your faults one to another, and pray one for another, that ye may be healed. The effectual fervent prayer of a righteous man availeth much."

This does not negate the place of medical help, but it puts sickness in its proper spiritual perspective, allowing many families to avoid unnecessary operations and costly medical bills.

MINISTRY CENTER

The early Church grew in numbers and effectiveness because each home was viewed as an extension of the local church. Early Christians would meet daily in various homes to exhort each other from God's Word, pray, and share meals together.

Today, homes abound with possibility for effective spiritual outreach. This outreach gives purpose and direction for funds spent in the home.

• *Home Bible studies*

Many neighbors and friends have been won to Christ and helped to spiritual growth through home Bible studies. Special classes can be conducted for men, women, couples, youth, children, professional groups, and families.

• *Missionary projects*

God may give a particular concern to a family for a missionary or mission field. This could involve correspondence during the year. If it is a home mission field, the family could make visits during the summer.

Missionary projects build fellowship in the family and provide clear direction for giving to the Lord's work.

• *Neighborhood witnessing*

A variety of opportunities are present in a neighborhood to demonstrate Christian love, understanding, and assistance, and to explain the Gospel. When we demonstrate Christian love, neighbors are encouraged to ask us for a reason for the hope that lies within us.

• *Visiting the fatherless and widows*

The growing reality of our society is that more and more families are being divided. This makes the outreach of Christian families even more necessary. God states that *"pure religion and undefiled before God and the Father is this, To visit the fatherless and widows . . ."* (James 1:27).

• *Home care for elderly parents*

In our throw-away society, the growing tendency is to put elderly parents in a nursing home.

The benefits of ministering to elderly parents in the home are not often recognized. Grandchildren are able to see the rewards of a Godly life or the consequences of youthful sins.

Family members are forced to develop more Godly attitudes as they respond to the difficult needs of the elderly.

The possibility of neglect or harmful care outside of the home is avoided. Grandchildren are taught loyalty and respect for their parents as they see their parents demonstrate those same qualities to their grandparents.

Relatives are drawn together for prayer and counsel as needs for care become more critical.

• *Superior way of life*

The most effective outreach comes as neighbors and friends observe all the functions taking place in your home and realize that you have a superior way of life. They will often share their problems and ask you for counsel.

REDUCE BILLS AND IMPROVE THE QUALITY OF YOUR LIFE

1. Shut off your television and learn how to communicate with each other.
2. Limit phone calls and learn how to write better letters.
3. Avoid prepared foods and dining out and learn more about cooking.
4. Replace home care services with family teamwork.
5. Decrease food bills by obeying Biblical guidelines for eating.
6. Reduce clothing costs by learning how to sew and how to care for clothes.
7. Reduce dental and medical bills by practicing dental hygiene and preventive medicine.
8. Reduce the use of the car and get more exercise by walking to nearby destinations.

WHAT HAPPENS WHEN A MOTHER WORKS OUTSIDE OF THE HOME

1. SHE VIOLATES SCRIPTURE

God intended for the home to be the center of a mother's world. In Titus 2:5, women are instructed to be "... *discreet, chaste, keepers at home, good, obedient to their own husbands, that the word of God be not blasphemed.*"

In I Timothy 5:14, younger women are instructed to "... *marry, bear children, guide the house, give none occasion to the adversary to speak reproachfully.*"

Solomon warned his son that one of the evidences of an evil woman was that "... *her feet abide not in her house*" (Proverbs 7:11).

2. SHE NEGLECTS HER CHILDREN

No one can fully take the place of the mother when children are young. There is no such thing as "quality time" in a child's world. The needs of children are as urgent as they are unscheduled; and God expects a mother, to whom He has entrusted a child, to care for that child.

3. SHE IS UNFULFILLED

The only way that a woman can find identity and meaning in her life is to discover and fulfill the purposes for which God made her.

Scripture clearly establishes the fact that God made the woman to be a "help meet" (helpful companion) to her husband. (See Genesis 2:18.) She will never find fulfillment by trying to copy a man's role.

4. SHE DAMAGES HER MARRIAGE

When a mother tries to establish her independence by working outside of her home, she deeply wounds the spirit of her marriage and the love between her and her husband.

Love is strengthened when there is a realization of how much each partner needs the other.

When we do not think that we need God, we lose our love for Him. When a mother does not think that she needs her husband or her children, she loses her love for them.

5. SHE MAY TRANSFER HER AFFECTIONS

When a wife works for another man, she actually displays toward him some of the attitudes of an ideal wife.

During working hours she is alert to her employer's needs and desires. She is flexible. Her expectations are minimal, and she is grateful for whatever he does to make her job easier.

Her grateful spirit encourages him to do even more for her. This prompts her to express more appreciation and admiration to him.

Soon she begins to compare her husband unfavorably with her employer, and this comparison leads to damage in her marriage relationship.

6. SHE FINDS HERSELF IN TWO COMPETING WORLDS

If a wife does find a job which she enjoys outside of the home, she will suddenly find that she is in two worlds—one at home and one at work. Each one will make demands and give rewards.

Since no one can serve two masters, she must ultimately decide which world will become her primary source for acceptance, approval, achievement, and fulfillment.

7. SHE SUFFERS DESTRUCTIVE PRESSURES

When a mother assumes employment outside of the home, she subjects herself to an additional set of pressures and tensions. These produce physical and emotional stresses.

Prolonged exposure to these stresses is causing many women to suffer physically, psychologically, and spiritually, and to transfer these pressures to their families.

8. SHE NEGLECTS VITAL HOME FUNCTIONS

If a mother gives her time, energy, and talent to a job outside of the home, it obviously means that she is less able to fulfill the God-given functions in her home simply for lack of time.

The priceless opportunities within a mother's home cannot be reclaimed once her children have grown up.

9. SHE SETS A BAD EXAMPLE FOR OTHERS

Some women may appear to function effectively in two worlds. By doing so, however, they provide a damaging example to other mothers who definitely cannot manage such a schedule.

10. SHE IS FINANCIALLY UNWISE

Many mothers feel that they have to work outside of the home in order to make ends meet. However, a careful evaluation of that second paycheck reveals that it is an unprofitable venture. On the other hand, a woman who develops the potential functions of her home and who practices wise buying can greatly increase the finances of the home.

The basis of "making ends meet" is not increasing income as much as it is decreasing bills by finding more efficient ways to utilize present resources.

THE MYTH OF A MOTHER'S PAYCHECK

The following costs have come from independent sources and accurately reflect the expenses which a wife and mother would incur by working outside the home.

Annual wage	**$14,000.00**
Monthly salary	**1,166.66**

EXPENSES (Monthly)

1. Federal income tax (15%)	$175.00
2. State income tax (3%)	35.00
3. Social Security tax (7%)	81.66
4. Tithe	117.00
5. Transportation* (400 miles @ 30¢ per mile)	120.00
6. Meals ($3 a day)	60.00
7. Restaurant and carry-out meals (From lack of time for preparation)	80.00
8. Extra clothes and cleaning	100.00
9. Forfeited savings on thrift shopping (10%)	116.60
10. Hairdresser	20.00
11. Employee insurance	15.00
12. Day care ($50 a week, one child)	200.00
13. "I owe it to myself" expenses	95.00
	$1215.26
Net Loss	(48.60)

*This does not include the additional costs of a second car, which might be needed because of the mother's job.

DO YOU PASS THE HOME DEVELOPMENT TEST?

TEST AREAS	QUESTIONS
1. Teaching center	Are you teaching Scriptural principles to your family?
2. Home maintenance	Is your house in need of repair?
3. Equipment repair	Is there broken equipment in your home?
4. Garbage quantity	Do you throw out leftover food or usable items?
5. Storage	Are your closets and shelves neat and orderly?
6. Unused items	Have you given to others the things that you no longer need?
7. Library books	Have you removed all unwholesome books and magazines from your home?
8. Background music	Do you play wholesome sacred and classical music?
9. Hospitality center	Is your home ready for guests at all times?
10. Craft center	Is your family developing practical skills?
11. Nurturing center	Do you practice preventive medicine?
12. Ministry center	Do your neighbors know that you are Christians?
13. Witnessing	Are you praying for specific individuals?
14. True religion	Are you assisting any widows or orphans?
15. Outside employment	Is your home a place of fulfillment for your wife?

Personal Commitment to Encourage Home Development

Because God has established the family and the home as the central unit of the Church and the nation, I purpose to develop the God-given potential of my home as taught in Scripture.

This means that I will encourage and assist my wife in a fulfilling ministry in our home, rather than encouraging her to work outside of the home.

Wife's agreement _____ Date _____

Husband's agreement _____ Date _____

HOW DID THE "PROPHET'S CHAMBER" COME INTO BEING?

Choose the correct answer for each question. This account is found in II Kings 4:8–37.

1. Years ago there was a great woman who lived in the town of
- ☐ **A.** Bethel.
- ☐ **B.** Shunem.
- ☐ **C.** Shushan.

2. Occasionally there passed by her house a Godly prophet named
- ☐ **A.** Elijah.
- ☐ **B.** Elisha.
- ☐ **C.** Daniel.

3. Whenever the prophet came by, she urged him to come in and
- ☐ **A.** Rest.
- ☐ **B.** Counsel.
- ☐ **C.** Eat.

4. One day she said to her husband, "Let us make a little
- ☐ **A.** House."
- ☐ **B.** Chamber."
- ☐ **C.** Tent."

5. She would furnish it with a bed, a table, a stool, and a
- ☐ **A.** Lamp.
- ☐ **B.** Lantern.
- ☐ **C.** Candlestick.

6. Her husband agreed, and thereafter the prophet always
- ☐ **A.** Used it.
- ☐ **B.** Stayed away.
- ☐ **C.** Remained.

7. One day, the prophet asked God to reward this woman and her husband by giving them
- ☐ **A.** Health.
- ☐ **B.** Money.
- ☐ **C.** A child.

8. The following year this woman and her husband had a
- ☐ **A.** Boy.
- ☐ **B.** Girl.
- ☐ **C.** Twins.

9. The child grew, but one day he had a severe
- ☐ **A.** Injury.
- ☐ **B.** Headache.
- ☐ **C.** Cough.

10. The mother held him on her knees until noon. Then he
- ☐ **A.** Recovered.
- ☐ **B.** Did not improve.
- ☐ **C.** Died.

11. So the mother saddled her donkey and rode to the
- ☐ **A.** Father.
- ☐ **B.** Doctor.
- ☐ **C.** Prophet.

12. When she arrived, she wanted the prophet to
- ☐ **A.** Pray.
- ☐ **B.** Come.
- ☐ **C.** Send help.

13. The prophet sent his servant after he gave him his
- ☐ **A.** Coat.
- ☐ **B.** Bible.
- ☐ **C.** Rod.

14. The servant used what he was given. The result was
- ☐ **A.** Healing.
- ☐ **B.** Improvement.
- ☐ **C.** Nothing.

15. Finally, the prophet arrived and stretched himself upon the boy. He recovered after sneezing
- ☐ **A.** Three times.
- ☐ **B.** Seven times.
- ☐ **C.** Once.

Answers: 1.B 2.B 3.C 4.B 5.C 6.A 7.C 8.A 9.B 10.C 11.C 12.B 13.C 14.C 15.B

HOW DOES GOD ILLUSTRATE THE POTENTIAL OF THE HOME?

☐ **1.** My home illustrates the potential of a learning center. I did not have the assistance of a father, yet the training that was given to me in my youth had far-reaching results for the cause of Christ. **?**

☐ **2.** The things that took place in my home demonstrate the potential of a hospitality center. God promises that if we entertain strangers, we may entertain angels without knowing it. We often entertained Someone of greater importance than angels. **?**

☐ **3.** My home became a health center. Late one night, I brought two severely wounded men into my house, bathed and dressed their wounds, and refreshed their spirits. God rewarded my family and me with salvation. **?**

☐ **4.** My home also illustrates a health center and a ministry center. I was caring for a very sick mother-in-law. Because I brought the Lord into my home, she was miraculously healed. She then used the home as a base of ministry. **?**

Whose home is described?

A. PETER'S HOME
(See Matthew 8:14–17.)

B. MARY AND MARTHA'S HOME *(See Luke 10:38–42.)*

C. TIMOTHY'S HOME
(See II Timothy 1:5.)

D. WIDOW'S HOME
(See II Kings 4:1–7.)

E. AQUILA AND PRISCILLA'S HOME *(See Acts 18:2; Romans 16:3.)*

F. PHILIPPIAN JAILOR'S HOME *(See Acts 16:33–34.)*

☐ **5.** My home illustrates the potential of a home industry. I did not believe I had anything of value in the house, but God had me take what I did have and use some other resources. He multiplied the results so that I was able to get out of debt. **?**

☐ **6.** Our home has been cited as an effective ministry center. In fact, we established the pattern for the growth of the early Church. Christians met in our home on a regular basis, and we strengthened them from God's Word. **?**

Answers: 1.C 2.B 3.F 4.A 5.D 6.E

WHO FAILED IN THE USE OF HIS HOME?

Match the statement with the best answer.

☐ **1.** This person failed to use his home as an effective learning center. The consequences were devastating to him, his two sons, and the nation.

☐ **2.** He used his home to show hospitality to a prophet of God; but to convince his guest to come, he deceived him with a lie. His guest was killed when he left the house.

☐ **3.** He asked that a relative visit his home to make a meal, but his real motive was to be immoral with his guest. His brother killed him for what he did.

☐ **4.** He used his home as a hospitality center, but failed to be the proper host. The Lord reproved him and praised another guest who did what the host should have done.

☐ **5.** His home failed as a learning center and a craft center when he made wine from his vineyard and became drunk. His son mocked him and was cursed by God.

☐ **6.** He wanted to buy a vineyard that was next to his house, but it was not for sale. He allowed his wife to seize it craftily. God destroyed him, his family, and all of his descendants.

☐ **7.** He turned his house into a health center for himself; but instead of first calling on the Lord, he trusted only in the doctors and died.

☐ **8.** He used his house as a place to hide the treasures which he had wrongfully gained. His disobedience caused many deaths.

☐ **9.** He used his house to entertain many guests, but he allowed sensual dancing to take place. This caused a tragic death.

☐ **10.** God blessed him with riches and wealth, but when visitors came to his house, he proudly showed them everything. This encouraged them to return and steal it all.

A. Noah
(See Genesis 9.)

B. Asa
(See II Chronicles 16:12–13.)

C. Amnon
(See II Samuel 13.)

D. Herod
(See Matthew 14:3–11.)

E. Achan
(See Joshua 7.)

F. The Old Prophet
(See I Kings 13.)

G. Simon
(See Luke 7:44.)

H. Eli
(See I Samuel 3–4.)

I. Hezekiah
(See II Kings 20:12–19.)

J. Ahab
(See I Kings 21:1–26.)

Answers: 1.H 2.F 3.C 4.G 5.A 6.J 7.B 8.E 9.D 10.I

ZACCHAEUS
A great restorer of funds

PUBLIC REJECTION

"... There was a man named Zacchaeus, which was the chief among the publicans, and he was rich. And ... he was little of stature. ...

"... [Jesus] said unto him, Zacchaeus ... to day I must abide at thy house. ... [The crowd] murmured, saying, That he was gone to be guest with a man that is a sinner" (Luke 19:2–7).

15 CHOOSE A GOOD NAME WHATEVER THE COST

"A good name is rather to be chosen than great riches, and loving favour rather than silver and gold" (Proverbs 22:1).

PUBLIC RESTITUTION

"And Zacchaeus stood, and said unto the Lord; Behold, Lord, the half of my goods I give to the poor; and if I have taken any thing from any man by false accusation, I restore him fourfold" (Luke 19:8).

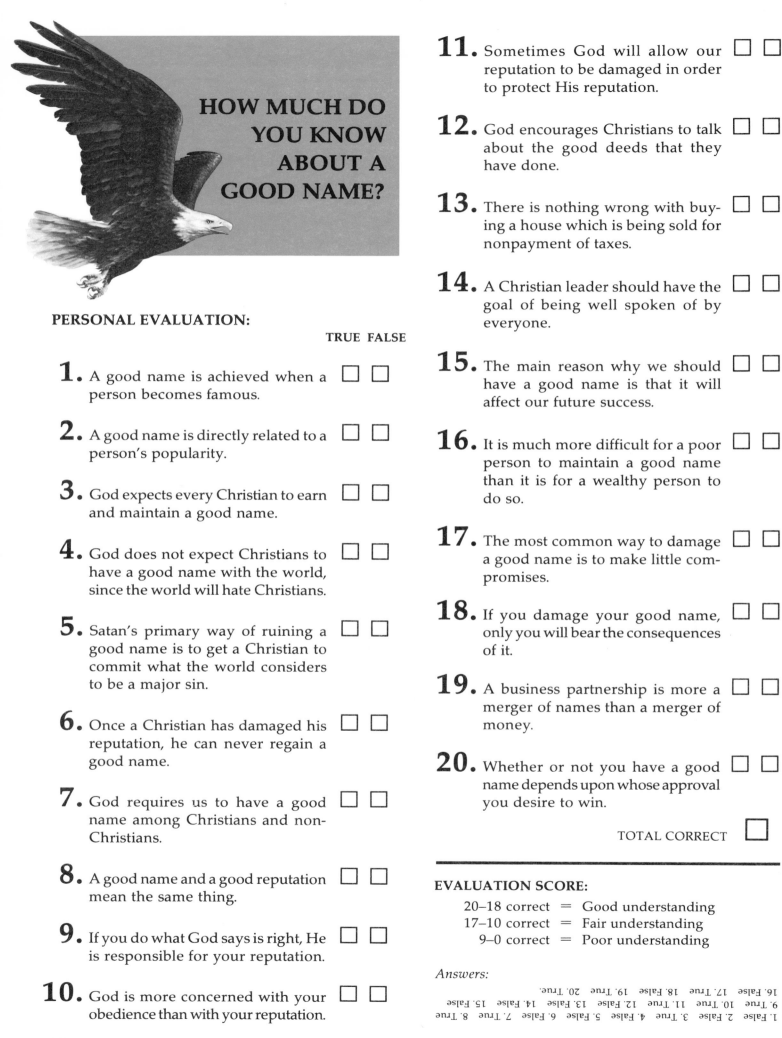

HOW MUCH DO YOU KNOW ABOUT A GOOD NAME?

PERSONAL EVALUATION:

TRUE FALSE

1. A good name is achieved when a person becomes famous. ☐ ☐

2. A good name is directly related to a person's popularity. ☐ ☐

3. God expects every Christian to earn and maintain a good name. ☐ ☐

4. God does not expect Christians to have a good name with the world, since the world will hate Christians. ☐ ☐

5. Satan's primary way of ruining a good name is to get a Christian to commit what the world considers to be a major sin. ☐ ☐

6. Once a Christian has damaged his reputation, he can never regain a good name. ☐ ☐

7. God requires us to have a good name among Christians and non-Christians. ☐ ☐

8. A good name and a good reputation mean the same thing. ☐ ☐

9. If you do what God says is right, He is responsible for your reputation. ☐ ☐

10. God is more concerned with your obedience than with your reputation. ☐ ☐

11. Sometimes God will allow our reputation to be damaged in order to protect His reputation. ☐ ☐

12. God encourages Christians to talk about the good deeds that they have done. ☐ ☐

13. There is nothing wrong with buying a house which is being sold for nonpayment of taxes. ☐ ☐

14. A Christian leader should have the goal of being well spoken of by everyone. ☐ ☐

15. The main reason why we should have a good name is that it will affect our future success. ☐ ☐

16. It is much more difficult for a poor person to maintain a good name than it is for a wealthy person to do so. ☐ ☐

17. The most common way to damage a good name is to make little compromises. ☐ ☐

18. If you damage your good name, only you will bear the consequences of it. ☐ ☐

19. A business partnership is more a merger of names than a merger of money. ☐ ☐

20. Whether or not you have a good name depends upon whose approval you desire to win. ☐ ☐

TOTAL CORRECT ☐

EVALUATION SCORE:

20–18 correct = Good understanding
17–10 correct = Fair understanding
9–0 correct = Poor understanding

Answers:

1. False 2. False 3. True 4. False 5. False 6. False 7. True 8. True 9. True 10. True 11. True 12. False 13. False 14. False 15. False 16. False 17. True 18. False 19. True 20. True.

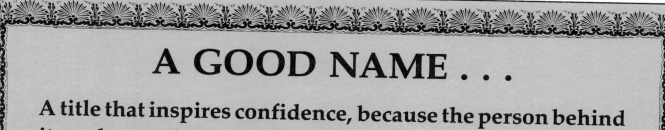

A GOOD NAME . . .

A title that inspires confidence, because the person behind it can be consistently depended upon to do what is legally and morally right, whatever the cost.

WHY A GOOD NAME IS ESSENTIAL

1. We represent God's name

As Christians, we are the only "Bible" that many people read. Every business transaction must therefore represent the truth of Scripture, or the reputation of the Lord will be damaged. *Ye are our epistle . . . known and read of all men" (II Corinthians 3:2).*

Has anyone rejected Christianity because of the way that you treated them in a business deal?

2. We honor our parents by it

The first commandment with a promise attached to it requires us to honor our father and mother. The promise is that only then will things go well for us. (See Ephesians 6:1–3.)

A name that is destroyed brings shame to the parents. *"Whoso keepeth the law is a wise son: but he that is a companion of riotous men shameth his father"* *(Proverbs 28:7).*

3. We pass it on to our children

More important than an inheritance of money is the heritage of a good name. Your children must bear the scorn and reaction or the praise and benefit of what your name represents. *"The memory of the just is blessed: but the name of the wicked shall rot"* *(Proverbs 10:7).*

4. We need it for business transactions

The foundation of a successful business is the reputation of the name behind it.

BASIC REQUIREMENTS TO EARN A GOOD NAME

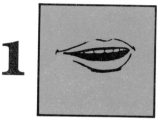 **1** **BE TRUE TO YOUR WORD**

Having a good name in business is primarily dependent upon the fulfillment of promises and commitments, whatever the cost. In this sense, a man's name is as good as his word. (See Psalm 15.)

God gives continual warning about making our words few and carefully chosen so that we can keep the promises that we make. We are to be swift to hear, but slow to speak. (See James 1:19.) *"Be not rash with thy mouth, and let not thine heart be hasty to utter any thing before God: for God is in heaven, and thou upon earth: therefore let thy words be few"* *(Ecclesiastes 5:2).*

MY VOWS AND PROMISES		Kept?
TO GOD	• Marriage vows	☐
	• Vows to serve God	☐
	• Daily Bible reading	☐
	• Tithes and offerings	☐
	• Other	☐
TO FAMILY	• Promises made to wife (Ask her to list them.)	☐
	• Promises made to children (Ask them for a list.)	☐
	• Promises to relatives (List them.)	☐
TO OTHERS	• Promises to friends	☐
	• Promises in business	☐
• Ask a trusted person to keep you accountable to fulfill each vow and promise. (See Hebrews 3:13.)		

2 RETURN BORROWED ITEMS

Scripture is very clear about the bad name that is earned when a person fails to return what was borrowed: *"The wicked borroweth, and payeth not again . . ."* (Psalm 37:21).

Borrowing among friends is usually done without careful records. It is often prompted by the urgency or need of the moment, with full intention to repay.

When the pressure eases, however, the items are forgotten by the borrower—but not by the lender. As time passes, the risk of damage, both to the borrowed items and to the friendship, continues to increase.

ITEMS I HAVE BORROWED	Repaid?
• Small amounts of money	☐
• Books	☐
• Tools	☐
• Food	☐
• Gas used in borrowed car or lawnmower	☐
• Pen or pencil	☐
• Clothes for special occasions	☐
• Equipment that I returned damaged	☐
• Items left by visitors	☐
• Other items that God brings to my mind	☐

3 USE "JUST WEIGHTS AND MEASURES"

God's eyes are upon every business transaction that we make. Dishonesty in selling or in buying is not only a sin against the person with whom we are dealing, but it is a sin against God and His economic order. God clearly tells us that He established just weights and measures. *"A just weight and balance are the Lord's: all the weights of the bag are his work"* (Proverbs 16:11).

Merchants in the marketplace would often use two sets of weights—one for buying and one for selling.

The weights that were used for buying were heavier than the weights used for selling. Obviously this was dishonest, because the amount of grain put on a scale to buy had to be more, while the grain put on a scale to sell would be less, in order to balance the weights.

God condemns this practice repeatedly in the Bible. *"A false balance is abomination to the Lord: but a just weight is his delight"* (Proverbs 11:1).

"Divers weights, and divers measures, both of them are alike abomination to the Lord" (Proverbs 20:10).

"Divers weights are an abomination unto the Lord; and a false balance is not good" (Proverbs 20:23).

A false weight or measure is not a large theft; in fact, it is a small theft repeated many times to many people. Yet, notice how severely God condemns and punishes the corruption of the marketplace for even a small unjust gain. *"Shall I count them pure with the wicked balances, and with the bag of deceitful weights? . . . Therefore also will I make thee sick. . . . Thou shalt eat, but not be satisfied. . . . Thou shalt sow, but thou shalt not reap; thou shalt tread the olives, but thou shalt not anoint thee with oil . . ."* (Micah 6:11–15).

LITTLE WAYS OF DISHONESTY	Guilty?
• Getting to work a few minutes late	☐
• Leaving work a few minutes early	☐
• Taking extra time for breaks	☐
• Not fulfilling expected services	☐
• Charging more than an item is worth	☐
• Failing to reveal defects	☐
• Reducing the quality of items	☐
• Making exaggerated claims	☐
• Not giving full amount of a purchase	☐
• Misusing "sick-day" policy	☐

Make a list of those whom you have cheated, and restore what was wrongly taken. *"Ye shall do no unrighteousness in judgment, in meteyard, in weight, or in measure. Just balances, just weights, a just ephah, and a just hin, shall ye have: I am the Lord your God . . ."* (Leviticus 19:35–36).

4 REJECT GAIN THAT COMES FROM ANOTHER'S LOSS

God condemns "unjust gain." He warns that those who receive it will gather it to their own hurt. *"And they lay wait for their own blood; they lurk privily for their own lives. So are the ways of every one that is greedy of gain; which taketh away the life of the owners thereof"* (Proverbs 1:18–19).

There will be severe and lasting damage to the name of any person who profits by another's loss.

GAIN AT ANOTHER'S LOSS	Guilty?
• Winning in a lottery or bingo game	☐
• Gaining through any form of gambling (races, cards, etc.)	☐
• Making, selling, or delivering liquor, cigarettes, harmful drugs, or pornography	☐
• Rewards for getting friends to buy high-priced items that they do not need	☐
• Taking advantage of the poor	☐

Although a way of getting money may be legal, it violates God's Word if it takes advantage of the poor. *"Blessed is he that considereth the poor: the Lord will deliver him in time of trouble. The Lord will preserve him, and keep him alive; and he shall be blessed upon the earth: and thou wilt not deliver him unto the will of his enemies"* (Psalm 41:1–2).

5 BE PUNCTUAL IN PAYING BILLS

A good name requires that bills be paid promptly. To withhold payment is to violate the clear instruction of Scripture: *"Say not unto thy neighbour, Go, and come again, and to morrow I will give; when thou hast it by thee"* (Proverbs 3:28). Notice that, in God's eyes, a payment is late one day after the work was finished.

There is good reason for this instruction. Those who are in business are often put in difficult financial circumstances. They depend upon the receipts that are owed to them so that they, in turn, can discharge their financial responsibilities.

When payment is late, the confidence and respect toward the one owing it is damaged. If there is inability to pay on time, the seller should be notified and special arrangements should be made.

HOW PROMPTLY DO YOU PAY BILLS?	Yes?
• Do I hold utility bills until the deadline to pay?	☐
• Do I wait 30 days to pay for items that were delivered?	☐
• Do I put money in the bank several days after writing checks on it?	☐
• Do I take advantage of grace periods in paying other bills?	☐
• Do I wait until the last day to pay my income taxes?	☐

To insure a good name in the matter of prompt payments, establish the practice of exchanging full payment for satisfactory services. This may require a special account for holding funds in trust so that they will not be spent for other items.

6 ASSOCIATE WITH WISE AND GODLY PEOPLE

Other people will evaluate our name on the basis of the company we keep. There is the continual danger of damaging a good name by wrong friendships. Scripture makes this quite clear. *"Be not deceived: evil communications corrupt good manners"* (I Corinthians 15:33).

Not only do our friends cause others to make judgments about our character, but they also influence us to make judgments about basic decisions in life. *"He that walketh with wise men shall be wise: but a companion of fools shall be destroyed"* (Proverbs 13:20).

Do all of your close friends have good reputations as wise and Godly people?

THREE KEY FACTORS
BEHIND A GOOD NAME

Just as gold is tried by fire, so a name will be tested by accusation and reaction. The Pharisees sought to tarnish the name of Jesus Christ by accusing Him of wrong association, breaking the Sabbath, and blasphemy.

Potiphar's wife tried to destroy Joseph's name by falsely accusing him of immorality.

Names that pass the test of fire give light and direction for generations to come.

1 MOTIVES

God warns that the secret motives of a man's heart will ultimately determine the quality and durability of his name.

If a person's secret desires are motivated by greed, pride, or sensuality, that person's thoughts and actions will sooner or later be influenced by them, and a good name will be destroyed. *"I the Lord search the heart, I try the reins, even to give every man according to his ways, and according to the fruit of his doings" (Jeremiah 17:10).*

On the other hand, if the secret motives of a person are to please the Lord and advance His kingdom, that person's name and reputation will be preserved even though he stumbles along the way. *"For a just man falleth seven times, and riseth up again: but the wicked shall fall into mischief" (Proverbs 24:16).*

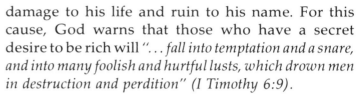

TEST OF MOTIVES	PURE MOTIVES	WRONG MOTIVES
1. Loss of possessions through catastrophes	Bless God	Curse God
2. Opportunity to gain at another's expense	Reject it	Justify it
3. False accusation in a business transaction	Forgive	Resent
4. Criticism for a wrong business decision	Make it right	Become bitter
5. Rejection or lack of recognition	Comfort in Scripture	Verbal reaction
6. Unresolved pressures and problems	Trust in the Lord	Frustration
7. Cheating by a Christian brother	Appeal	Sue

If a man has a secret desire to be rich, he will be attracted to people and schemes that will bring damage to his life and ruin to his name. For this cause, God warns that those who have a secret desire to be rich will *". . . fall into temptation and a snare, and into many foolish and hurtful lusts, which drown men in destruction and perdition" (I Timothy 6:9).*

If a person's secret motive is to set his affection on things above rather than on the things in the earth, he is able to endure the loss of temporal things with insight and spiritual gain. *"But what things were gain to me, those I counted loss for Christ. Yea doubtless, and I count all things but loss for the excellency of the knowledge of Christ Jesus my Lord: for whom I have suffered the loss of all things, and do count them but dung, that I may win Christ" (Philippians 3:7–8).*

2 CONSCIENCE

Right motives are the foundation of a clear conscience, and a clear conscience is the foundation of a good name.

To have a clear conscience means to be assured in our heart that no one can point a finger at us and say that we have wronged them and never tried to make it right. This kind of inward reassurance is our most effective defense against any attack on our name. *"Having a good conscience; that, whereas they speak evil of you, as of evildoers, they may be ashamed that falsely accuse your good conversation in Christ" (I Peter 3:16).*

A clear conscience gives inward motivation to maintain good works when your name is under attack. It is through the perseverance of good works that God's reward is gained and a good name is established. *"Having your conversation honest among the Gentiles: that, whereas they speak against you as evildoers, they may by your good works, which they shall behold, glorify God in the day of visitation" (I Peter 2:12).*

3 PRIORITIES

Motives reveal our true goals, and priorities reveal our values. Motives are tested by our response to money, and priorities are tested by our response to time.

Our priorities let other people know whether money and possessions are more important to us than our spiritual and family responsibilities and our outreach to others.

When a man's priorities are out of order, he destroys the relationships that will do the most to build and maintain a good name. It is perhaps in this area, more than any other, that daily decisions are made which ultimately result in choosing a good name rather than great riches.

MEASURING PRIORITIES

1. WITH GOD
☐ Quoting Scripture as you go to sleep
☐ Reading the Bible daily
☐ Using Scripture to conquer temptations
☐ Spending time each day in prayer
☐ Searching out Scriptural answers
☐ Reading Christian classics

2. WITH FAMILY
☐ Having a weekly "date" with your wife
☐ Studying a book with your wife
☐ Working on home repairs
☐ Having long-range family goals and plans
☐ Teaching your family Scriptural principles
☐ Taking your family to church
☐ Maintaining life notebooks

3. WITH OTHERS
☐ Explaining God's truth to others
☐ Being efficient and productive at work
☐ Getting sufficient food, sleep, and exercise
☐ Keeping up on current events

- When our priorities are right, God will give us more productive days.
- When our priorities are right, God will give us favor with Him and with others.
- When our priorities are right, God will give us direction for daily decisions.
- When our priorities are right, God will give us peace and good health.
- Our priorities are right when we honor the Lord with the first fruits of all our increase: *"So shall thy barns be filled with plenty . . ."* (Proverbs 3:10).

RIGHT PRIORITIES

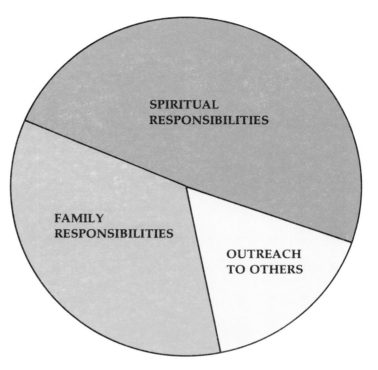

SPIRITUAL RESPONSIBILITIES

FAMILY RESPONSIBILITIES

OUTREACH TO OTHERS

Priorities are *not* determined by how much time you spend on them but by how difficult it would be to distract you from fulfilling them.

WRONG PRIORITIES

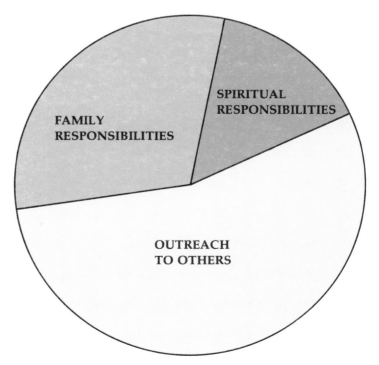

FAMILY RESPONSIBILITIES

SPIRITUAL RESPONSIBILITIES

OUTREACH TO OTHERS

SATAN'S METHOD OF DESTROYING A MAN'S NAME . . .

Every day we experience temptations to compromise God's standards.
The temptation is to increase our gain, but the active result is losing a good name.

Little compromises are usually made on the basis that they will never be discovered; and, even if they are, there will be no significant consequences. Both of these ideas are totally inaccurate.

DISHONEST BILLING

A man hired a landscaper to work at his office and his home. When the work was completed, the landscaper cheerfully informed the man, "I'm putting the work I did at your home on your company bill, and that way you can write it off as a business expense."

The man thanked the landscaper for his desire to save him money but explained that he could not do that. He wanted two bills so that he could pay his share of the job.

The landscaper remarked, "I had heard that you were a Christian and a very honest man. Now I know that the reports are true."

Compromises occur when we try to adjust our moral or ethical standards so that we will be accepted, or at least not ridiculed, by people who do not live by Scriptural standards. In reality, these very people secretly ridicule us when we compromise God's standards.

IMMORALITY

A businessman was invited by an influential associate to go with a group of business leaders on a hunting trip. He replied, "I want to go with you, but I don't really hunt." The associate lowered his voice and explained, "You don't need to hunt— we're going to get some women and whiskey and have a good time."

The businessman graciously rejected the offer, even though it meant losing important business contacts. He said, "I love my wife so much that I would not have any desire to do that."

God gave this businessman great financial success. Six years later the associate visited him. With a tearful voice he said, "My father died. I leaned on him for everything. Now that he's gone, I need someone to trust and depend on. Of all the people that I know, there is only one man whom I totally trust, and that is you."

CHEATING ON TAXES

An agent of the Internal Revenue Service examined the financial records of a wealthy businessman.

The agent asked the man if his car was used for business or for pleasure, since it was listed as a deduction. The agent was assured that it was used only for business.

Later, God prompted the businessman to re-evaluate the honesty of that statement. The more that he thought about it, the more he realized that it was used for personal business as well as company business.

The next day the businessman said to the I.R.S. agent, "I need to correct a statement that I gave to you yesterday. My car is used for private business as well as company business. I was wrong in deducting the total amount of the car's expenses. That was not honest."

The agent concluded that if the businessman was that honest in one area, he could trust him with the rest. Instead of conducting an extensive audit, the agent asked the executive to explain the Christian life to him, and then the agent took steps to discover the Christian faith for himself.

COOPERATION WITH EVIL

The owner of a shopping center was told by one of his investors that they would be giving a lease to a liquor lounge. The owner explained his personal convictions against liquor. However, the investor convinced him to go along with it, as the money was desperately needed. The owner felt a twinge of conscience but agreed to do it.

The remodeling for the lounge cost the owner more than he expected. The day the lounge was scheduled to open, its manager had a mental breakdown. A few days later, a bomb blew up the lounge, causing extensive damage to other buildings in the shopping center.

The owner learned a costly lesson about compromise and cooperation with evil.

The opportunity to compromise usually comes to a man when he is facing extreme needs. He believes that by compromising he will relieve the pressure. What he does not realize is that the pressure is God's test of his character; and if he compromises, he will not only fail the test, but he will also multiply his future problems.

MISUSING GOD'S MONEY

King Asa was under attack. He devised a clever way to defeat his enemy. His plan, however, required a few little compromises.

He used money that had been dedicated to God to arrange a partnership with an ungodly king.

His plan worked, but God spelled out the consequences. ". . . *Because thou hast relied on the king of Syria, and not relied on the Lord thy God, therefore is the host of the king of Syria escaped out of thine hand. . . . Herein thou hast done foolishly: therefore from henceforth thou shalt have wars*" (II Chronicles 16:7, 9).

Compromises are little departures from God's standards that can be easily overlooked as not important. However, one who is committed to a good name realizes that little inconsistencies reveal the true character of a man and lead to big tragedies.

"*For the eyes of the Lord run to and fro thoughout the whole earth, to shew himself strong in the behalf of them whose heart is perfect toward him . . .*" (II Chronicles 16:9).

A man's ability to reject compromise opens the way for God to bless both him and those who are influenced by his example.

INDIRECT IMMORALITY

After going nearly two years without sales, a land developer was offered an unusually high price for property which he and his vice president owned.

The vice president exclaimed, "Look at how God is blessing us because we are attempting to run our business according to Scriptural principles!"

The president suddenly realized something and replied, "We can't sell our property to that grocery chain, because they sell pornography."

The vice president objected, "But they sell cigarettes and sugar there, too, and they are not good for people either. We cannot be responsible for what they sell."

The president explained, "Cigarettes damage the body, but pornography destroys the soul. By making it available in this area, we share the responsibility of all that it causes people to do. Remember, we dedicated that property to God. Would *He* sell it for pornography?"

The vice president reluctantly cooperated with the president. They added a clause to the contract which prohibited the sale of any pornography.

When the vice president nervously reported this to the buyers, he was surprised and humbled when they said, "We expected that from your boss. That won't hinder our purchase."

When a man purposes ahead of time to reject compromise of any kind, he avoids the path of the ungodly man and the strange woman. (See Proverbs 2:12, 16.)

RESTORE A GOOD NAME

1. **Realize that a good name must be earned.**

"A good name is rather to be chosen than great riches . . ." (Proverbs 22:1).

2. **Have genuine repentance before God.**

On the basis of salvation through Christ, confess and forsake every violation of God's law.

"If we confess our sins, he is faithful and just to forgive us our sins, and to cleanse us from all unrighteousness" (I John 1:9).

3. **Clear your conscience with people whom you have wronged.**

Make a list of those who have been wronged by your violation of God's principles. Ask them if they would forgive you, and then make proper restitution to them.

"And herein do I exercise myself, to have always a conscience void of offence toward God, and toward men" (Acts 24:16).

4. **Consistently do good to others.**

"Having a good conscience; that, whereas they speak evil of you, as of evildoers, they may be ashamed that falsely accuse your good conversation in Christ" (I Peter 3:16).

"A REAL MAN!"

The president of a construction company hired a plumbing contractor. Before the job was completed, the contractor explained that because of unforseen village restrictions, the job would cost more.

The president replied, "It's your job to know the village codes. We signed a contract, and I'm not paying any more money than what I agreed upon."

Six years later, a new associate said to the president of the construction company, "You've told us that you want to maintain a good name and that we should tell you if we ever meet someone who feels that you have wronged them. When I let bids out on our new building, a certain plumbing contractor told me that if it's your building, he would never bid on it."

The president had forgotten the incident, and now that he was more experienced in building, he realized that the plumbing contractor had been right and he had been wrong.

He went to the contractor, confessed his wrong, asked forgiveness, and gave him a check for the full amount plus interest for six years. The stunned contractor pounded the desk, stood up, reached his hand out, and exclaimed, "I want to shake the hand of a real man!"

Personal Commitment to a Good Name

Because God's reputation is directly affected by my actions, I purpose to establish a good name, whatever the cost. I will not hide behind legal technicalities, bankruptcy provisions, or rationalizations to justify damage to others.

I will admit where I have been wrong and make proper restitution wherever necessary.

I plan to have a clear conscience on this matter by _____ (Date).

DO YOU KNOW HOW TO EARN A GOOD NAME?

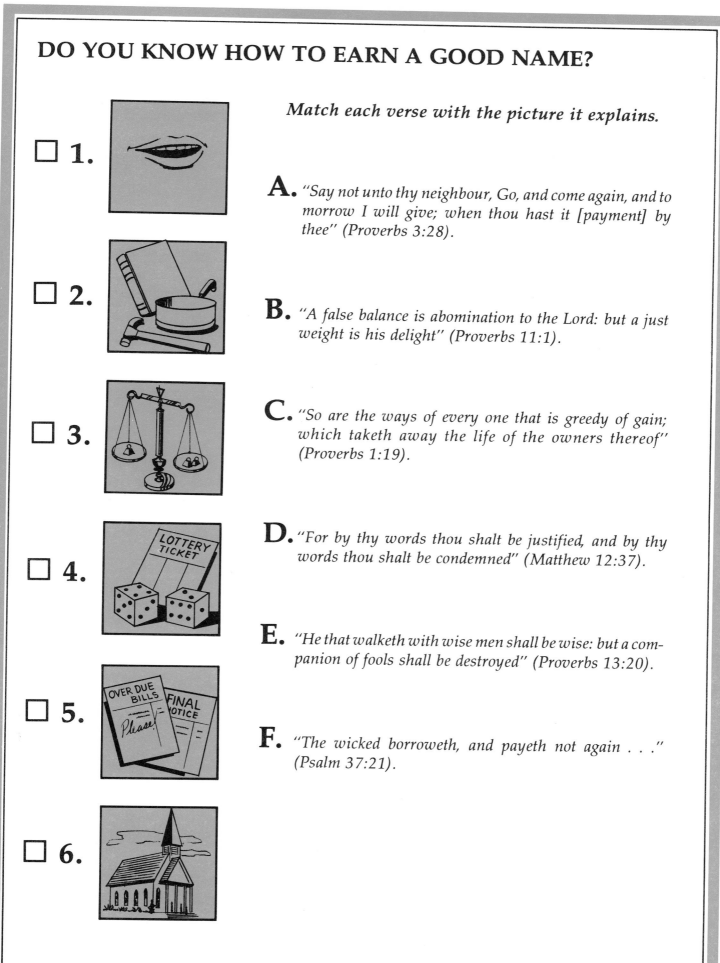

Match each verse with the picture it explains.

☐ **1.**

☐ **2.**

☐ **3.**

☐ **4.**

☐ **5.**

☐ **6.**

A. *"Say not unto thy neighbour, Go, and come again, and to morrow I will give; when thou hast it [payment] by thee" (Proverbs 3:28).*

B. *"A false balance is abomination to the Lord: but a just weight is his delight" (Proverbs 11:1).*

C. *"So are the ways of every one that is greedy of gain; which taketh away the life of the owners thereof" (Proverbs 1:19).*

D. *"For by thy words thou shalt be justified, and by thy words thou shalt be condemned" (Matthew 12:37).*

E. *"He that walketh with wise men shall be wise: but a companion of fools shall be destroyed" (Proverbs 13:20).*

F. *"The wicked borroweth, and payeth not again . . ." (Psalm 37:21).*

Answers: 1.D 2.F 3.B 4.C 5.A 6.E

WHO IN THE BIBLE HAD A GOOD NAME?

A. Timothy

B. Stephen

C. Cornelius

D. Ananias

E. Demetrius

F. Titus' friend

Match each quotation with the person to whom it refers.

☐ **1.** He was *". . . a just man, and one that feareth God, and of good report among all the nation . . ."* (Acts 10:22).

☐ **2.** He was one of *". . . seven men of honest report, full of the Holy Ghost and wisdom . . ."* (Acts 6:3).

☐ **3.** He *". . . was well reported of by the brethren . . ."* (Acts 16:2).

☐ **4.** He had a *". . . good report of all men, and of the truth itself . . ."* (III John 12).

☐ **5.** He was one *". . . whose praise is in the gospel throughout all the churches"* (II Corinthians 8:18).

☐ **6.** He was *". . . a devout man according to the law, having a good report of all the Jews . . ."* (Acts 22:12).

DO YOU COMPREHEND THE FULL SCOPE OF A GOOD NAME?

Match each of God's requirements for church leaders with its definition.

☐ **1.** Endures difficult situations without giving God deadlines to remove them

☐ **2.** Is alert to every danger that would damage his testimony

☐ **3.** Enjoys sharing his home and table with others

☐ **4.** Rejects the goal of becoming rich

☐ **5.** Has been a Christian several years and is mature

☐ **6.** Is able to effectively communicate God's truth

☐ **7.** Refuses to become involved in any wrong habit

☐ **8.** Is faithful to the words and spirit of his marriage vows

☐ **9.** Demonstrates wise leadership at home

☐ **10.** Has living proof that he is a good leader at home

☐ **11.** Can look every person in the eye without guilt

☐ **12.** Does not desire for himself that which belongs to others

☐ **13.** Is approachable, reasonable, and willing to make peace

☐ **14.** Is well-respected by people who are not Christians

☐ **15.** Shows good manners and orderliness in all of his actions

☐ **16.** Does not resort to force when frustrated

☐ **17.** Is serious-minded and displays sound reasoning

A. Blameless

B. Husband of one wife

C. Vigilant

D. Sober

E. Of good behavior

F. Given to hospitality

G. Apt to teach

H. Not given to wine

I. No striker

J. Not greedy of filthy lucre

K. Patient

L. Not a brawler

M. Not covetous

N. Ruleth well his own house

O. Children in subjection

P. Not a novice

Q. Good report of them which are without

(See I Timothy 3:1–13.)

CALEB

A leader who did the impossible because he saw the invisible

HE CLAIMED WHAT GOD HAD PROMISED

"Now therefore give me this mountain, whereof the Lord spake in that day, . . . if so be the Lord will be with me, then I shall be able to drive them [the giants] out, as the Lord said" (Joshua 14:12).

16 LEARN THE SECRETS OF PRAYING FOR MONEY

"And this is the confidence that we have in him, that, if we ask any thing according to his will, he heareth us: And if we know that he hear us, whatsoever we ask, we know that we have the petitions that we desired of him" (I John 5:14–15).

GOD'S PROVISION REQUIRES SPIRITUAL WARFARE

"Hebron therefore became the inheritance of Caleb . . . because that he wholly followed the Lord God of Israel" (Joshua 14:14).

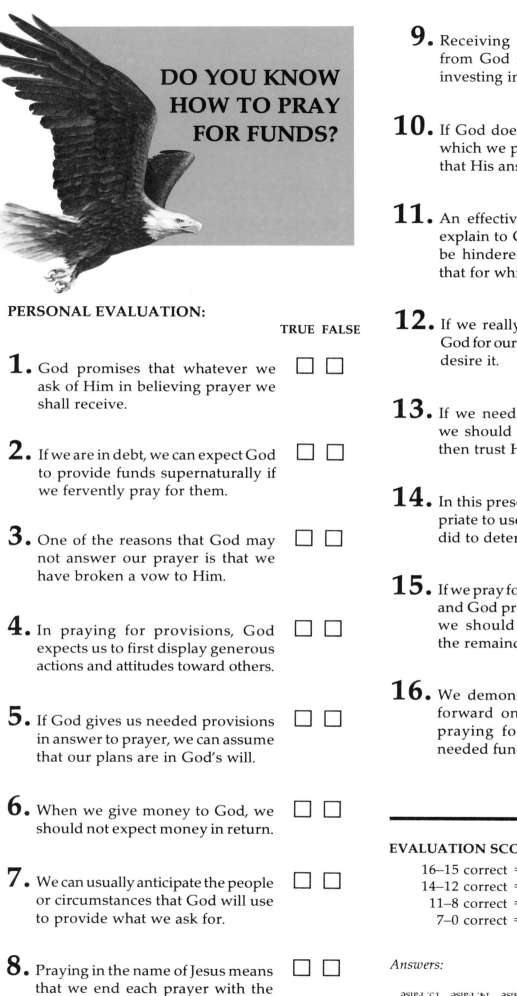

DO YOU KNOW HOW TO PRAY FOR FUNDS?

PERSONAL EVALUATION:

TRUE FALSE

1. God promises that whatever we ask of Him in believing prayer we shall receive. ☐ ☐

2. If we are in debt, we can expect God to provide funds supernaturally if we fervently pray for them. ☐ ☐

3. One of the reasons that God may not answer our prayer is that we have broken a vow to Him. ☐ ☐

4. In praying for provisions, God expects us to first display generous actions and attitudes toward others. ☐ ☐

5. If God gives us needed provisions in answer to prayer, we can assume that our plans are in God's will. ☐ ☐

6. When we give money to God, we should not expect money in return. ☐ ☐

7. We can usually anticipate the people or circumstances that God will use to provide what we ask for. ☐ ☐

8. Praying in the name of Jesus means that we end each prayer with the words "in Jesus' name." ☐ ☐

9. Receiving unexpected provision from God is a by-product of first investing in the lives of others. ☐ ☐

10. If God does not give us the items which we pray for, we can assume that His answer is "no." ☐ ☐

11. An effective basis of appeal is to explain to God how our goals will be hindered if we do not receive that for which we are praying. ☐ ☐

12. If we really want something from God for ourselves, we must earnestly desire it. ☐ ☐

13. If we need provisions from God, we should only ask one time and then trust Him to work it out. ☐ ☐

14. In this present day, it is not appropriate to use a "fleece" like Gideon did to determine God's will. ☐ ☐

15. If we pray for one amount of money and God provides a lesser amount, we should continue praying for the remainder. ☐ ☐

16. We demonstrate faith by moving forward on a program and then praying for God to supply the needed funds. ☐ ☐

TOTAL CORRECT ☐

EVALUATION SCORE:

16–15 correct = Understanding of God
14–12 correct = Awareness of God
11–8 correct = Confusion in Prayer
7–0 correct = Disillusionment about God

Answers:

1. False 2. False 3. False 4. True 5. False 6. True 7. False 8. False 9. True 10. False 11. False 12. False 13. False 14. False 15. False 16. False

BASIC PRINCIPLES OF PRAYING FOR MONEY

1 WE MUST BE IN "RIGHT STANDING" WITH GOD

God gives rain, sunshine, breath, and health to the non-Christian as well as to the Christian. However, the first words of the Lord's prayer must be true before we can expect God to hear special petitions. He must be *our* Father who is in heaven.

We become members of His family by faith and trust in the Lord Jesus Christ for our personal salvation. Only then are we in "right standing."

2 OUR REQUEST MUST BE BASED ON THE NAME OF CHRIST

We do not expect to buy shoes at a restaurant, nor would we expect to find hamburgers sold in a shoe store.

When Christ taught us to pray in His name, He was referring to the character and the functions for which His name stands.

For example, He is the light of the world and in Him is no darkness at all. (See I John 1:5.) If we ask Him to bless a "shady" business deal He will have no part of it. Instead of blessing such a transaction, He will expose it, because that is what the light does to whatever it touches.

Our request for bread, however, is consistent with His name because He is the bread of life. (See John 6:35.) Christ the Son is the full expression of His heavenly Father.

3 WE MUST BASE OUR APPEAL ON GUARDING GOD'S REPUTATION

When we pray for money or provision, we must clearly explain to God how His reputation will be benefited if we receive it and damaged if we do not.

This is the meaning of the second phrase in the prayer which Christ taught: *". . . Hallowed be thy name" (Matthew 6:9).*

God is committed to protecting His own reputation. When the Syrians lost a battle to Israel, their officers concluded, *". . . Their gods are gods of the hills; therefore they were stronger than we; but let us fight against them in the plain, and surely we shall be stronger than they" (I Kings 20:23).*

When they said that, God replied, *". . . Because the Syrians have said, The Lord is God of the hills, but he is not God of the valleys, therefore will I deliver all this great multitude into thine hand, and ye shall know that I am the Lord" (I Kings 20:28).*

When we pray for God to provide, we must base our petition on His will as it is clearly revealed in His Word. We must give Him an opportunity to provide before we move ahead with a financial venture. It is wrong to enter into a financial obligation and then ask God or others to provide the money so that God's reputation will not be damaged.

Moses effectively appealed to God not to destroy the nation of Israel because doing so would damage His reputation.

Nehemiah successfully appealed to God and the king for all that he needed to rebuild the walls. He based his prayer on a clear promise in God's Word.

"Lest the land whence thou broughtest us out say, Because the Lord was not able to bring them into the land which he promised them, and because he hated them, he hath brought them out to slay them in the wilderness" (Deuteronomy 9:28).

The real test of this appeal is whether we are desiring to protect God's reputation or our own reputation.

For example, if we buy a car that we cannot afford, God is not going to protect His reputation by providing the money for our payments. In fact, it will protect His reputation if we were to sell the car and buy one which we can afford.

THE AUTHORITY OF OUR APPEAL MUST BE GOD'S WORD

The correct application of God's name and character is understood by rightly dividing the Word of God. *". . . For thou hast magnified thy word above all thy name"* (Psalm 138:2).

One of the names of Jesus is "Counselor." Thus, we can rightfully pray for counsel in making a business decision. However, the Scripture gives precise direction on how to get that counsel:

- *". . . The commandment of the Lord is pure, enlightening the eyes"* (Psalm 19:8).
- *"Hearken unto thy father that begat thee, and despise not thy mother when she is old"* (Proverbs 23:22).

"Remember, I beseech thee, the word that thou commandedst thy servant Moses, saying, If ye transgress, I will scatter you abroad among the nations: But if ye turn unto me, and keep my commandments . . . yet will I gather them from thence, and will bring them unto the place that I have chosen. . . . Now these are thy servants and thy people, whom thou hast redeemed by thy great power, and by thy strong hand" (Nehemiah 1:8–10).

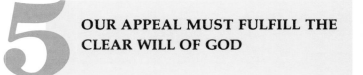

OUR APPEAL MUST FULFILL THE CLEAR WILL OF GOD

". . . Thy will be done in earth, as it is in heaven" (Matthew 6:10).

When we understand God's will in relation to our money, possessions, priorities, and attitudes, we will have a clear basis for effective praying.

For example, it is God's will that we move toward holiness of life. (See I Thessalonians 4:3.) However, if we ask for money or possessions that will hinder Godly living, we are not praying according to His will.

God's will is that we learn patience, and patience comes through tribulation. (See Romans 5:1–4.) It is also God's will that we give thanks in all things. (See I Thessalonians 5:18.)

Therefore, if we pray for God to remove a situation that He has designed to teach us patience, we are not praying according to God's will.

Daniel discerned that it was God's will for His people to return to the promised land. This was the basis of his successful prayer.

"... I Daniel understood by books the number of the years ... in the desolations of Jerusalem.... Now therefore, O our God, hear the prayer of thy servant.... O my God, incline thine ear, and hear; open thine eyes, and behold our desolations, and the city which is called by thy name: for we do not present our supplications before thee for our righteousnesses, but for thy great mercies. O Lord, hear; O Lord, forgive; O Lord, hearken and do; defer not, for thine own sake, O my God: for thy city and thy people are called by thy name" (Daniel 9:2, 17–19).

6 WE MUST SEPARATE BASIC NEEDS FROM PROJECT FUNDS

God has promised to provide for our food and clothing. However, sometimes a Christian will presumptuously enter into a major financial obligation and then expect God to provide the necessary funds for it. When God then provides any funds for food or clothing, this provision is looked upon as evidence of His approval of the entire obligation.

In reality, God is only reassuring that Christian that He loves him and that he is His child. Sometimes God's goodness is even for the purpose of bringing that Christian to repentance. (See Romans 2:4.)

Paul made a very clear separation between funds for personal living and funds for public ministry. We must do the same.

Paul established that he had the Scriptural right to receive money from his ministry. However,

to avoid any criticism, he purposed not to receive those funds because he knew that his doing so would hinder the Gospel. (See I Corinthians 9:9–14.) He knew that it was God who called him to his ministry and that it would be wrong to start a ministry for the purpose of supporting himself. Therefore, Paul wanted to avoid any hint of wrong motives.

7 WE MUST FOLLOW SCRIPTURAL PRINCIPLES IN OBTAINING FUNDS

God makes direct application of harvest laws to the obtaining of special funds. "... He which soweth sparingly shall reap also sparingly; and he which soweth bountifully shall reap also bountifully" (II Corinthians 9:6).

• Sowing must come before reaping.

Paul invested his life and God's Word in the churches which he established. Years later they gave gifts to him so that he could continue his ministry with others. (See Philippians 4:10.)

Christ healed and taught the multitudes. As a response to transformed lives, various disciples ministered to Him from their resources. (See Mark 15:41; Luke 8:3.)

Before a Christian can expect financial support, he must have effectively sown in the hearts and lives of many people.

• Reaping requires patience.

There is a significant time period between sowing the seed and reaping the harvest. During that period the sower cannot be sure of the results. In fact, he goes through the death of a vision, yet he has hope of fruit for his labor. (See John 12:24.) "Cast thy bread upon the waters: for thou shalt find it after many days" (Ecclesiastes 11:1).

• The size of the harvest is determined by the quality of the soil and the quality and quantity of the seed.

A farmer's entire success depends upon his knowledge of when, how, and where to plant seed. Each harvest becomes his "report card."

Similarly, God has called and ordained us that we should go forth and bear much fruit, and that our fruit should remain. (See John 15:8, 16.)

Even a widow's support by the church is to be based on her wide sowing of ministry in the lives of others. *"Well reported of for good works; if she have brought up children, if she have lodged strangers, if she have washed the saints' feet, if she have relieved the afflicted, if she have diligently followed every good work"* (I Timothy 5:10.)

8 WE MUST NOT LIMIT GOD'S WAYS OF PROVIDING

It is very easy for us to try to anticipate how God is going to supply the funds or items that we need.

The disappointing results will be a wrong focus on people, a temptation to show favoritism, and a resentment when we are disappointed by the people to whom we were looking for assistance. *". . . He that followeth after vain persons shall have poverty enough"* (Proverbs 28:19). *"My brethren, have not the faith of our Lord Jesus Christ, the Lord of glory, with respect of persons"* (James 2:1).

God's desire to supply through unexpected sources gives further meaning to His instruction in Luke 6:33–35: *"And if ye do good to them which do good to you, what thank have ye? for sinners also do even the same. . . . Do good, and lend, hoping for nothing again; and your reward shall be great. . . . "*

God wants our focus to remain on Him for all of our provisions. For this reason, He will often provide what we need through totally unexpected sources. If He provides less than what we ask, we should re-examine our needs.

THE CHURCH THAT SURPRISED AN ENTIRE COMMUNITY

When a pastor and his wife came to serve a newly-formed congregation, they learned that a building committee had been formed and the congregation had already voted to borrow $650,000 to build their first building.

The pastor encouraged the people to trust God to provide a church building without borrowing.

The people cautiously agreed to follow his plan. On a given day they totalled the amount which each family could give in cash.

The total was announced. It was only $21,000! The people were discouraged; however, the pastor assured them, "God has tested our faith, now He will test our obedience."

A few weeks later, a visitor approached the pastor and asked, "Could you use a church?"

The visitor explained, "I bought some land and it has a very good church on it. If you can move it, you can have it free."

The cost of moving the church was $21,000!

Not only was the congregation given a church building, but the entire community was given a powerful message of a miracle-working God.

9 IF WE GIVE MONEY, WE MUST NOT EXPECT MONEY IN RETURN

Many Christians have been disillusioned by giving an amount of money to God and expecting that He will give money back.

They have seen or heard that He did it for others, and since God is no respecter of persons, they assumed that He would also do it for them.

The problem is that they saw God's actions but did not understand His ways. God's way is to return to us in like kind as we have given.

By giving to God we do not sow money—we sow faith; therefore, we will reap greater faith. Faith is a spiritual ability to discern what God intends to do in and through our lives. By faith Noah built an ark, and by faith Moses rejected Egypt. (See Hebrews 11.)

It may be that God will provide funds, but we should not count on them. Instead of funds, He may provide the actual items we need, new or used. God caused the shoes of the Israelites to last for forty years, and He gave them manna every morning.

10 TO RECEIVE FUNDS, WE MUST NOT SEEK OUR OWN WILL

It is all too easy for us to use human effort to try to accomplish God's work. The net result is conflict and discouragement.

In order to seek God's will and not our own, we must balance our expectations.

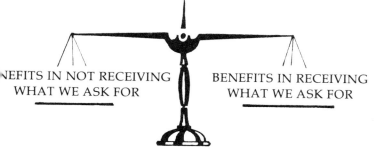

NEFITS IN NOT RECEIVING WHAT WE ASK FOR   BENEFITS IN RECEIVING WHAT WE ASK FOR

When we have just as many reasons for thanking God for not receiving something as we have for receiving something, then we are free to allow God to perform His perfect will.

George Mueller founded many orphanages in England during the 1800's. His underlying purpose was to demonstrate to Christians how God could provide funds in direct answer to prayer. He received millions of dollars in this way.

GEORGE MUELLER'S METHODS FOR DETERMINING THE WILL OF GOD

1. I seek to get my heart into such a state that it has no will of its own in a given matter. When you're ready to do the Lord's will, whatever it may be, nine-tenths of the difficulties are overcome.

2. Having done this, I don't leave the result to feeling or simply impression. If I do so, I leave myself liable to great delusion.

3. I seek the will of the Spirit of God through, or in connection with, God's Word. The Spirit and the Word must be combined. If I look to the Spirit alone without the Word, I lay myself open to great delusions also. If the Spirit guides us, He'll do it according to the Scriptures, not contrary to them.

4. Next, I take into account providential circumstances. These often plainly indicate God's will in connection with His Word and Spirit.

5. I ask God in prayer to reveal His will to me.

6. Thus, through prayer, the study of the Word, and reflection, I come to a deliberate judgment, according to the best of my ability and knowledge.

If my mind is thus at peace, and continues after two or three more petitions, I proceed accordingly.

I have found this method always effective in trivial or important issues.

KNOW WHY GOD DOES NOT ANSWER PRAYER

REASONS	NAMES OF CHRIST	EXPLANATORY SCRIPTURES
1. Breaking a vow	**Truth**	*Ecclesiastes 5:4–6; Malachi 2:13–16*
2. Dishonoring parents	**Counselor**	*Exodus 20:12; Ephesians 6:1–3*
3. Secret sin	**Light**	*Psalm 66:18; Proverbs 15:29*
4. Pride	**Lamb of God**	*Psalm 10:17; James 4:6*
5. Lustful motives	**Holiness**	*James 4:1–4; Galatians 5:17*
6. Desiring to be rich	**Savior**	*Proverbs 28:22; Job 31:7–8*
7. Committing adultery	**Love**	*Proverbs 5:10; Job 31:9–12*
8. Unbelief	**The Way**	*Matthew 13:58; Luke 17:19*
9. Unforgiving spirit	**Redeemer**	*Matthew 6:14–15; Matthew 5:7*
10. Repaying evil for good	**Prince of Peace**	*Proverbs 17:13; Proverbs 28:10*

Son of God • Son of Man • Creator • Word • King of Kings • First Born
Love • Light • Rock • Water • Door • The Life • The Truth • The Way
• Jes... Bread of Life • Redeemer • Wisdom of God •

Personal Commitment to Pray Scripturally for Provisions

In order to glorify God and to strengthen the faith of my family, I will maintain a prayer journal listing our requests on one side and God's answers on the other side.

I will remove any known hindrances to God's answering prayer.

Date _____

WHO WAS SUCCESSFUL IN APPEALING TO GOD?

Match each statement with the right person.

☐ **1.** I was able to save a whole nation because I reminded God that His reputation would be damaged if the nation was destroyed.

?

☐ **2.** God answered my appeal for funds to rebuild. I based my prayer on a promise that I found in God's Word.

?

☐ **3.** I prayed that God would prosper His people by bringing a remnant back to their promised land. My prayer was based on what I discerned from Scripture to be God's will.

?

☐ **4.** God answered my prayers for personal funds and ministry funds through the people in whose lives I had invested God's Word.

?

☐ **5.** I asked the Lord about a need for paying taxes. He supplied the money in a very unusual way. He had me catch a fish and get a coin out of its mouth.

?

A. Daniel
(See Daniel 9:2–19.)

B. Peter
(See Matthew 17:24–27.)

C. Moses
(See Deuteronomy 9:25–28.)

D. Nehemiah
(See Nehemiah 1:6–10.)

E. Abraham
(See Genesis 21:1–8.)

F. Paul
(See Philippians 4:10.)

☐ **6.** I appealed to God for a son. After many years, I came to the place of having no will of my own. Following this, God supernaturally gave me a son.

?

Answers: 1C 2D 3A 4F 5B 6E

WHAT DO WE LEARN FROM PRAYERS THAT GOD DID NOT ANSWER?

Match each prayer with the lesson it teaches.

☐ 1. ESAU

He prayed to recover the birthright which he had sold to his brother. *". . . He found no place of repentance, though he sought it carefully with tears" (Hebrews 12:17).*

☐ 2. BALAAM

He prayed for permission to go with King Balak and curse the nation of Israel. God refused him on two separate occasions. (See Numbers 22.)

☐ 3. KING SAUL

He prayed for direction in battle, but God did not answer him; so he disguised himself and went to consult a witch. (See I Samuel 28:7–25.)

☐ 4. KING DAVID

He prayed for three years that God would end a famine. Finally, God told him that He could not answer his prayer because King Saul had murdered the Gibeonites. (See II Samuel 21:1–9.)

☐ 5. THE RICH MAN

He prayed that God would send a messenger to warn his relatives of the torments of hell. God explained that if they rejected the Scriptures, they would not believe any messenger. (See Luke 16:19–31.)

☐ 6. PAUL

He prayed three times that God would remove a thorn in his flesh. God explained that the thorn was given to him for a purpose. (See II Corinthians 12:7–10.)

A. A physical infirmity is not only a mark of God's ownership but a means of receiving more of His grace. God's grace is of eternal value because it provides the desire and the power to do His will. A humiliating infirmity conquers pride.

B. Before God answers prayer, full restitution must be made. The need for restitution may go back many years, even to the sins of others who preceded us.

C. God has provided clear warning through His Word. Those who reject the Scriptures harden their hearts to any further teaching from God. Even if He displays a miracle, those who reject the Scriptures will not believe.

D. Decisions have lasting consequences. Many are irreversible. That is why early training and reverence for God are so vital. Without them, the things of this world become more important than the things of God.

E. If we seek counsel from God but have envy and hatred in our heart, God will not hear us. If we seek any other means of direction, we only add to our confusion and judgment.

F. When God clearly says "no" once, we should accept it as being final. If we ask again, He may give us the desire of our hearts but send leanness into our souls.

Answers: 1.D 2.F 3.E 4.B 5.C 6.A

DO YOU KNOW THE PRINCIPLES OF PRAYING FOR PROVISION?

Match each word or phrase to its most precise definition.

☐ **1.** Right standing

☐ **2.** The name of Christ

☐ **3.** God's reputation

☐ **4.** God's Word

☐ **5.** God's will

☐ **6.** Separating funds

☐ **7.** Laws of the harvest

☐ **8.** Unexpected sources

☐ **9.** Sowing faith

☐ **10.** No will of our own

☐ **11.** Tempting God

☐ **12.** A fleece

A. Appealing on the authority of what God has said

B. Not expecting money if we give money to God

C. Forcing God to give after we have indebted ourselves

D. Avoiding the dangers of guessing how God will provide

E. Basing our prayers on Christ's character and attributes

F. Allowing God to direct through specific circumstances

G. Balancing expectations so we can thank God for "yes" or "no"

H. Making sure that we are members of God's family

I. Explaining how our request will protect God's name

J. Receiving based on the quality and quantity of giving

K. Discerning whether God is showing love or direction

L. Asking God to fulfill the goals that we know He has

DANIEL
The most influential political advisor in history

HE MADE WISE DECISIONS BASED ON GODLY CONVICTIONS

"But Daniel purposed in his heart that he would not defile himself with the portion of the king's meat, nor with the wine which he drank . . ." (Daniel 1:8).

17 AVOID BUSINESS PARTNERSHIPS

"Watch ye, stand fast in the faith, quit you like men, be strong" (I Corinthians 16:13).

HE WAS GREATLY HONORED BY GOD

"Then this Daniel was preferred above the presidents and princes, because an excellent spirit was in him . . ." (Daniel 6:3). Daniel displayed this excellent spirit through the reigns of four kings.

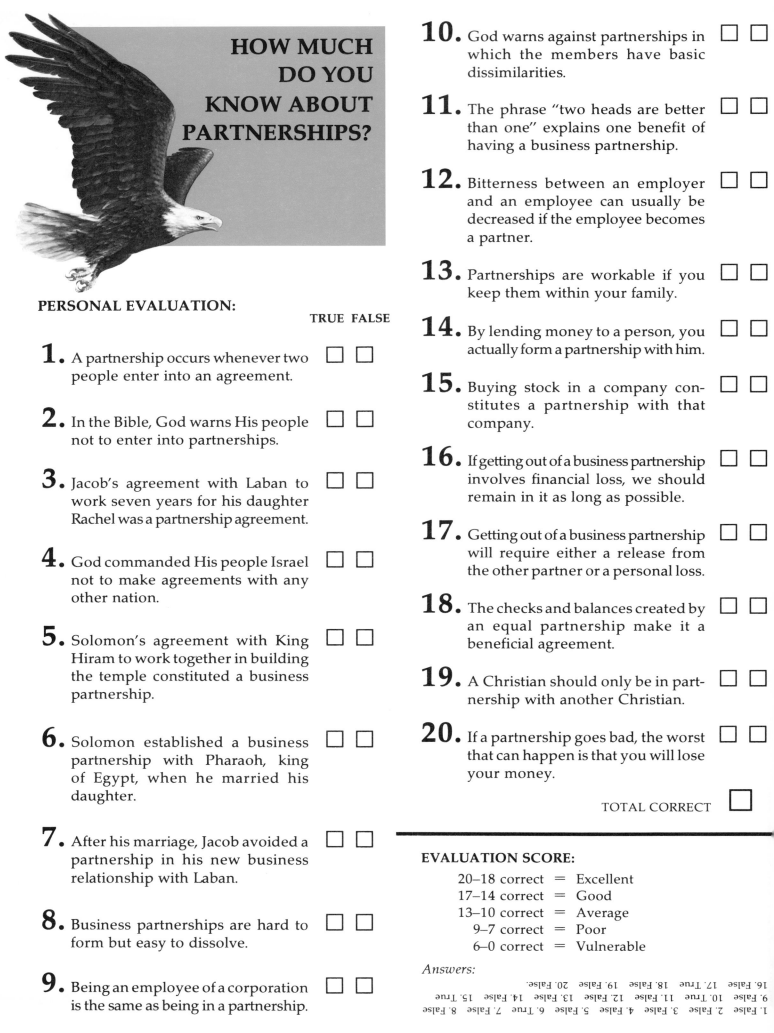

HOW MUCH DO YOU KNOW ABOUT PARTNERSHIPS?

PERSONAL EVALUATION:

TRUE FALSE

1. A partnership occurs whenever two people enter into an agreement.

2. In the Bible, God warns His people not to enter into partnerships.

3. Jacob's agreement with Laban to work seven years for his daughter Rachel was a partnership agreement.

4. God commanded His people Israel not to make agreements with any other nation.

5. Solomon's agreement with King Hiram to work together in building the temple constituted a business partnership.

6. Solomon established a business partnership with Pharaoh, king of Egypt, when he married his daughter.

7. After his marriage, Jacob avoided a partnership in his new business relationship with Laban.

8. Business partnerships are hard to form but easy to dissolve.

9. Being an employee of a corporation is the same as being in a partnership.

10. God warns against partnerships in which the members have basic dissimilarities.

11. The phrase "two heads are better than one" explains one benefit of having a business partnership.

12. Bitterness between an employer and an employee can usually be decreased if the employee becomes a partner.

13. Partnerships are workable if you keep them within your family.

14. By lending money to a person, you actually form a partnership with him.

15. Buying stock in a company constitutes a partnership with that company.

16. If getting out of a business partnership involves financial loss, we should remain in it as long as possible.

17. Getting out of a business partnership will require either a release from the other partner or a personal loss.

18. The checks and balances created by an equal partnership make it a beneficial agreement.

19. A Christian should only be in partnership with another Christian.

20. If a partnership goes bad, the worst that can happen is that you will lose your money.

TOTAL CORRECT

EVALUATION SCORE:

20–18 correct = Excellent
17–14 correct = Good
13–10 correct = Average
9–7 correct = Poor
6–0 correct = Vulnerable

Answers:

1. False 2. False 3. False 4. False 5. False 6. True 7. False 8. False 9. False 10. True 11. False 12. False 13. False 14. False 15. True 16. False 17. True 18. False 19. False 20. False.

208

THREE DETERMINING FACTORS OF A PARTNERSHIP

Types Of Partnerships	**1.** Who Is Legally Responsible?	**2.** Who Is Final Authority?	**3.** Who Pays For Expenses & Losses?	Biblical Examples
Limited Partnership	Senior Partner	Senior Partner	All Partners	Sarah and Hagar (See Genesis 16:1–6.)
General Partnership (Joint venture)	All Partners	No One (Unless appointed)	All Partners	Jehoshaphat and Ahab (See II Chronicles 18.)

OTHER TYPES OF BUSINESS RELATIONSHIPS

Seller to Buyer	Seller (Responsible for representations and warranties)	None	Seller	Abraham Buying Field of Ephron (See Genesis 23:10–20.)
Employer to Employee	Employer	Employer	Employer	Jacob Working for Laban (See Genesis 29–30.)
Lender to Borrower	Both (As defined by contract)	Lender	Borrower (Pays interest) Lender (Suffers any loan loss)	Bond-Servants (See Nehemiah 5:5.)
Trade Association to Members	Officers	Officers	Limited to Funds of Association	Gentile Collection to Jewish Christians (See I Corinthians 16:1-3.)
Corporation to Employees	Board of Directors	Board of Directors	Limited to Corporate Funds and Assets	Local Church (See Hebrews 13:17.)
Family Business (Father and son)	Father	Father	Family Members	David and Solomon (See I Chronicles 28:11–21.)

EIGHT DANGERS IN BUSINESS PARTNERSHIPS

A PARTNERSHIP JEOPARDIZES YOUR REPUTATION

One of the obvious motivations of a business partnership is to get a greater return on your investments. God warns, however, that a good name is more important than great wealth. *"A good name is rather to be chosen than great riches, and loving favour rather than silver and gold"* (Proverbs 22:1).

In forming a partnership, you become identified with the reputation of your partner(s). You may acquire their friends, but you will also inherit their enemies.

As the partnership continues, you will become identified with each decision that your partner makes, both on and off the job. Because you are in partnership, you do not have full control over these decisions.

God blessed King Jehoshaphat with *"... riches and honour in abundance ..."* (II Chronicles 18:1). He had a good name. However, when he formed a partnership with wicked King Ahab, he greatly damaged his reputation. Rather than receiving riches and honor, Jehoshaphat received the rebuke and wrath of God.

God's spokesman, Jehu, stated, *"... Shouldest thou help the ungodly, and love them that hate the Lord? therefore is wrath upon thee from before the Lord"* (II Chronicles 19:2).

A PARTNERSHIP HINDERS YOUR FREEDOM TO OBEY GOD

God wants every man to be free to follow Scriptural direction in regard to business decisions.

In a partnership, you delegate partial authority for these decisions to others who may not understand or appreciate Scriptural financial principles.

God had marvelous plans and direction for Abraham. When God called him, the instructions were very explicit. *"... Get thee out of thy country, and from thy kindred, and from thy father's house, unto a land that I will shew thee"* (Genesis 12:1).

Instead of obeying, Abraham formed a partnership of sorts by bringing several relatives along with him, including Lot. The immediate consequence of this decision was the waste of several years of progress. (See Genesis 11:31–32.)

The long-range consequence of this "partnership" is vividly illustrated in the following chronology.

GENERATIONS OF ABRAHAM AND LOT

ABRAHAM   LOT

- Leaves Abraham because of conflict and moves to Sodom.
- Captured by Amalekites.
- Rescued by Abraham.
- Flees Sodom with his remaining daughters.
- Daughters have incest with Lot. Ammon and Moab born.
- Moab becomes a nation and an enemy to Abraham's children.
- King of Moab hires Balaam to curse Israel, and introduces Israel to Baal worship, which ultimately causes Israel's captivity.

"... These caused the children of Israel, through the counsel of Balaam, to commit trespass against the Lord ..." (Numbers 31:16).

A PARTNERSHIP USUALLY IGNORES GOD-GIVEN LIMITATIONS

4

A PARTNERSHIP OFTEN ENDS IN BITTERNESS

If God calls a person to accomplish a certain task, He will either give him the ability to do it himself, or He will give him the financial resources to hire the skill and assistance that are needed.

The lack of ability or resources is usually a motivation for a person to form a partnership. God, however, may have intended this lack as a signal to pray and receive from Him what is needed.

God may also have intended this lack of funds or abilities to be a message to wait, which is a vital part of God's way of working. He gives us a "vision" and then takes us through the "death of a vision" in order to prepare us for His ultimate supernatural fulfillment of that "vision."

During our "death of a vision," Satan usually appears as an angel of light. He prompts us to fulfill God's goals with human effort. If we follow his leading, we may achieve our goal but miss God's will. Instead of blessing, there will be continual conflict.

This pattern is clearly illustrated in Sarah's "partnership" with Hagar.

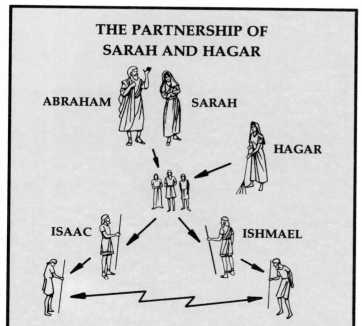

THE PARTNERSHIP OF SARAH AND HAGAR

ABRAHAM   SARAH

HAGAR

ISAAC   ISHMAEL

Sarah had a husband but no children, so she used Hagar to gain a son. As soon as Hagar was with child, she despised Sarah. Later Ishmael, Hagar's son, despised Sarah's son, Isaac; and today the descendants of Ishmael (Arabs) have continuing conflict with the descendants of Isaac (Jews).

There are several reasons why partnerships tend to breed bitterness.

First of all, each partner will have certain expectations of the other and of the business. When these expectations are not fulfilled, the tendency is to look for someone to blame.

Second, there will be constant comparison of each other. This is inevitable, because each one will be evaluating the company and the factors that are making it profitable or unprofitable.

It is very easy for one partner not to be aware of what the other partner is actually contributing; or he may feel that he is investing more money, effort, or skill into the business than his partner is.

If one partner takes time off for personal needs, the other partner may resent the fact that the profits from his own labors must be shared, especially if he is not able to take equal time off.

Third, each partner will have different values and ideas as to what is essential for success. If one partner spends money for remodeling, and the other partner feels that the money was needed for new equipment, there will be an underlying current of resentment.

Fourth, the families of each partner will also be forming judgments and making comments about the other. If these comments are negative, they become seeds of destruction in the relationship. *"The words of a talebearer are as wounds, and they go down into the innermost parts of the belly"* (Proverbs 18:8).

". . . A whisperer separateth chief friends" (Proverbs 16:28).

Fifth, the possible conflicts with each other can be multiplied if there are any employees.

Differing personalities usually cause employees to like one boss better than another. If special favors are given by one partner to the employees in order to gain favor, the other partner will resent such action.

The bitterness that can result from a partnership is well documented in Scripture. One example is Jacob's business partnership with Laban.

During the first fourteen years of Jacob's working relationship with Laban, he was the employee and Laban was the employer. At that point, Jacob asked Laban to send him away. Laban urged him to maintain the employer-employee relationship by saying, ". . . *Appoint me thy wages, and I will give it*" (Genesis 30:28).

Jacob replied that he did not want wages. He wanted a share in the profits. Laban agreed; but after seven years, Jacob bitterly complained about how he had to also stand behind the losses. "*That which was torn of beasts . . . I bare the loss of it; of my hand didst thou require it, whether stolen by day, or stolen by night*" (Genesis 31:39).

While the competition continued between Laban and Jacob, Laban's two daughters also turned against their father in resentment. "*And Rachel and Leah answered and said unto him . . . Are we not counted of him strangers? for he hath sold us, and hath quite devoured also our money*" (Genesis 31:14–15).

5 AN EQUAL PARTNERSHIP WILL PRODUCE CONFLICTS AMONG EMPLOYEES

When each partner has equal authority, the employees have two equal bosses.

God assures us that such a structure will result in division. "*No man can serve two masters: for either he will hate the one, and love the other; or else he will hold to the one, and despise the other . . .*" (Matthew 6:24).

Christ applied this principle to those who try to serve God and money. However, it has valid application to other situations where equal-authority structures exist.

God understands human nature; He designed it. He knows that our responses will be consistent under given conditions in any relationship, whether it be a business partnership or a marriage partnership.

When there are two equal authorities in a marriage, division and competition will result among the children, just as it will in a business partnership among the employees.

This principle, that "no man can serve two masters," is also clearly demonstrated in God's account of Jacob and Esau. The parents were divided over their two sons. Esau looked to his father for approval and direction, while Jacob looked to his mother for approval and direction. (See Genesis 27:1–46.)

6 A PARTNERSHIP FORCES YOU TO SHARE ANY CHASTENING WHICH GOD GIVES TO YOUR PARTNER

God uses financial loss as one means of severely disciplining those who violate His laws. For example, an adulterer is reduced to a meager income because of God's judgment. (See Proverbs 6:26.) A drunkard and a glutton also come to poverty. (See Proverbs 23:21.)

If your partner is openly or secretly violating God's laws, then you will share in his loss when God brings discipline upon him.

This is exactly what happened to Jehoshaphat when he joined with Ahab. God was going to punish Ahab with death in battle. Before the battle, Ahab said to Jehoshaphat, ". . . *I will disguise myself, and enter into the battle; but put thou on thy robes. . . . And it came to pass, when the captains of the chariots saw Jehoshaphat, that they said, Surely it is [Ahab]. . . . And they turned aside to fight against him: and Jehoshaphat cried out*" (I Kings 22:30–32).

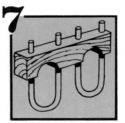

7 A PARTNERSHIP OF "DIVERS KINDS" VIOLATES SCRIPTURE

One of God's basic principles involves the need for compatibility and harmony between that which is united. He warns in Scripture that certain partnerships are not only incompatible but, if attempted, will produce detrimental results.

A farmer is warned not to sow his vineyard with different kinds of seed. (See Deuteronomy 22:9.) One consequence is a decrease in crop yield.

A seamstress is warned not to make a garment of different fibers, such as wool and linen. (See Deuteronomy 22:11.)

God also warned the Israelites not to yoke different types of animals together, such as an ox and a donkey. (See Deuteronomy 22:10.) One of the obvious consequences of this is uneven plowing, as well as uneven burden.

God applies this same principle to a Christian's being linked together with a non-Christian. "*Be ye not unequally yoked together with unbelievers: for what fellowship hath righteousness with unrighteousness? and what communion hath light with darkness?*" (II Corinthians 6:14).

This is such an important point that God continues to emphasize it in the following verses: *"And what concord hath Christ with Belial? or what part hath he that believeth with an infidel? And what agreement hath the temple of God with idols? for ye are the temple of the living God; as God hath said, I will dwell in them, and walk in them; and I will be their God, and they shall be my people. Wherefore come out from among them, and be ye separate, saith the Lord . . ."* (II Corinthians 6:15–17).

8 A PARTNERSHIP OF "SURETY" VIOLATES SCRIPTURE

God consistently warns against becoming surety for anyone. (See Chapter 13.) By entering into a partnership, you become surety for your partner. Whatever decisions he makes, you must stand behind.

One of the strong motivations of a partnership is the security that comes by mutual commitment. It is ironic, however, that the very security that we desire in business is lost in a partnership, because of the insecurity of becoming surety for another.

Instead, God wants us to depend upon Him for our security; and in return, He wants to bless us in such a way that others will recognize His work in our life and business.

This was the concluding point of God's rebuke to Asa for his partnership with Ben-hadad.

> *"For the eyes of the Lord run to and fro throughout the whole earth, to shew himself strong in the behalf of them whose heart is perfect toward him . . ."*
> (II Chronicles 16:9).

Many partnerships are based on business potential, and character deficiencies are overlooked. Often a partner will be congenial to begin with, especially if he is looking to the partnership for his success. However, pressures will come in a partnership, and under pressure the true character of a man is revealed.

One of the most destructive character deficiencies in any business relationship is anger. God warns us not to make even close friendships with an angry man, much less a binding partnership! *"Make no friendship with an angry man; and with a furious man thou shalt not go"* (Proverbs 22:24).

THE SPECIAL DANGER OF GIVING TO THE RICH

"He that oppresseth the poor to increase his riches, and he that giveth to the rich, shall surely come to want" (Proverbs 22:16).

WHY "GIVING TO THE RICH" LEADS TO POVERTY

1. The rich do not need your gifts; so in giving to the rich, your motive is that of expecting something in return.

2. The things that you expect from a rich person are probably essential to your success; otherwise, you would not give away something which has value to you.

3. Most rich men are very cautious and very slow to give things away. They tend to hoard their assets. *". . . He heapeth up riches . . ."* (Psalm 39:6).

4. Rich men are sensitive about people who expect to get things from them. The rich usually figure out how they can get more than they give. *". . . Eat and drink, saith he to thee; but his heart is not with thee"* (Proverbs 23:7).

5. While waiting for the rich to give you what you want or need, financial pressures and deadlines will increase for you. If you do finally get something from the rich, there will usually be strings attached to it which will be to your detriment. *"The morsel which thou hast eaten shalt thou vomit up, and lose thy sweet words"* (Proverbs 23:8).

"He that tilleth his land shall have plenty of bread: but he that followeth after vain persons shall have poverty enough" (Proverbs 28:19).

GET OUT OF A WRONG BUSINESS PARTNERSHIP

1. Review the terms of your commitment to your business partner.

"For by thy words thou shalt be justified, and by thy words thou shalt be condemned" (Matthew 12:37).

2. Be prepared for the possibility of suffering financial loss.

"A good name is rather to be chosen than great riches . . ." (Proverbs 22:1).

3. Work out an appeal based on a just settlement.

". . . He that ruleth over men must be just, ruling in the fear of God" (II Samuel 23:3).

4. Examine your motives for the partnership and for wanting to get out of it. Ask for God's forgiveness and pray for God to prepare the heart of your partner.

"For if we would judge ourselves, we should not be judged. But when we are judged, we are chastened of the Lord, that we should not be condemned with the world" (I Corinthians 11:31–32).

5. Go to your partner and humbly appeal for an equitable release.
   A. Offer to buy him out. (Be willing to pay more than it is worth.)
   B. Offer to sell. (Be willing to take less.)
   C. Ask if the partnership could be sold. (Cooperate in "going the second mile.")

"My son, if thou be surety for thy friend, if thou hast stricken thy hand with a stranger, Thou art snared with the words of thy mouth. . . . Go, humble thyself. . . . Give not sleep to thine eyes, nor slumber to thine eyelids. Deliver thyself. . ." (Proverbs 6:1–5).

6. If release is not given, wait for God to make it possible.

". . . He . . . sweareth to his own hurt, and changeth not. . . . He that doeth these things shall never be moved" (Psalm 15:4–5).

Personal Commitment to Avoid Partnerships

Based on the clear Scriptural reasons for avoiding business partnerships, I purpose not to enter into one.

If I am already in a business partnership, I will take Scriptural steps to be honorably released from it.

Date _____

DO YOU KNOW WHAT IS TRUE AND FALSE ABOUT PARTNERSHIPS?

Mark each of the following statements true or false.

TRUE FALSE

1. A business partnership is a legal agreement to share the expenses, profits, and losses of a business venture. ☐ ☐

2. A business partnership jeopardizes your reputation. ☐ ☐

3. A business partnership hinders your ability to obey God. ☐ ☐

4. A business partnership often ignores God-given limitations. ☐ ☐

5. A business partnership usually ends in bitterness. ☐ ☐

6. A business partnership will produce conflicts among employees. ☐ ☐

7. A business partnership forces you to share God's judgment with your partner. ☐ ☐

8. A business partnership of "divers kinds" violates Scripture. ☐ ☐

9. A business partnership is becoming surety, which violates Scripture. ☐ ☐

Answers: 1.True 2.True 3.True 4.True 5.True 6.True 7.True 8.True 9.True

WHOSE BUSINESS PARTNERSHIPS DID NOT WORK?

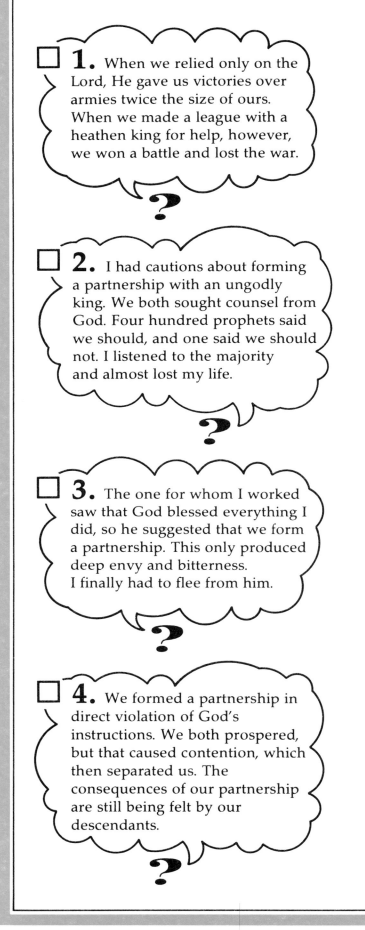

1. When we relied only on the Lord, He gave us victories over armies twice the size of ours. When we made a league with a heathen king for help, however, we won a battle and lost the war.

2. I had cautions about forming a partnership with an ungodly king. We both sought counsel from God. Four hundred prophets said we should, and one said we should not. I listened to the majority and almost lost my life.

3. The one for whom I worked saw that God blessed everything I did, so he suggested that we form a partnership. This only produced deep envy and bitterness. I finally had to flee from him.

4. We formed a partnership in direct violation of God's instructions. We both prospered, but that caused contention, which then separated us. The consequences of our partnership are still being felt by our descendants.

Match each description with the persons involved.

A. JACOB AND LABAN
(See Genesis 30:27–43.)

B. ABRAHAM AND LOT
(See Genesis 13.)

C. ISRAEL AND THE GIBEONITES
(See Joshua 9.)

D. JEHOSHAPHAT AND AHAB
(See II Chronicles 18.)

E. ASA AND BEN-HADAD
(See II Chronicles 16:1–9.)

F. SOLOMON AND PHARAOH
(See I Kings 3:1.)

5. The ultimate business partnership is marrying your partner's daughter. I made such a partnership with a foreign ruler; and ultimately, it cost me my relationship with the Lord and my ability to pass on my riches to future generations.

6. Our army had just suffered a demoralizing military experience; so when a foreign nation offered to be our partner, we agreed. Three days later, we discovered that we had been tricked.

Answers: 1E 2D 3A 4B 5F 6C

CAN YOU PRECISELY IDENTIFY BUSINESS RELATIONSHIPS?

Match each business relationship with the precise term which it illustrates.

☐ **1. THE VINEYARD OWNER**
(See Matthew 20:1–16.)
He contracted with a group of laborers to harvest his crop.

☐ **2. KING DAVID**   (See I Chronicles 28.)
He worked with his son to build the temple.

☐ **3. GENTILE CHURCHES**
(See I Corinthians 16:1–3.)
They collected an offering for the Jewish Christians in Jerusalem.

☐ **4. KING JEHOSHAPHAT**
(See II Chronicles 18:1.)
He went out to battle with King Ahab.

☐ **5. KING AHAB**   (See I Kings 21:1–16.)
He allowed his wife to get Naboth's vineyard.

☐ **6. BARNABAS**   (See Acts 4:36–37.)
He was a member of the church at Antioch.

☐ **7. RULERS IN JERUSALEM**
(See Nehemiah 5:1–5.)
They made contracts with the builders of the wall.

☐ **8. JOSEPH**   (See Genesis 41:56–57.)
He sold corn during the famine.

A. Seller to buyer

B. Employer to employee

C. Lender to borrower

D. Association to members

E. Individual to corporation officers

F. Family business/ Father to son

G. Controlling partner to another partner

H. Equal partner to equal partner

HE CONVEYED GOD'S WARNING TO A SLOTHFUL FATHER

"For I [the Lord] have told him that I will judge his house for ever for the iniquity which he knoweth; because his sons made themselves vile, and he restrained them not" (I Samuel 3:13).

18 IDENTIFY AND CONQUER SLOTHFULNESS

> ". . . This we commanded you, that if any would not work, neither should he eat" (II Thessalonians 3:10).

HE CHALLENGED A SLOTHFUL NATION

> ". . . I will teach you the good and the right way: Only fear the Lord, and serve him in truth with all your heart: for consider how great things he hath done for you" (I Samuel 12:23–24).

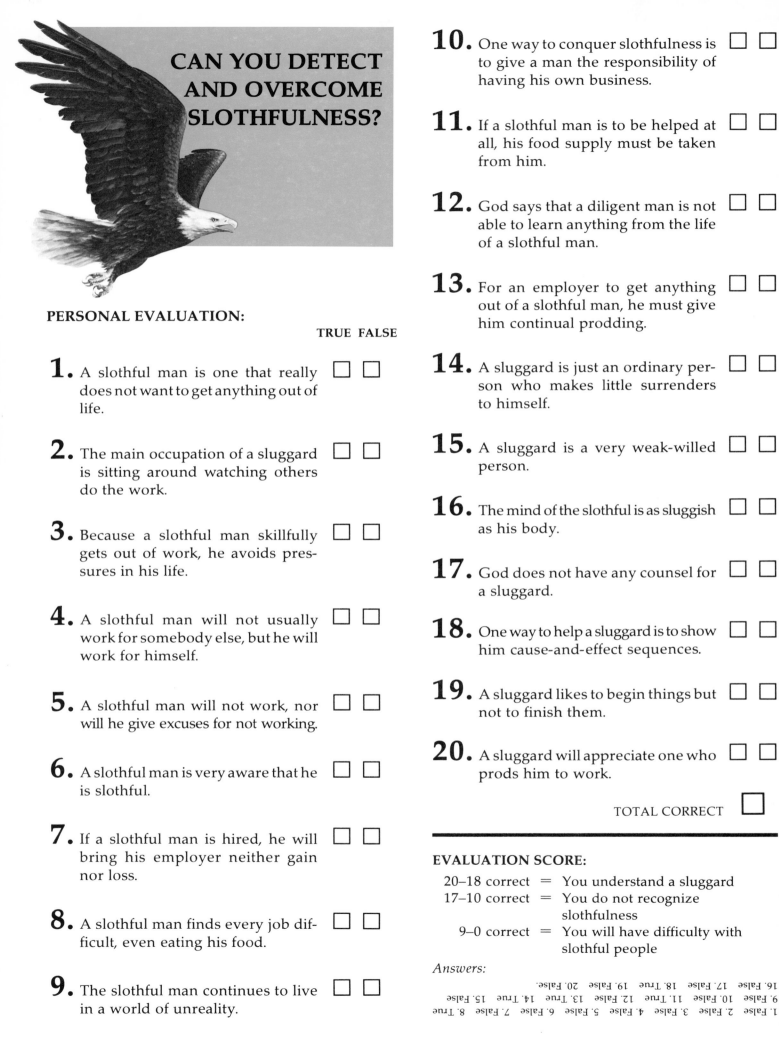

CAN YOU DETECT AND OVERCOME SLOTHFULNESS?

PERSONAL EVALUATION:

TRUE FALSE

1. A slothful man is one that really does not want to get anything out of life.

2. The main occupation of a sluggard is sitting around watching others do the work.

3. Because a slothful man skillfully gets out of work, he avoids pressures in his life.

4. A slothful man will not usually work for somebody else, but he will work for himself.

5. A slothful man will not work, nor will he give excuses for not working.

6. A slothful man is very aware that he is slothful.

7. If a slothful man is hired, he will bring his employer neither gain nor loss.

8. A slothful man finds every job difficult, even eating his food.

9. The slothful man continues to live in a world of unreality.

10. One way to conquer slothfulness is to give a man the responsibility of having his own business.

11. If a slothful man is to be helped at all, his food supply must be taken from him.

12. God says that a diligent man is not able to learn anything from the life of a slothful man.

13. For an employer to get anything out of a slothful man, he must give him continual prodding.

14. A sluggard is just an ordinary person who makes little surrenders to himself.

15. A sluggard is a very weak-willed person.

16. The mind of the slothful is as sluggish as his body.

17. God does not have any counsel for a sluggard.

18. One way to help a sluggard is to show him cause-and-effect sequences.

19. A sluggard likes to begin things but not to finish them.

20. A sluggard will appreciate one who prods him to work.

TOTAL CORRECT

EVALUATION SCORE:

20–18 correct = You understand a sluggard
17–10 correct = You do not recognize slothfulness
9–0 correct = You will have difficulty with slothful people

Answers:

1. False 2. False 3. False 4. False 5. False 6. False 7. False 8. True 9. False 10. False 11. True 12. False 13. True 14. True 15. False 16. False 17. False 18. True 19. False 20. False.

SEVEN SYMPTOMS OF A SLOTHFUL MAN

WHICH ONE IS THE SLOTHFUL MAN?

1. HE DOES *NOT* BELIEVE THAT HE IS SLOTHFUL

Slothfulness is a by-product. It is not a goal which the slothful seek after. Furthermore, it is completely rationalized in the mind of the sluggard. Thus, a slothful person will reject the label of being a sluggard.

He will assure you that he would be very willing to work if there were fewer obstacles in his path. He is only waiting for more favorable working conditions. In the meantime, he rehearses the reasons why he is unable to begin the projects which he knows must be done.

These reasons include the false notion that too much work injures one's health, that there is an easier way to do things, and that he is smart if he finds them. He reminds himself of the dangers of overexertion and the possibility of blunting his lifestyle by unnecessary labor. He is quick to explain his views to any who wonder why he is not working at the moment. *"The sluggard is wiser in his own conceit [eyes] than seven men that can render a reason"* (Proverbs 26:16).

2. HE MAKES *LITTLE* SOFT CHOICES IN LIFE

Slothfulness comes on gradually. It happens to normal people who begin making little surrenders in daily decisions.

These little surrenders seem totally harmless—staying in bed just a little longer, taking a little more rest during the day, waiting a few more minutes before starting a project, or spending a little more time in idle chatter. *"Yet a little sleep, a little slumber, a little folding of the hands to sleep: So shall thy poverty come as one that travelleth, and thy want as an armed man"* (Proverbs 6:10–11).

These daily surrenders come from making the soft choices in life, such as a refusal to be subject to adverse working conditions. *"The sluggard will not plow by reason of the cold; therefore shall he beg in harvest, and have nothing"* (Proverbs 20:4).

Soon the little choices which are carefully reasoned away become a habit of life. *"Slothfulness casteth into a deep sleep; and an idle soul shall suffer hunger"* (Proverbs 19:15).

3. HE DOES NOT VALUE THE IMPORTANCE OF TIME OR SEASONS

The sluggard is not a self-starter. To him one day is as good as another. What he does not do today can just as easily be done tomorrow.

The sluggard does not understand the value of time or the control of seasons. His basic philosophy is to live for the moment and let the future take its own course.

The slothful person does not consider that he must one day give account to God for the way that he has used his time. He looks at nightfall as a justifiable reason for sleep, not for examining whether he has earned it.

He looks at winter as an intrusion upon his life, not a time during which he can enjoy the fruit of his labors. Therefore, the sluggard loses the freedom to make his own choices and becomes a slave of the diligent, by whose industry he will be kept alive. *"The hand of the diligent shall bear rule: but the slothful shall be under tribute"* (Proverbs 12:24).

4. HE WILL NOT FINISH TASKS

A slothful person is lethargic in everything he does. Each job becomes a mountain in his path, not a door of opportunity.

If he is visited by success, he does not recognize or value it. It simply means more work. Thus, he allows opportunities to slip by and half-completed jobs to spoil. *"The slothful man roasteth not that which he took in hunting: but the substance of a diligent man is precious"* (Proverbs 12:27).

Even the maintenance of what he has becomes a burden to him. *"By much slothfulness the building decayeth; and through idleness of the hands the house droppeth through"* (Ecclesiastes 10:18). *"I went by the field of the slothful . . . And, lo, it was all grown over with thorns, and nettles had covered the face thereof, and the stone wall thereof was broken down"* (Proverbs 24:30–31).

Answer to question on Page 221:

The symptoms of a slothful man are not usually recognizable by outward appearance.

5. HE LIVES IN A WORLD OF WISHFUL THINKING

When the sluggard is not sleeping, he is desiring to do things and to get things. The tension between his restless mind and his inactive body produces destructive frustrations. *"The desire of the slothful killeth him; for his hands refuse to labour. He coveteth greedily all the day long . . ."* (Proverbs 21:25–26).

His desires are also destructive because they are related to his own sensual pleasures. These indulgences in turn produce more sluggishness. *"A slothful man hideth his hand in his bosom, and will not so much as bring it to his mouth again"* (Proverbs 19:24). *"As the door turneth upon his hinges, so doth the slothful upon his bed"* (Proverbs 26:14).

6. HE BRINGS PAINFUL DAMAGE TO HIS EMPLOYERS

A slothful employee is not just unproductive, he is destructive. His presence on the job is worse than his absence from it. His lack of initiative and follow-through becomes very costly to those who are counting on him. *"He also that is slothful in his work is brother to him that is a great waster"* (Proverbs 18:9).

At first, employers may try to adapt to his slothfulness by transferring him to a less strategic position. This damages his self-esteem and prompts him to give reasons why things did not work out as they should have, thus creating disloyalty and spreading discontent. *"As vinegar to the teeth, and as smoke to the eyes, so is the sluggard to them that send him"* (Proverbs 10:26).

7. HE IS THE VICTIM OF SELF-INDUCED FEARS

Slothfulness results in fears which are then reinforced by more slothfulness. These fears are based on the fact that a sluggard is a realist—up to a point. He knows that he must have a source of food. Rather than stealing it, he will beg for it. His lack of food is a result of making the soft choices and of the fears which rationalized his choices. *"The slothful man saith, There is a lion without, I shall be slain in the streets"* (Proverbs 22:13). As an escape from his fears, he will resort to more sleep.

HOW SLOTHFULNESS DEVELOPS

A discouraged wife wondered if her family would ever be free from financial pressures. She was working to help support the family, because her husband could never seem to get the right employment. On two occasions he had used the family savings for businesses which had failed.

The following sequence defines the causes which produced their financial pressures.

God's reproofs for slothfulness are very painful. A sluggard has trouble all through his life. For this reason, we must conquer slothfulness in ourselves and avoid hiring a sluggard. *"The way of the slothful man is as an hedge of thorns . . ."* (Proverbs 15:19).

INWARD CAUSES	RESULTING CONFLICTS	RELATED SCRIPTURE
1. During his youth, the husband had his personal *wants* fulfilled without any effort on his part.	He found ways to manipulate people and facts in order to get what he wanted. Conflicts with his conscience resulted.	*"The desire of the slothful killeth him; for his hands refuse to labour. He coveteth greedily all the day long . . ."* (Proverbs 21:25–26).
2. After sliding through school, he searched for the easy job that paid maximum wages for minimum effort.	His slothfulness caused strong reaction from those who were responsible for his production.	*"He also that is slothful in his work is brother to him that is a great waster"* (Proverbs 18:9).
3. Pressure from employers caused him to start his own business and to be his own boss.	He willingly believed "get rich quick" schemes and went into debt to finance his new venture.	*"He that hasteth to be rich hath an evil eye, and considereth not that poverty shall come upon him"* (Proverbs 28:22).
4. In order to insure success, he bought expensive clothes and cars and gave gifts to rich friends.	His wife reacted to his extravagance and tried to warn him about his business associates.	*". . . He that giveth to the rich, shall surely come to want"* (Proverbs 22:16).
5. After failing in business, he is now forced to get a job in order to pay back his debts.	His heart and mind are not in his work; thus, he is under greater pressure now than in previous jobs.	*". . . The slothful shall be under tribute"* (Proverbs 12:24).
6. He views his job as temporary and keeps looking for the "big opportunity" of a position that brings money and prestige.	His lack of achievement and his financial pressures seriously damage his self-image. He views labor with contempt.	*"In the sweat of thy face shalt thou eat bread . . ."* (Genesis 3:19).

HOW TO CONQUER SLOTHFULNESS

There is hope for the sluggard, based on the fact that God gives instructions to him and about him. There are also other Scriptural principles that directly relate to slothfulness, from youth to adulthood.

1. COUNTERACT SLOTHFULNESS WITH HUNGER

God's primary cure for slothfulness is hunger. *". . . If any would not work, neither should he eat"* *(II Thessalonians 3:10).*

This is consistent with the requirement which God established after Adam and Eve sinned. *"In the sweat of thy face shalt thou eat bread, till thou return unto the ground . . ." (Genesis 3:19).*

There is value in every person's experiencing hunger, especially one who tends to be slothful. A beginning point in conquering slothfulness would be a three-day fast, for the purpose of studying God's principles and examples of diligence. (See Matthew 6:16–18.)

2. LEARN THE PRINCIPLES OF DILIGENCE

The ultimate goal of a slothful person must be to develop diligence. This is precisely the instruction of God. *"Go to the ant, thou sluggard; consider her ways, and be wise" (Proverbs 6:6).*

The ant illustrates the basic characteristics which are lacking in those who are slothful—initiative, self-direction, respect for seasons, the ability to finish jobs, and the foresight that is necessary in planning for the future.

After studying the ant, it would be wise to read the biographies of great Christians in order to learn how their diligence was developed by obedience to God's Word.

3. REALIZE THAT SLOTHFULNESS DEVELOPS IN STAGES

Slothfulness is not confined to just a few or a certain type of persons. Anyone can become its victim. Its gradual development begins unnoticed; and if left unchecked, slothfulness will disable those who obey its promptings.

- LATENT SLOTHFULNESS

Latent slothfulness is the inward tendency to reject God's requirement for diligent labor. This tendency requires instant obedience to the promptings of the Holy Spirit.

- INITIAL SLOTHFULNESS

Initial slothfulness is selecting the soft choices in daily decisions. This type of slothfulness requires accountability to others for the completion of projects.

- DISABLING SLOTHFULNESS

Disabling slothfulness is allowing little surrenders each day to become a habitual way of life. This slothfulness requires the discipline of going without food in order to clarify goals and to reach objectives.

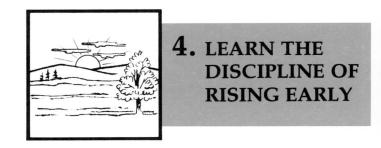

4. LEARN THE DISCIPLINE OF RISING EARLY

The definition of the Hebrew word translated *diligently* is "to be up early at a task."

This discipline strikes at the very heart of slothfulness. *"How long wilt thou sleep, O sluggard? when wilt thou arise out of thy sleep?" (Proverbs 6:9).*

If necessary, be accountable to others for getting up at a given time. Resist the temptation to get just a little more sleep. Do not even learn how to use the "doze" button on your alarm clock. When you wake up, get up!

A practical way to establish accountability for rising early is to have someone call you on the telephone, or you agree to call someone when you are up, or you plan to meet someone for a time of devotions.

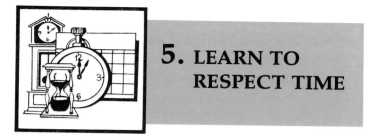

5. LEARN TO RESPECT TIME

GOD'S WARNINGS ON SLEEP

A proper amount of sleep is essential for good health. Lack of sleep is one of the consequences of business problems or of doing evil. However, God's primary concern for sleep is not that we get too little, but that we get too much.

• BEWARE OF THE BONDAGE OF SLEEP

"As the door turneth upon his hinges, so doth the slothful upon his bed" (Proverbs 26:14).

• BEWARE OF SLEEP THAT DISABLES

"Slothfulness casteth into a deep sleep; and an idle soul shall suffer hunger" (Proverbs 19:15).

• BEWARE OF LOVING SLEEP

"Love not sleep, lest thou come to poverty . . ." (Proverbs 20:13).

• BEWARE OF SLEEP THAT ROBS

"Yet a little sleep, a little slumber, a little folding of the hands to sleep: So shall thy poverty come as one that travelleth; and thy want as an armed man" (Proverbs 24:33–34).

• BEWARE OF SLEEP THAT DISAPPOINTS GOD

"How long wilt thou sleep, O sluggard? when wilt thou arise out of thy sleep?" (Proverbs 6:9).

• BEWARE OF A LITTLE EXTRA SLEEP

"Yet a little sleep, a little slumber, a little folding of the hands to sleep: So shall thy poverty come as one that travelleth, and thy want as an armed man" (Proverbs 6:10–11).

• BEWARE OF INAPPROPRIATE SLEEP

"He that gathereth in summer is a wise son: but he that sleepeth in harvest is a son that causeth shame" (Proverbs 10:5).

Life is a race against time. We will only win the race if we realize the following:

- Time is limited.
- Death is certain.
- The second coming of Christ is even more certain.
- The maximum number of productive years is established by God.

   "The days of our years are threescore years and ten; and if by reason of strength they be fourscore years, yet is their strength labour and sorrow; for it is soon cut off, and we fly away" (Psalm 90:10).

- Days must be counted.

   "So teach us to number our days, that we may apply our hearts unto wisdom" (Psalm 90:12).

- Time requires accountability.
- Time is entrusted to us for God's work.

   ". . . The night cometh, when no man can work" (John 9:4).

- Time is unrecoverable.

There are several practical projects that will reinforce our respect for time and guard us from wasting it.

For one week, keep a detailed record of what you do every fifteen minutes. At the end of the week, go back and evaluate how many of the 168 hours were used for sleeping, eating, resting, entertainment, and conversations, and how many hours were used for productive work and achievement. The results may shock you. Thereafter, keep a daily journal of goals and achievements.

TIME

. . . is no respecter of persons: No one receives more hours in a day than another.

. . . is not recoverable: Every hour that is lost is gone forever.

"Go to the Ant, Thou Sluggard . . ."

"Go to the ant, thou sluggard; consider her ways, and be wise: Which having no guide, overseer, or ruler, Provideth her meat in the summer, and gathereth her food in the harvest" (Proverbs 6:6–8).

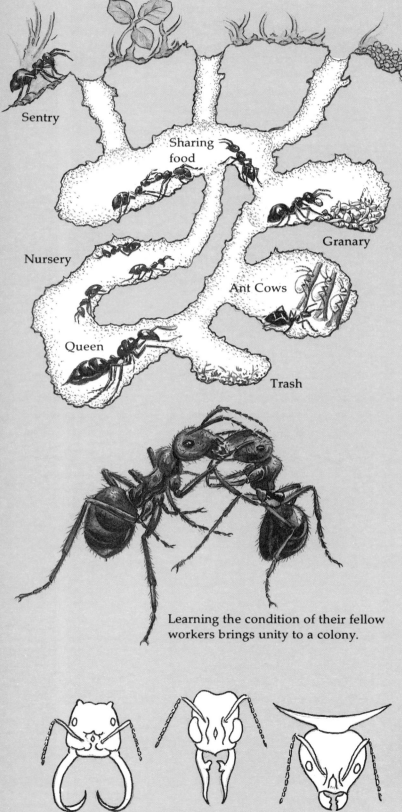

Sentry

Sharing food

Nursery

Granary

Ant Cows

Queen

Trash

Learning the condition of their fellow workers brings unity to a colony.

The many faces of the ant.

THE GOVERNMENT OF THE ANT

WHO PERSUADES ANTS TO WORK?

While the queen ant is the center of attention and the mother of most of the ants in a colony, she is not the chief ruler. Instead, work is initiated by servant-leaders who lead by example. These servant-leaders are older ants who begin each new activity in the colony by doing the work themselves. Younger ants imitate the servant-leaders and join in the task at hand. There are no supervisors, chiefs, or officers among the ants.

WHAT CHARACTERISTIC OF LEADERSHIP MUST AN ANT HAVE?

The worker ants that search for food leave a trail of tiny drops that contain a scent common to the whole colony. Other workers follow this trail to locate food and return to the nest. It is important that a scout never mislead its fellow workers by crossing over its own trail. To do so would confuse the followers and cause them to travel in circles until they died from exhaustion.

HOW DO ANTS PROVIDE FOR THEIR "POOR"?

There are no "poor" ants in an ant colony. Ants readily share their food with one another without concern for themselves. This generosity is possible because of a social stomach, or crop, that stores food before it is digested. When two ants meet, the food from the crop is brought up and shared. Those who have an abundance of food voluntarily give to those with less, until all have shared equally.

HOW DO ANTS REPORT NEWS?

Although researchers are not clear on how this process fully operates, it is evident that the food from the social stomach carries with it chemicals that report information about what is happening in every part of the nest. Food picked up from the nursery workers includes a nursery report on the conditions there. Food shared by scouts communicates what new sources of food are being brought back to the nest. This sharing of food acts just like a newspaper to keep everyone in the nest informed about the conditions of their fellow workers.

DO ANTS HAVE A KNOWLEDGE OF GOOD AND EVIL?

Ants determine the difference between good and evil strangers by their sense of smell. When two ants approach one another, they carefully touch each other with their antennae to determine whether they are friend or foe. If friendly, they caress one another and share food. If not, they either flee or defend themselves.

THE INDUSTRY OF THE ANT

DO ANTS REALLY HARVEST CROPS?

Up until the late 1800's, many thought that Solomon had exaggerated the industry of the ant. In 1871, however, a species of ant was found that not only harvests grain but also winnows it and treats it to prevent germination during storage. Harvester Ants have also been known to carry spoiled seeds to dumping grounds, where they sprout and create small fields which are cultivated and later harvested. The grain is stored in large underground granaries, where it is actually milled and converted to a type of bread.

WHAT SACRIFICE WILL ANTS MAKE TO SALVAGE DAMAGED PROVISIONS?

If water creeps into a granary of the Harvester Ant, the seeds must be dried or they will rot. The ants carry every seed to the surface, where it is dried in the sun and then returned to a fresh storage place. In a large colony, this task may take days.

HOW ARE ANTS LIKE DAIRY FARMERS?

An insect called the aphid secretes a sweet sticky substance called honeydew, which is greatly prized by the ant. Just as dairy farmers maintain herds of cows, ants maintain herds of aphids. Certain worker ants act as "cow herders" and look after the aphids by moving them from plant to plant and by protecting them from predators. In the fall, the worker ants collect the aphid eggs and guard them over the winter. In the spring, the newly hatched aphids are then brought out of the ant nest and placed on plants to feed.

HOW DO ANTS PRESERVE THE MILK THEY GATHER?

The milk of the aphid is stored in large tanks, just as dairy farmers store cow's milk. Ants, however, use living tanks. A few workers are allowed to gorge themselves until they become so large that they are unable to move. They hang suspended from the ceiling of the nest until the milk is needed. They are then pumped dry to feed the rest of the colony.

WHAT CROPS DO ANTS RAISE?

Several species of ants are fungus farmers. They gather leaves and grass which are chewed into a moist mash and stored in fields deep inside the nest. The fungus that grows from this compost is harvested by the ants for food. Some of the underground fields, which are cultivated to keep out undesirable fungi, have been measured to be over 100 square meters in area.

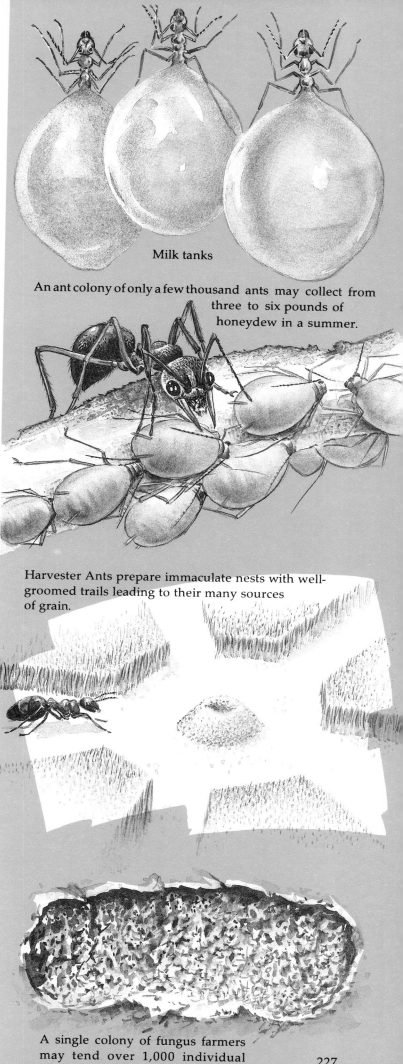

Milk tanks

An ant colony of only a few thousand ants may collect from three to six pounds of honeydew in a summer.

Harvester Ants prepare immaculate nests with well-groomed trails leading to their many sources of grain.

A single colony of fungus farmers may tend over 1,000 individual gardens, some larger than a football.

227

What God Reveals About the Ant

"There be four things which are little upon the earth, but they are exceeding wise: The ants are a people not strong, yet they prepare their meat in the summer" (Proverbs 30:24–25).

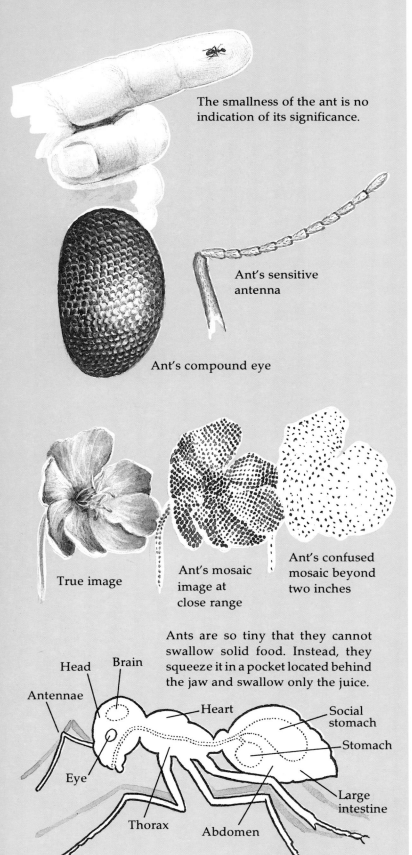

The smallness of the ant is no indication of its significance.

Ant's sensitive antenna

Ant's compound eye

True image

Ant's mosaic image at close range

Ant's confused mosaic beyond two inches

Ants are so tiny that they cannot swallow solid food. Instead, they squeeze it in a pocket located behind the jaw and swallow only the juice.

Head — Brain — Heart — Social stomach — Stomach — Large intestine — Abdomen — Thorax — Eye — Antennae

228

THE DETAIL OF THE ANT

WHY DOES GOD CALL THE ANT LITTLE?

In comparison to the things of the earth, the ant is indeed little. Even the largest of the queens is not over two inches in length. The pharaoh ant is smaller than the dot of an "i" and weighs perhaps less than a thousandth of an ounce. The average ant is so tiny that its life can be ended with the slightest pressure of a human's toe.

The ant's size, however, is no reflection on its significance. Over 8,000 species of ants have been identified, more species than any other insect or animal; and the total number of ants on the face of the earth is staggering. No other creature the size of the ant exhibits so much energy or organization.

WHEN DO ANTS CARE ABOUT THEIR APPEARANCE?

Ants returning from the field are very concerned about their cleanliness. They are greeted by younger worker ants at the entrance to the nest. These younger ants lick the older ones clean in a manner similar to a drive-through car wash. The antennae are given special attention because of the many segments which must be kept clean. If the joints of the segments become sticky and clogged with dirt, the ant may lose the use of its major sensory organ.

WHEN ARE THE ANT'S EYES A HANDICAP?

Most ants have compound eyes. Compound eyes are made up of hundreds of fixed eyelets, each with its own non-focusing lens and light receiver. Because of this, the ant sees a mosaic rather than a single image. At close range, the mosaic resembles the true image. At greater distances, the mosaic becomes a confused pattern of light which the ant's mind cannot sort out. Beyond even an inch, the ant is virtually blind, except for an awareness of light and dark.

HOW DOES THE ANT FIND ITS WAY IN A JUNGLE OF GIANTS?

While almost useless for vision, the ant's eyes are polarized like sunglasses. This enables the ant to determine the position of the sun, even on cloudy days. Ants use the sun's position as a reference for navigation, just as sailors use the stars. By walking in a direction which keeps the sun at the same angle, the ant is able to walk in a straight line through any maze of grass and sticks. If an ant is covered for a period of time by a box and then released, it will deviate from its original course by the exact angle that the sun moved during the ant's entrapment.

HOW DO ANTS HEAR WITHOUT EARS?

Like most insects, ants have no ears. Yet they hear by sensing sound vibrations through their feet, antennae, and tiny hairs that cover their legs and body.

Ants even sing to one another by rubbing parts of their abdomen together to create a high-pitched hum. Other ants hear these vibrations through the ground and often become excited and work more vigorously.

THE STRENGTH OF THE ANT

HOW MUCH CAN THE ANT LIFT?

Although by human standards the ant is very weak, compared to its own weight the ant is stronger than any man. A Leaf Cutting Ant may carry up to 50 times its own weight over a hundred yards. That is equivalent to a 200-pound man carrying five tons on his back for a distance of seventeen miles. The real strength of the ant, however, lies not in its individual performance but in its cooperative strength. In a single summer, a large colony may excavate 30,000 to 40,000 pounds of earth to make its nest and carry 5,000 pounds of material back into the nest for food.

HOW FAR DOES THE ANT WALK IN A DAY?

The ant may make as many as four round trips a day to food sources which may be over 400 feet from the nest. That is roughly equivalent to a man's walking sixty-eight miles. If the ant had the stride of a man, it would be capable of bursts of speed in excess of sixty-five miles an hour and would walk normally at a speed of twenty miles per hour.

HOW LONG CAN THE ANT WORK?

Bees live only five or six weeks before they work themselves to death. Ants live and work for years before wearing out. Young ants usually begin working as assistants in the nursery and then move to other jobs as they grow older. By the time a worker reaches the age of five or six years, it is considered old and takes on the role of a servant-leader in the colony.

WHICH ANT IS STRONGER THAN AN OX?

If an animal is tied and cannot otherwise flee, it can easily be overcome and pulled to the ground by a species of ant called the Driver Ant. These ants migrate in long columns, eating every piece of flesh in their path. There have been reports of caged leopards being reduced to bones overnight; and an elephant that could not escape was completely consumed in three days. Even the mighty ox is no match for the Driver Ant if it cannot flee.

WHY MUST THE ANT PREPARE FOOD IN SUMMER?

The activity of the ant, like other insects, is affected by the temperature. As the nest cools in the fall, ants become weaker and are unable to provide for themselves. Therefore they must gather food during the warm months while they have the strength to do so. Ants apparently are not bothered by freezing weather, because they hibernate during the coldest months. In the spring, as temperatures warm, they become active long before food is plentiful and must rely on what has been stored the previous summer.

Man vs. Ant

A leaf with legs?

Ounce for ounce, a man would need a bulldozer to match the combined strength of a colony of ants.

A column of Driver Ants may be so long that it takes over two weeks for the column to pass.

229

BE COMMITTED TO DILIGENCE

ITS REQUIREMENTS

1. Be diligent to remember the truths that God has shown you. (See Deuteronomy 4:9.)

2. Be diligent to teach God's Word to your children and grandchildren. (See Deuteronomy 6:7.)

3. Be diligent to keep all of God's commandments. (See Deuteronomy 6:17.)

4. Be diligent to guard your affections. (See Proverbs 4:23.)

5. Be diligent to add to your faith. (See II Peter 1:5.)

6. Be diligent to make your calling and election sure. (See II Peter 1:10.)

7. Be diligent to minister to other Christians. (See Hebrews 6:10–12.)

8. Be diligent in seeking the Lord. (See Hebrews 11:6.)

9. Be diligent to remove roots of bitterness. (See Hebrews 12:15.)

10. Be diligent to avoid swindlers and frauds. (See Proverbs 23:1–3.)

11. Be diligent to know the condition of those under your spiritual care. (See Proverbs 27:23.)

ITS REWARDS

1. You will be rich.
". . . The hand of the diligent maketh rich" (Proverbs 10:4).

2. You will be given authority.
"The hand of the diligent shall bear rule . . ." (Proverbs 12:24).

3. You will enjoy your possessions.
". . . The substance of a diligent man is precious" (Proverbs 12:27).

4. You will be fulfilled.
". . . The soul of the diligent shall be made fat" (Proverbs 13:4).

5. You will be creative and resourceful.
"The thoughts of the diligent tend only to plenteousness . . ." (Proverbs 21:5).

6. You will obtain favor.
"He that diligently seeketh good procureth favour . . ." (Proverbs 11:27).

7. You will be given honor.
"Seest thou a man diligent in his business? he shall stand before kings . . ." (Proverbs 22:29).

Personal Commitment to Conquer Slothfulness

I purpose to know the symptoms of slothfulness and to develop discipline by refusing to make those little daily surrenders which lead to slothfulness. I also purpose to make the most of each day which God entrusts to me.

Date _____

CAN YOU DETECT THE SYMPTOMS OF A SLUGGARD?

Match each piece in the puzzle with the verse it illustrates.

☐ **1.** *"As the door turneth upon his hinges, so doth the slothful upon his bed"* (Proverbs 26:14).

☐ **2.** *"The sluggard will not plow by reason of the cold; therefore shall he beg in harvest, and have nothing"* (Proverbs 20:4).

☐ **3.** *"... The field of the slothful ... was all grown over with thorns, and nettles had covered the face thereof, and the stone wall thereof was broken down"* (Proverbs 24:30–31).

☐ **4.** *"The slothful man roasteth not that which he took in hunting . . ."* (Proverbs 12:27).

☐ **5.** *"By much slothfulness the building decayeth; and through idleness of the hands the house droppeth through"* (Ecclesiastes 10:18).

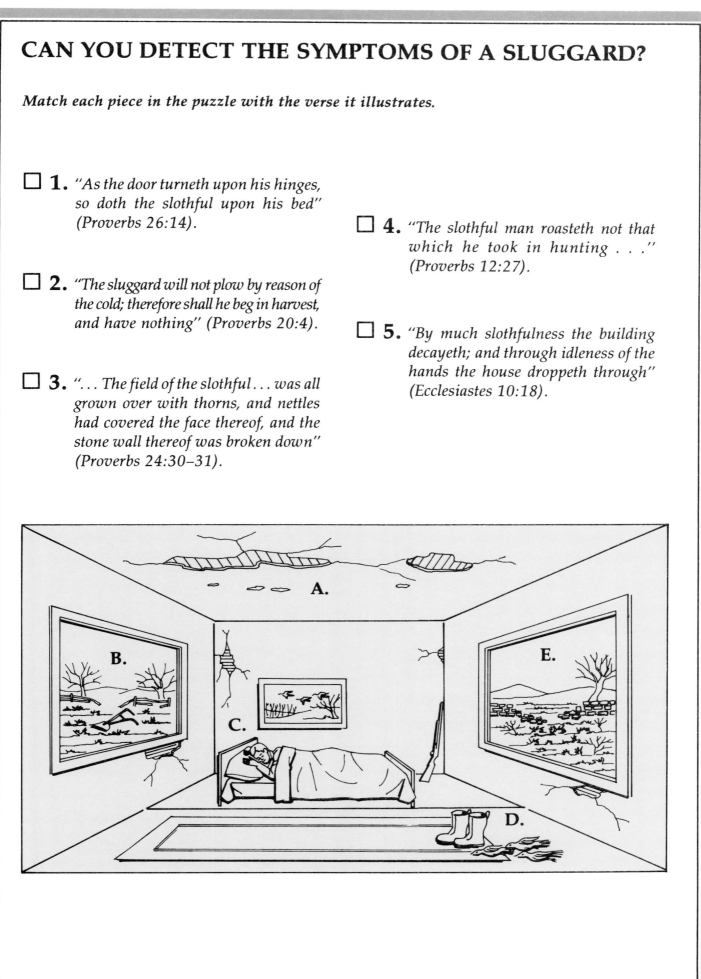

Anwers: 1C 2B 3E 4D 5A

WHO PASSED THE "SLEEP TEST" IN THE BIBLE?

Match each statement with the person to whom it refers.

A. DARIUS
(See Daniel 6:18–19.)

B. MOSES
(See Exodus 8:20; 9:13.)

C. ABRAHAM
(See Genesis 22:3.)

D. SAMUEL
(See I Samuel 9:26.)

E. JOSHUA
(See Joshua 6:12; 8:10.)

F. JESUS
(See Mark 1:35.)

G. GIDEON
(See Judges 6:38.)

H. JOB
(See Job 1:5.)

☐ 1. I got up very early in the morning, so that I could get alone with My heavenly Father.

☐ 2. I was not alert to the schemes of wicked men. As a result, an innocent man was condemned. I spent the night fasting and waiting for his deliverance.

☐ 3. I had a great deal of responsibility. However, I regularly got up early in the morning to pray for my family.

☐ 4. God promised me continuous victories in battle. In spite of this reassurance, it was my practice to get up early in the morning and begin my campaigns.

☐ 5. I needed direction from God for a major decision. I asked God to work out certain circumstances, and I got up early in the morning to check them out.

☐ 6. God asked me to perform a very difficult task—surrendering my most cherished affection. I got up early in the morning to begin carrying it out.

☐ 7. God gave me the responsibility of communicating His truth to the ruler of the land. In order to effectively carry this out, I got up early in the morning.

☐ 8. God asked me to anoint the ruler of the nation. I got up early in the morning in order to carry out His instructions.

Answers: 1.F 2.A 3.H 4.E 5.G 6.C 7.B 8.D

WHO FAILED THE "SLEEP TEST" IN THE BIBLE?

Match each statement with the person it best describes.

☐ **1.** God warned me that my task was both dangerous and delicate. He gave me precise instructions for my journey. I made the mistake of stopping to rest under an oak tree, and it cost me my life. Who am I?

☐ **2.** It was the time that leaders go out to battle. Instead, I stayed home to get a little more sleep. It was obvious that I did not need it because I could not sleep; so I went for a walk and fell into terrible sin. Who am I?

☐ **3.** I was startled by the words, "O sleeper, get up and call on your God." This was a rebuke to me, but it revealed that my slothfulness was a by-product of my rebellion against God. He severely disciplined me. Who am I?

☐ **4.** I, too, was slothful in praying. Rather than being spiritually alert as I should have been, I fell asleep. As a consequence, I fell into the very temptation that I was warned about. Who am I?

☐ **5.** I had a habit of falling asleep when I should have been fleeing from temptation. My enjoyment of inappropriate sleep cost me my spiritual and physical vision. Who am I?

☐ **6.** I fell asleep at a time when I should have been listening to instruction. My sleep was so sound that I caused a shocking incident and disrupted the meeting. Who am I?

☐ **7.** My slothfulness was compounded by drunkenness. At a time of great danger to my family, I was sleeping. When I woke up, God punished me with a heart attack. Who am I?

☐ **8.** A slothful person does not anticipate future needs, and that was precisely my problem. Because of it, I lost the opportunity of a lifetime. Who am I?

A. Jonah
(See Jonah 1:6.)

B. Eutychus
(See Acts 20:9.)

C. David
(See II Samuel 11:2.)

D. Samson
(See Judges 16:19.)

E. Nabal
(See I Samuel 25:36–38.)

F. Peter
(See Matthew 26:40–43.)

G. A foolish virgin
(See Matthew 25:5.)

H. Unnamed prophet
(See I Kings 13:14–24.)

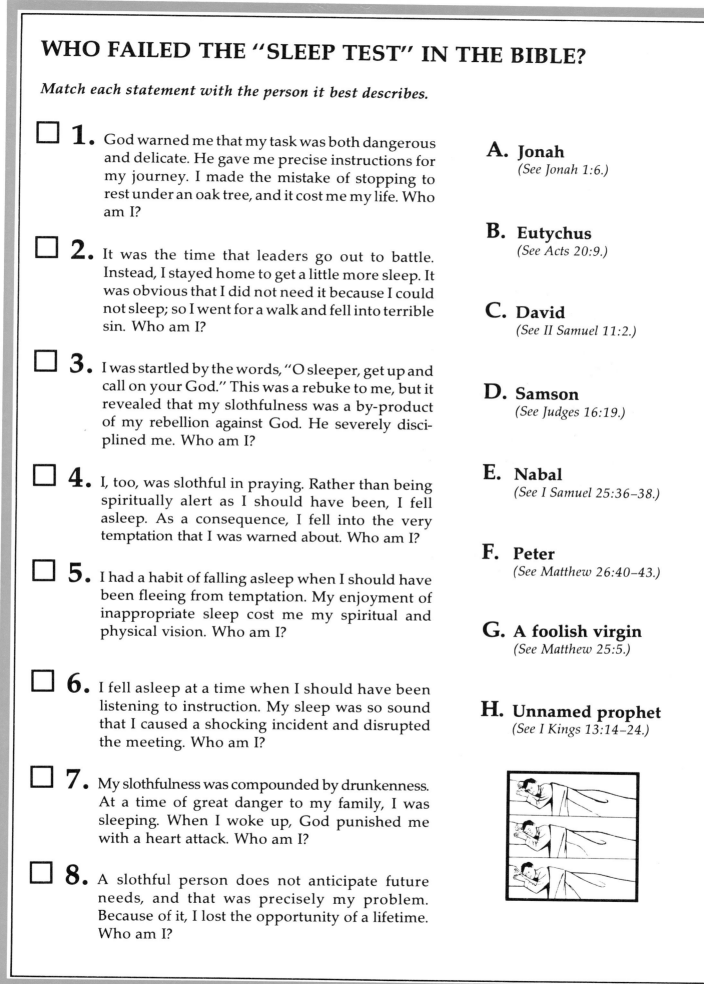

Answers: 1.H 2.C 3.A 4.F 5.D 6.B 7.E 8.G

JOSEPH
A great achiever through serving

LISTENING REQUIRES A SERVANT'S HEART

"...Whosoever will be great among you, shall be your minister: And whosoever of you will be the chiefest, shall be servant of all" (Mark 10:43–44).

19 LISTEN TO THE CAUTIONS OF YOUR WIFE

"As an earring of gold, and an ornament of fine gold, so is a wise reprover upon an obedient ear" (Proverbs 25:12).

A SERVANT'S REWARD

"A wise man will hear, and will increase learning; and a man of understanding shall attain unto wise counsels" (Proverbs 1:5).

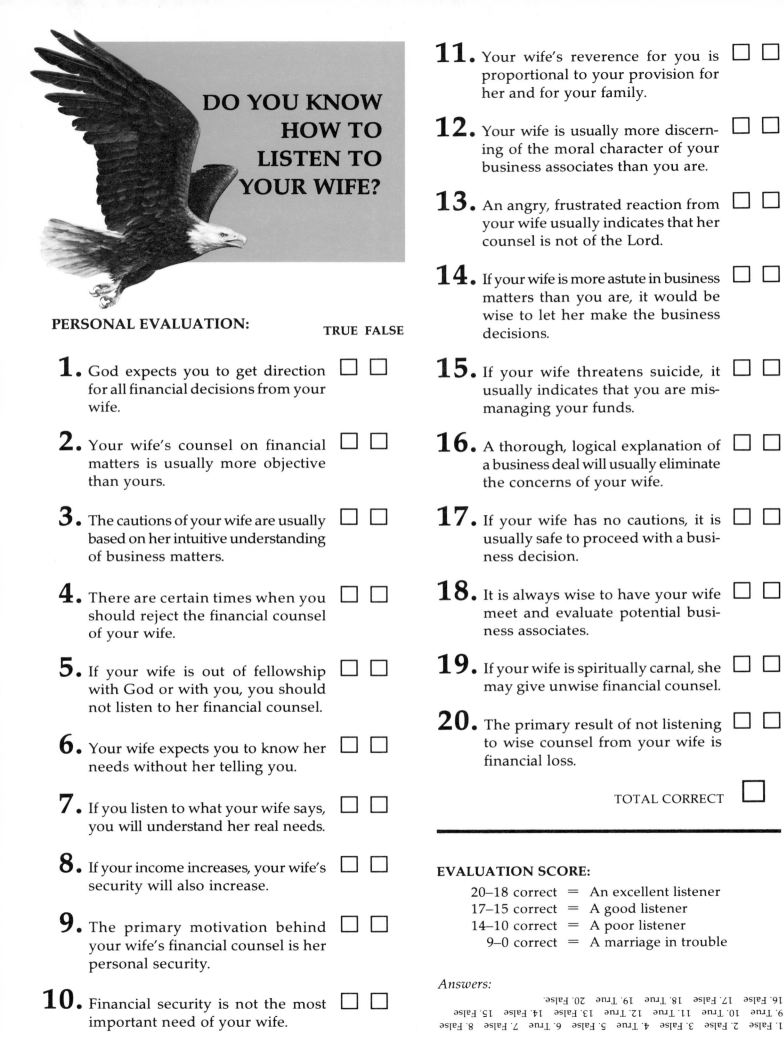

DO YOU KNOW HOW TO LISTEN TO YOUR WIFE?

PERSONAL EVALUATION:

TRUE FALSE

1. God expects you to get direction for all financial decisions from your wife. ☐ ☐

2. Your wife's counsel on financial matters is usually more objective than yours. ☐ ☐

3. The cautions of your wife are usually based on her intuitive understanding of business matters. ☐ ☐

4. There are certain times when you should reject the financial counsel of your wife. ☐ ☐

5. If your wife is out of fellowship with God or with you, you should not listen to her financial counsel. ☐ ☐

6. Your wife expects you to know her needs without her telling you. ☐ ☐

7. If you listen to what your wife says, you will understand her real needs. ☐ ☐

8. If your income increases, your wife's security will also increase. ☐ ☐

9. The primary motivation behind your wife's financial counsel is her personal security. ☐ ☐

10. Financial security is not the most important need of your wife. ☐ ☐

11. Your wife's reverence for you is proportional to your provision for her and for your family. ☐ ☐

12. Your wife is usually more discerning of the moral character of your business associates than you are. ☐ ☐

13. An angry, frustrated reaction from your wife usually indicates that her counsel is not of the Lord. ☐ ☐

14. If your wife is more astute in business matters than you are, it would be wise to let her make the business decisions. ☐ ☐

15. If your wife threatens suicide, it usually indicates that you are mismanaging your funds. ☐ ☐

16. A thorough, logical explanation of a business deal will usually eliminate the concerns of your wife. ☐ ☐

17. If your wife has no cautions, it is usually safe to proceed with a business decision. ☐ ☐

18. It is always wise to have your wife meet and evaluate potential business associates. ☐ ☐

19. If your wife is spiritually carnal, she may give unwise financial counsel. ☐ ☐

20. The primary result of not listening to wise counsel from your wife is financial loss. ☐ ☐

TOTAL CORRECT ☐

EVALUATION SCORE:

- 20–18 correct = An excellent listener
- 17–15 correct = A good listener
- 14–10 correct = A poor listener
- 9–0 correct = A marriage in trouble

Answers:

1. False 2. False 3. False 4. True 5. False 6. True 7. False 8. False 9. True 10. True 11. True 12. True 13. False 14. False 15. False 16. False 17. False 18. True 19. True 20. False.

ATTENTIVENESS

Being alert to God's warnings through the spoken and unspoken cautions of your wife

BASIC INSIGHTS TO UNDERSTAND AND ACT UPON A WIFE'S CAUTIONS

1 A wife often has inexplicable cautions regarding financial decisions

When God designed the husband and wife to come together in one flesh, His purpose was for the wife to provide valuable assistance in the basic areas of the husband's life.

Accordingly, God gives to the wife an alertness and understanding that He does not initially give to the husband. In this way, the husband recognizes his need for his wife and is motivated to maintain a oneness of spirit in order not to miss God's direction through her.

There are several Scriptural examples of God's giving vital information to the wife first. He told Manoah's wife that she would have a son, and how she was to rear him, before He told Manoah. (See Judges 13:1–15.) He appeared to Mary before He explained Christ's birth to Joseph. (See Matthew 1:18–25.)

2 A wife has special alertness to the moral aspects of a business relationship

The wife of a prosperous landowner in Shunem accurately discerned the Godly character of Elisha and urged her husband to assist him. (See II Kings 4:8–9.)

The wife of a governing ruler in Jerusalem discerned the innocent character of Jesus and warned her husband not to deliver Him over to judgment. (See Matthew 27:19.)

These Scriptural examples serve to illustrate the significant ability of a wife to discern the character of those with whom her husband is dealing.

A wife may not understand technical business procedures, but she can often discern the moral character of a business agreement or associate.

If a man is considering an important business decision, it would be very wise for him to explain it to his wife and, if possible, to have her meet the person or persons involved.

If a husband invites a potential business associate to have dinner with him and his wife, she will be especially sensitive to the following four areas:

- Moral impurity (by watching his eyes)
- Pride (by sensing his ambitions)
- Worldliness (by evaluating his appearance and attitudes)
- Insincerity (by listening to his words).

3 A wife can express her cautions from four conflicting viewpoints

If a wife sees that her husband is about to make a business decision, she has four possible responses:

- Mental ("It sounds logical; I think it will work.")
- Emotional ("I feel very nervous about the business decision that you are going to make.")
- Volitional ("I have decided to trust God to work through you in this matter.")
- Spiritual ("I am sure that God is wanting to teach me some lessons through whatever happens.")

Most husbands become confused when their wives switch from one perspective to another. However, God explains that counsel in the heart of a person is like deep water, but a man of understanding will draw it out. (See Proverbs 20:5.) To draw out your wife's counsel means that there is oneness of spirit, not just verbal approval.

If a husband relies on only one of his wife's perspectives, she will later blame him if the decision turns out to be incorrect. The classic illustration of this involves Sarah's response to Abraham.

Thinking that she would never have children of her own, Sarah told her husband to have a child with Hagar, who was Sarah's Egyptian handmaid. When Abraham followed her logic and conflicts arose, Sarah blamed him for an unwise decision. *"And Sarai said unto Abram, My wrong be upon thee..."* (Genesis 16:5).

4 A wife has a basic human need for security

God describes the wife as "the weaker vessel" in I Peter 3:7. She is to be protected and cared for by her husband. If in her later years her husband dies, she is to be cared for by family members and, ultimately, by the church. (See I Timothy 5:1–16.)

This is what God intended. Unfortunately, family members and churches often fail to fulfill their God-given responsibilities toward widows. Many times they are not able to do so because of financial bondage due to unwise decisions.

The knowledge of this failure on the part of family members and churches puts the wife in an awkward position. Fearing the financial insecurity of widowhood, she tries to warn her husband of financial danger, or she may attempt to take financial matters into her own hands.

Abigail recognized the danger that was about to destroy her family because of her husband's rude response to David's messengers. Her husband was totally oblivious to the danger. (See I Samuel 25:3–38.)

To express it a different way, a wife becomes alarmed when she sees cracks in the ceiling. A husband becomes alarmed when the roof caves in!

It is to a man's credit to listen to his wife's early warnings, thereby avoiding the greater damages. *"A prudent man forseeth the evil, and hideth himself: but the simple pass on, and are punished"* (Proverbs 22:3).

5 A wife is not as concerned about the amount of her husband's earnings as she is about his management of it

A doctor was puzzled because of his wife's concern over their financial status. Their attractive home was paid for, they owned two cars and several valuable properties, and he earned an annual income of over $100,000.

His wife finally explained the source of her deep concern. The doctor made impulsive business decisions. As long as ample funds were coming in, bad investments were covered. However, his wife realized that one major unwise decision could wipe out all of the assets which they owned.

Her deeper concern was that her husband resisted her cautions and counsel and was confident that he alone was able to make all of the business decisions.

6 A wife loses her feeling of self-worth when her husband rejects her financial cautions

When a husband rejects the cautions of his wife, he is communicating any number of messages to her:

- You are not very intelligent.
- I do not value you as a person.
- Your judgment is not to be trusted.
- You are not very important to me.
- I do not respect you.
- You are not capable of understanding.
- Other people's ideas are more important than yours are.

Every one of these messages damages the self-image of a wife. They cause her to conclude that she is of no value when it comes to financial matters. In addition to damaging his wife's self-image, the husband is also rejecting her God-given role of being a helpmeet to her husband.

The injury to a wife's self-esteem is made even more painful when she must share the consequences of her husband's poor judgment in financial decisions.

7 A wife's agreement with a business decision does not in itself make it right

There may be times when a husband should not follow the counsel of his wife. For example, any counsel that violates God's Word is wrong, even though the wife is fully in favor of it.

Sapphira agreed with her husband to misrepresent the sale price of their land, and both she and her husband were judged. (See Acts 5:1–11.)

AS HE RAN PAST HIS WIFE, HE SHOUTED, "HOW DID YOU KNOW?"

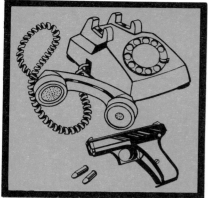

The following true account provides vivid reinforcement of the need for every man to listen to the God-given cautions of his wife.

The testimony of a businessman:

One day, a friend said to me, "I've got a great investment. Why don't we go into it together?"

It looked good, so I agreed and gave him several thousand dollars. That evening I told my wife about it.

"Oh, I wish you hadn't done that," she said. "I sense that he is not as Godly as he appears on the outside."

I reacted, "Now that's not right! This guy has been the chairman of the deacon board."

My wife replied, "Well, there's just something that a woman knows about a man, and one of those things is that he does not have moral freedom. I can tell by the way he looks at women."

"Well, I don't think you're right," I responded. "But even if you are right, and even if he does have a problem, that doesn't have anything to do with his investments."

"But how can God bless a man like that?" my wife asked. "And if you are in a partnership with him, how can He bless that partnership?"

Well, I just ignored her cautions. There was no way this deal could miss.

A few months later this man called up and said, "I've got bad news. The deal fell through and you lost your money. I can't understand why it didn't work."

*   *   *

Several months later, I hired a new man. I soon discovered that he was an alcoholic. Every once in a while he would disappear for three or four days after first calling in sick.

One day I said to him, "If you miss work like this again, you will have fired yourself." He agreed.

Several weeks later he didn't show up again. On Monday I came home and said to my wife, "Honey, he's doing it again! I'll bet he's on another drinking spree." Tuesday night I told my wife, "That guy is just an alcoholic. He's a bum. He's no good. I've just got to get him out of the office." While eating dinner on Wednesday night I said, "Honey, that does it. He has fired himself. I'm through with him."

My wife gently asked, "Have you called him?"

"No," I replied. "I'm not going to call him. I told him if he did it, he's through. I don't need to call him. I mean it's over, period."

"Why don't you go call him?" my wife asked.

"I'm not going to call him," I insisted. "I wouldn't call him for anything. He's through, and that's it."

We ate a little more, and pretty soon she said, "I really feel that you ought to call him."

I got all worked up and excited and said, "I'm not going to call him. Will you leave it alone? The subject is dead!"

My three-year-old daughter started crying. "Daddy, you are talking so ugly to Mommy. You need to ask Mommy to forgive you."

So I smiled and looked across the table and said, "Honey I'm sorry I talked so roughly to you. Would you forgive me?"

She said, "Yes, I will."

Then under my breath, I hissed, "And would you leave it alone?"

We continued eating. A minute later my wife bravely persisted, "I've just got to ask you—what if he's going to commit suicide?"

"Commit suicide? That's never been in the picture. It's never been talked about. He just loves alcohol." I got up and stormed over to the phone. "All right, I'm going to call him just for you." I dialed and let it ring. It rang about seven times. On the eighth ring, just to "rub it in," I yelled into the kitchen, "There's eight rings. There's nine. There's ten. See, he's out buying some more booze. I told you."

All of a sudden he answered the phone. In a deep voice that I could hardly recognize, he said, "Hello."

"What are you doing, drinking again?" I asked.

In a low, gutteral voice he answered, "Yes, I am."

"That's what I thought," I sneered. "That's what you deserve."

"Oh, please!" he cried, "I just put a bullet in my gun and cocked it. I was waiting for the phone to quit ringing so I could kill myself, but it just wouldn't quit ringing."

Chills went up and down my spine! "Put the gun down! I'm coming right over!" As I ran past my wife, I shouted, "How did you know?"

"I don't know," she said. "It was just something inside of me. Something kept saying, 'What if he's going to kill himself?'"

I raced to his home with my pastor. We were able to help sober him up. Later, he received Christ as his personal Savior. Today he is a different person, living with his family, and doing very well.

Used by permission

THE WISDOM OF LISTENING TO YOUR WIFE

A $100,000 PROFIT!

A very happy smile greeted the president of a small company when one of his salesmen announced that he had just lined up a sale that would bring a commission of $100,000. A few years earlier, the staff of this company had attended a Seminar in Basic Youth Conflicts and many of them had become Christians. Business was good that year; but by the following year, the changing economy had reduced their profits drastically. This sale was badly needed.

ENTHUSIASM DIMMED BY THE CAUTIONS OF A WIFE

That evening the company president excitedly told his wife about the deal they were making with an investment group. He explained that a large number of prominent Christians in their town were involved in it.

Later on that evening his wife asked, "Honey, would you explain again how that deal is going to be worked out?"

With a tinge of irritation he answered, "I explained it to you once."

"Honey, why are you angry?" she asked.

"I don't know why I'm angry," he replied, and then he thought, "Maybe I'd better check this whole thing out again."

For months he and his staff had sought to build every business decision on the principles of Scripture. They had been studying the book of Proverbs to find wisdom on financial matters. Now, as the company president looked more deeply into this business deal, he realized that there was a violation of some Scriptural principles.

The following day he approached his salesman and explained that he was not free to go ahead with the deal. Would the salesman be willing to drop it, even though each of them would lose $50,000 of the commission? The president explained his

wife's cautions; and then, to his surprise, the salesman reported that his mother and girlfriend also had expressed cautions about the deal. Both men agreed that they would not move ahead until they felt free to do so.

SCORNFUL LAUGHTER

Together they approached the director of the investment group and explained that they were not able to proceed with the deal. They told him that they wanted to return the $100,000 note in exchange for a letter of release. The investment director scornfully laughed and assured them that they were making a big mistake.

About six months later that investment group, which was composed of Christian leaders and businessmen of the community, discovered that they had been swindled by their director. He had taken several hundred thousand dollars of their money and left town. He was an established businessman and leading church member, and his theft had devastating effects on his church and destroyed his marriage. Lawyers were hired and a complete investigation was made. Every company and person involved in the business deal became liable and had lawsuits filed against them. One lawyer told this company president, "It looks like everyone is going to be sued, except you. We are absolutely amazed that you got out of this when you did. How did you know to get out?"

The president explained that he purposed to run his business entirely on the principles of Scripture, and that doing so also involved paying attention to the cautions of those around him, especially the cautions of his wife.

THE REWARD OF LISTENING

The law firm which conducted the investigation was so impressed by the honesty of this company president that they began giving him their business and referring others to him. Not only did he avoid a costly lawsuit, but he made more money on commissions from these references than he had lost in the other commission.

Used by permission

LISTENING REQUIRES A ONENESS OF SPIRIT

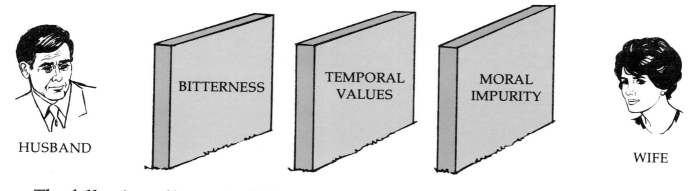

HUSBAND   BITTERNESS   TEMPORAL VALUES   MORAL IMPURITY   WIFE

The following offenses build barriers between husband and wife and hinder the wife from communicating God-given cautions.

1. Awareness that she is not first in his life

The purpose of the head of a family is to be aware of, and meet, the needs of his family. When a husband is preoccupied with other people, possessions, or activities, his wife begins to doubt his love. She then becomes insecure.

2. Failure to recognize and appreciate attempts to please him

A wife loses her creativity, or else she looks for recognition from other sources, when her husband is insensitive and fails to admire or praise her for the special little things that she does to try to please him.

3. Unfavorable comparison with other women

A wife is deeply hurt when her husband admires the appearance or abilities of other women. She is prompted to jealousy and self-rejection.

4. Lack of spiritual leadership

Every wife has a deep longing for her husband to show interest in the things of God. When a husband is lacking in spiritual leadership, his wife feels insecure and is motivated to seek spiritual leadership from others.

5. Rejection of her opinions

A husband tends to evaluate his wife's opinion through his frame of reference rather than through the immediate needs which she sees.

6. Lack of personal discipline

When a man fails to conquer anger and moral impurity, his wife loses her admiration and respect for him; and his attempts to correct her faults are met with silence or reaction.

7. Inadequate preparation for changes

When a man receives a job transfer and has to move his family, his wife needs to mentally and emotionally move before she actually relocates. Inadequate time to do this produces frustration and resentment.

8. Inconsistency in discipline

When a husband takes sides with the children against his wife, he divides his family and teaches them to be disloyal to him.

9. Attempts to correct in public

A wife's self-image is deeply damaged when her husband uses jokes or cutting remarks in front of other people in order to make some correction in her life. Rather than correcting her faults, his wife becomes resentful.

10. Unwillingness to ask forgiveness

A wife reacts to her husband's pride when he refuses to admit failure or ask forgiveness when he knows that he is wrong.

MAKE FINANCIAL DECISIONS TOGETHER

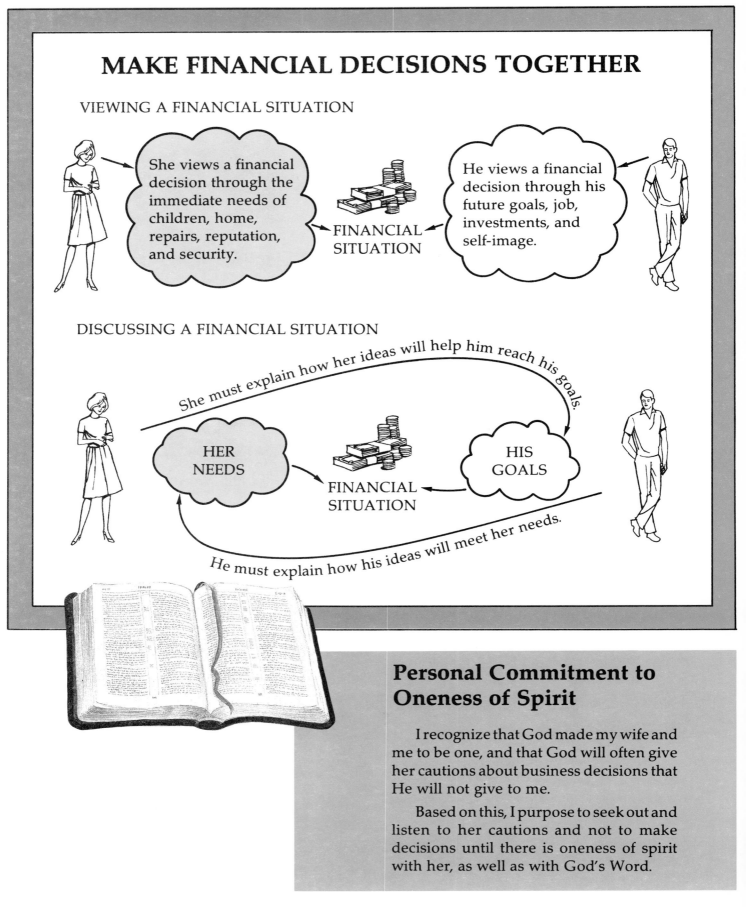

VIEWING A FINANCIAL SITUATION

She views a financial decision through the immediate needs of children, home, repairs, reputation, and security.

FINANCIAL SITUATION

He views a financial decision through his future goals, job, investments, and self-image.

DISCUSSING A FINANCIAL SITUATION

She must explain how her ideas will help him reach his goals.

HER NEEDS

FINANCIAL SITUATION

HIS GOALS

He must explain how his ideas will meet her needs.

Personal Commitment to Oneness of Spirit

I recognize that God made my wife and me to be one, and that God will often give her cautions about business decisions that He will not give to me.

Based on this, I purpose to seek out and listen to her cautions and not to make decisions until there is oneness of spirit with her, as well as with God's Word.

Present decisions that need to be made:

_____

_____

_____

242

WHO FOLLOWED THE WRONG COUNSEL OF A WIFE?

Just as the wife should never obey instructions that violate God's Word,
so the husband should never follow counsel that contradicts God's commands.

Match each command with the husband who failed to obey it.

☐ **1.** *"So shall not the inheritance of the children of Israel remove from tribe to tribe: for every one of the children of Israel shall keep himself to the inheritance of the tribe of his fathers."*

☐ **2.** *"And I will make of thee a great nation, and I will bless thee, and make thy name great. . . ."*

☐ **3.** *"And the Lord God commanded the man, saying, Of every tree of the garden thou mayest freely eat: But of the tree of the knowledge of good and evil, thou shalt not eat of it. . . ."*

☐ **4.** *"Neither shall he multiply wives to himself, that his heart turn not away. . . ."*

A. **Adam**
(See Genesis 2:16–17;
3:1–7.)

C. **Solomon**
(See Deuteronomy 17:17;
I Kings 11:4–8.)

B. **Abraham**
(See Genesis 12:2; 16.)

D. Ahab
(See Numbers 36:7;
I Kings 21:7.)

Match the wrong counsel of each wife to the husband who listened to it.

☐ **5.** If you follow my plan, you can fulfill the promise that God made to you. **?**

☐ **6.** Get up and eat, and I will give you what you want. **?**

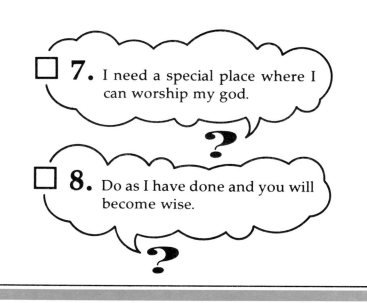

☐ **7.** I need a special place where I can worship my god. **?**

☐ **8.** Do as I have done and you will become wise. **?**

WHO GAVE THEIR HUSBANDS WISE COUNSEL?

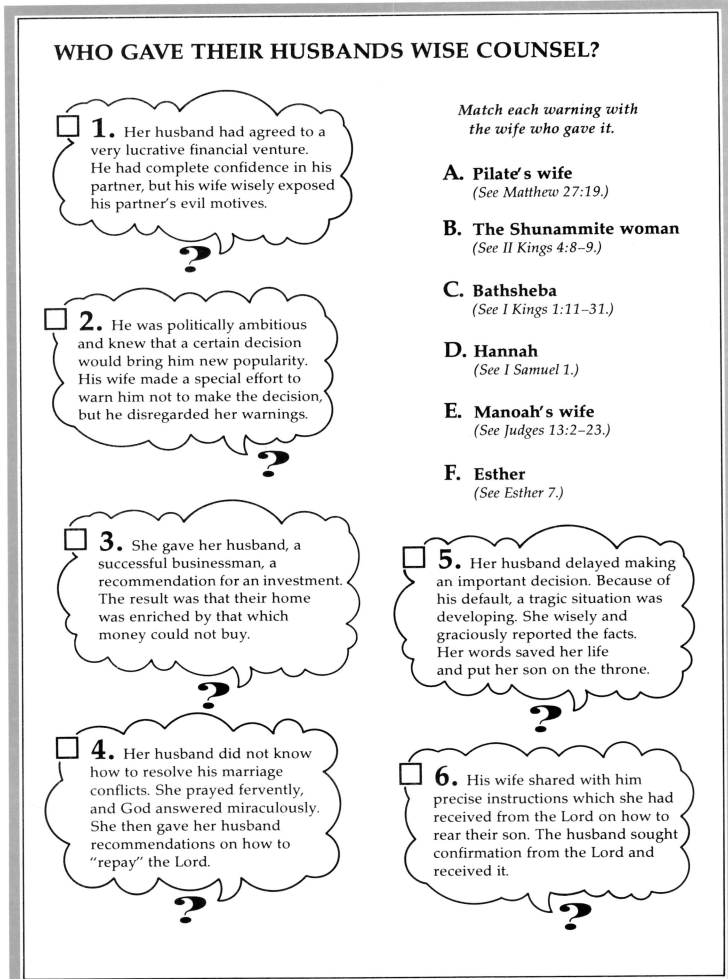

1. Her husband had agreed to a very lucrative financial venture. He had complete confidence in his partner, but his wife wisely exposed his partner's evil motives.

2. He was politically ambitious and knew that a certain decision would bring him new popularity. His wife made a special effort to warn him not to make the decision, but he disregarded her warnings.

3. She gave her husband, a successful businessman, a recommendation for an investment. The result was that their home was enriched by that which money could not buy.

4. Her husband did not know how to resolve his marriage conflicts. She prayed fervently, and God answered miraculously. She then gave her husband recommendations on how to "repay" the Lord.

5. Her husband delayed making an important decision. Because of his default, a tragic situation was developing. She wisely and graciously reported the facts. Her words saved her life and put her son on the throne.

6. His wife shared with him precise instructions which she had received from the Lord on how to rear their son. The husband sought confirmation from the Lord and received it.

Match each warning with the wife who gave it.

A. Pilate's wife
(See Matthew 27:19.)

B. The Shunammite woman
(See II Kings 4:8–9.)

C. Bathsheba
(See I Kings 1:11–31.)

D. Hannah
(See I Samuel 1.)

E. Manoah's wife
(See Judges 13:2–23.)

F. Esther
(See Esther 7.)

Answers: 1.F 2.A 3.B 4.D 5.C 6.E.

WHY WERE THESE WIVES UNABLE TO GIVE WISE COUNSEL?

Match each wrong decision with the reason which hindered the wife from giving wise counsel to her husband.

☐ **1. Abraham and Sarah**
Abraham decided to take his wife's counsel and have a son by Hagar. (See Genesis 16:1–3.)

☐ **2. Isaac and Rebekah**
Isaac decided to show favoritism toward Esau, his oldest son. (See Genesis 25:23; 27:1–46.)

☐ **3. Ahab and Jezebel**
Ahab decided to let his wife take Naboth's vineyard by whatever means she chose. (See I Kings 16:31.)

☐ **4. Ahasuerus and Esther**
Ahasuerus agreed to slaughter all the Jews in order to enrich his treasury and rid the land of "dissidents." (See Esther 4:5–9.)

☐ **5. Haman and Zeresh**
Haman took his wife's counsel and built a 75-foot-high gallows upon which to hang Mordecai. (See Esther 5:9–14.)

☐ **6. Herod and Herodias**
Herod decided to fulfill his wife's request to behead John the Baptist. (See Mark 6:17–28.)

☐ **7. Ananias and Sapphira**
Ananias decided to lie about the price he received for selling his land. (See Acts 5:1–2.)

☐ **8. Agrippa and Bernice**
Agrippa decided not to become a Christian after having the Gospel clearly explained to him by Paul. (See Acts 25:23–26:32.)

WHY NO RIGHT COUNSEL WAS GIVEN

A. She was unequally yoked with her husband, since he was an Israelite and she was a Baal worshiper.

B. She was struggling with guilt over her immoral relationship.

C. She needed reassurance that she was not standing in the way of his spiritual goals.

D. She loved the pomp of public office.

E. She was focusing on the need for temporal security and public praise, rather than on God's provision.

F. She took up an offense for her husband.

G. She did not learn about the situation until a binding decision had already been made.

H. Because she did not see spiritual leadership in her husband, she took matters into her own hands.

Answers: 1C 2H 3A 4G 5F 6B 7E 8D

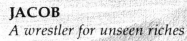

JACOB
A wrestler for unseen riches

RESTITUTION AND WRESTLING

After initiating restitution with an offended brother, Jacob wrestled all night with an angel. He won a blessing of power with God and with man. (See Genesis 32:24–28.)

20 PREPARE NOW FOR A LASTING HERITAGE

"But lay up for yourselves treasures in heaven, where neither moth nor rust doth corrupt, and where thieves do not break through nor steal: For where your treasure is, there will your heart be also" (Matthew 6:20–21).

GENERATIONS OF BLESSING

Jacob passed on a Godly heritage to his descendants and also to every Christian who partakes of his spiritual riches. (See Isaiah 58:14.)

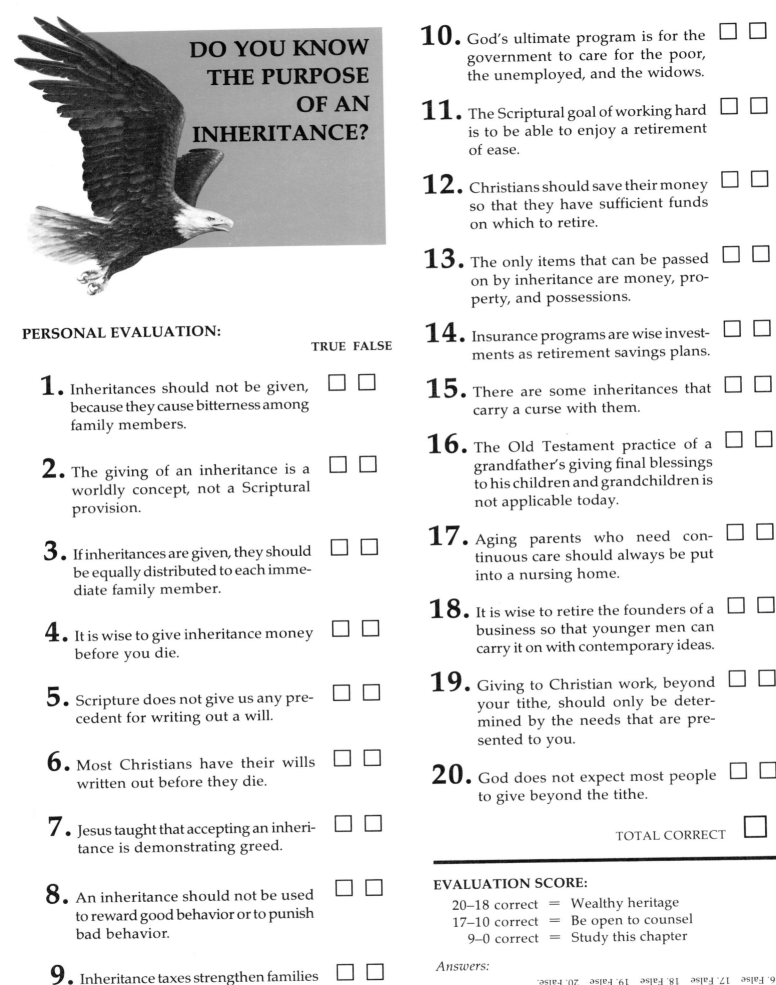

DO YOU KNOW THE PURPOSE OF AN INHERITANCE?

PERSONAL EVALUATION:

TRUE FALSE

1. Inheritances should not be given, because they cause bitterness among family members. ☐ ☐

2. The giving of an inheritance is a worldly concept, not a Scriptural provision. ☐ ☐

3. If inheritances are given, they should be equally distributed to each immediate family member. ☐ ☐

4. It is wise to give inheritance money before you die. ☐ ☐

5. Scripture does not give us any precedent for writing out a will. ☐ ☐

6. Most Christians have their wills written out before they die. ☐ ☐

7. Jesus taught that accepting an inheritance is demonstrating greed. ☐ ☐

8. An inheritance should not be used to reward good behavior or to punish bad behavior. ☐ ☐

9. Inheritance taxes strengthen families by allowing the government to distribute the money equally. ☐ ☐

10. God's ultimate program is for the government to care for the poor, the unemployed, and the widows. ☐ ☐

11. The Scriptural goal of working hard is to be able to enjoy a retirement of ease. ☐ ☐

12. Christians should save their money so that they have sufficient funds on which to retire. ☐ ☐

13. The only items that can be passed on by inheritance are money, property, and possessions. ☐ ☐

14. Insurance programs are wise investments as retirement savings plans. ☐ ☐

15. There are some inheritances that carry a curse with them. ☐ ☐

16. The Old Testament practice of a grandfather's giving final blessings to his children and grandchildren is not applicable today. ☐ ☐

17. Aging parents who need continuous care should always be put into a nursing home. ☐ ☐

18. It is wise to retire the founders of a business so that younger men can carry it on with contemporary ideas. ☐ ☐

19. Giving to Christian work, beyond your tithe, should only be determined by the needs that are presented to you. ☐ ☐

20. God does not expect most people to give beyond the tithe. ☐ ☐

TOTAL CORRECT ☐

EVALUATION SCORE:

20–18 correct = Wealthy heritage
17–10 correct = Be open to counsel
9–0 correct = Study this chapter

Answers:

1. False 2. False 3. False 4. True 5. False 6. False 7. False 8. False 9. False 10. False 11. False 12. False 13. False 14. False 15. True 16. False 17. False 18. False 19. False 20. False.

TEN BASIC FACTORS OF A WEALTHY HERITAGE

Few men today even begin to comprehend the far-reaching potential and responsibility which they have in raising up the foundations of many Godly generations. This is done by passing on a valuable heritage.

1 PASS ON A GOOD NAME

The most valuable asset that you have to pass on to your children is a good name. *"A good name is rather to be chosen than great riches..."* (Proverbs 22:1).

A good name is the by-product of consistently demonstrating Godly character, such as honesty, diligence, kindness, sincerity, purity, loyalty, generosity, self-control, dependability, faith, love, humility, and orderliness.

A good name is also the result of significant achievement. Lasting achievement involves those things which you allow God to accomplish through your life, such as leading your own family to salvation and spiritual maturity, helping many others find salvation, and motivating Christians to grow spiritually.

If your good name has been falsely accused, there are several important steps to take.

- Verify the facts by properly appealing to the one who has falsely accused you.

- If there is partial blame, ask for forgiveness and make restitution as far as you can.

- Reconfirm your name by being zealous unto good works.

"Having your conversation honest among the Gentiles: that, whereas they speak against you as evildoers, they may by your good works, which they shall behold, glorify God in the day of visitation" (I Peter 2:12).

2 TRANSFER A GODLY CAUSE AND BASIC LIFE TEACHING

God commands fathers to accept the responsibility of teaching their children and their grandchildren. *"... Teach them [to] thy sons, and thy sons' sons..."* (Deuteronomy 4:9). *"... Teach them diligently unto thy children..."* (Deuteronomy 6:7).

The motivation for learning must be based on an active involvement in a contest between good and evil, God's truth and Satan's deception.

In this spiritual warfare you must carefully explain the lessons that God has taught you, and you must tell how those lessons have helped you to learn basic Scriptural principles as well as Godly character, convictions, and standards.

A vital and valuable means of conveying this material will be your own life notebook and family yearbooks. These books will be lasting treasures that will tell how God taught you the principles of self-acceptance, obedience to authority, clear conscience, genuine forgiveness, yielding rights, moral freedom, purpose in life, and financial freedom.

These books will be valuable resources on how you learned specific character qualities, how your Scriptural convictions were tested, what standards are essential to you and will be to your children, and what skills will be important for their success. Included in your family books should be family pictures and other related materials.

"Happy is the man that findeth wisdom... For the merchandise of it is better than... fine gold... and all the things thou canst desire are not to be compared unto her.... She is a tree of life to them that lay hold upon her..." (Proverbs 3:13–15, 18).

". . . Wise men die, likewise the fool and the brutish person perish, and leave their wealth to others. Their inward thought is, that their houses shall continue for ever, and their dwelling places to all generations; they call their lands after their own names" (Psalm 49:10–11).

ACKNOWLEDGE THE SINS OF YOUR FOREFATHERS

3

Children and grandchildren benefit from the character and achievement of their parents. They also suffer the consequences of the sins and weaknesses of their parents. *". . . I the Lord thy God am a jealous God, visiting the iniquity of the fathers upon the children unto the third and fourth generation of them that hate me" (Exodus 20:5).*

Medical problems, physical features, and personality traits can be passed on by both parents, but the destructive consequences of sin are primarily passed on by the father.

It was by the sin of Adam that transgression entered into the world. *"Wherefore, as by one man sin entered into the world, and death by sin; and so death passed upon all men . . ." (Romans 5:12).*

Not only is sin passed on by the forefathers, but the children were a physical part of the fathers when those sins were committed. God establishes this point when he explains that Levi, the great grandson of Abraham, was a part of Abraham's action of paying tithes to Melchizedek, because Levi was in Abraham's loins. (See Hebrews 7:10.)

Based upon this truth, God teaches that all of us sinned in Adam. (See Romans 5:12–19.) For this reason also, Scripture teaches the need for us to acknowledge the sins of our forefathers. *"We acknowledge, O Lord, our wickedness, and the iniquity of our fathers: for we have sinned against thee" (Jeremiah 14:20).* This is repeated many places in Scripture, such as Psalm 106:6: *"We have sinned with our fathers, we have committed iniquity, we have done wickedly."*

When we become Christians, we are forgiven of all our sin. However, inherited physical, psychological, and spiritual weaknesses and tendencies must be recognized and overcome by the disciplines of walking in God's Spirit.

It is important to explain to your children in a clear yet discreet manner the special temptations which they may face because of the failures of previous generations.

Emphasize to your children that there will be constant limitations on them because of inherited weaknesses. Emphasize that these limitations are actually standards that everyone should have.

SINS OF FOREFATHERS	REQUIRED DISCIPLINES
1. **Moral impurity**	Be pure in thought, action, and friendships
2. **Drunkenness and drug abuse**	Abstain totally from alcoholic beverages and habit-forming drugs
3. **Lying and deception**	Be totally honest, and have a clear conscience
4. **Occult involvement**	Cleanse your home and bind Satan
5. **Pride and rejection**	Yield rights and never divorce

UNDERSTAND GOD'S PURPOSES FOR AN INHERITANCE

The primary purpose of the inheritance is to strengthen the family unit; and then, through the family, the basic social needs of the community are cared for.

Excessive taxation of inheritances weakens the family and the community. It transfers capital from the family to the state. Attempts by the state to solve social problems become more and more ineffective as the family becomes weaker.

• *Final means of discipline*

Scripture gives ample evidence that the promise of inheritance is to be a strong deterrent to rebellion and an equally strong reward for obedience to God's laws.

Jacob's first-born son, Reuben, was immoral. Therefore, he lost the double portion of inheritance which he should have received. (See Genesis 49:3–4.)

Joseph, however, was loyal and obedient to his father, and he earned his father's favor and the double portion of inheritance. (See Genesis 48:22.)

A father must explain that an inheritance is not a right, but a responsibility, and that spiritual failure will only reveal that a son or daughter is not capable of fulfilling that responsibility.

If inheritance money is given to a rebellious child, it will most certainly be used for purposes that are directly contrary to God's objectives.

• *Provision for the sick and elderly*

Inheritance is to be a ready reserve for medical needs. The very character of the family is strengthened as it discharges its responsibility to its sick and needy members.

Scripture severely condemns the failure to carry out this function. *"But if any widow have children or nephews, let them learn first to shew piety at home, and to requite their parents: for that is good and acceptable before God. . . . But if any provide not for his own, and specially for those of his own house, he hath denied the faith, and is worse than an infidel"* (I Timothy 5:4, 8).

• *A resource for education and business*

God designed the family to assume the primary responsibility for educating the children. The parents are to use the home as the basic classroom.

What they are not able to teach at home is to be carefully delegated to qualified teachers. *". . . A child . . . is under tutors and governors until the time appointed of the father"* (Galatians 4:1–2).

Businesses that grow out of a family's efforts will tend to have greater quality and craftsmanship, because the entire family name is affected by their products.

Capital investments for equipment and improvement should come from family resources rather than outside interest. By borrowing, the family becomes servant to the lender.

• *Provision for a home*

Buying a home should be an investment in an appreciating item and does not need to constitute personal debt. Many couples, however, are increasing their faith by seeing God provide a home without going into debt. Each story is a unique message of God's supernatural power to provide.

God outlines a key factor in the provision of a home in Proverbs 19:14. *"House and riches are the inheritance of fathers: and a prudent wife is from the Lord."* In other words the parents are to assist the children in the provision of a home. In our day this may require a reassessment of other financial priorities. For example, it may be wise for parents to encourage their children to earn their own money for higher education if such education is in God's will. The parents would then use the money that they would have spent for the college education for a home instead. Many who have worked their way through school or have waited until they earned the money have gotten more out of their education because they have approached it with more maturity and a greater sense of relating what they have learned to the real world in which they must live.

• *Assistance for the poor*

When families are spiritually and financially strong, they, through the local church, can become a community's most effective welfare agency.

They are able to provide jobs, be examples, and give to the poor and needy. This ministry to the poor is clearly taught as a family and church responsibility in Scripture.

God commands, *". . . Deal thy bread to the hungry, and . . . bring the poor that are cast out to thy house . . ."* (Isaiah 58:7).

In the New Testament, widows are evaluated on the basis of their ministry to the poor, among other things. *"If she have lodged strangers . . . if she have relieved the afflicted . . ."* (I Timothy 5:10).

5 PREPARE AN INSTRUCTIVE WILL FOR YOUR FAMILY

The potential of a will goes far beyond the disposal of property. To be done correctly, a will requires much thought, prayer, and preparation.

A will can be a carefully compiled document, drawn from what God has taught you over the years and what you want your family to learn for years to come. God gave us two "wills" when He gave us the Old and New Testaments. They contain history, chronology, practical instruction, and future direction.

As you prepare your own will, there will undoubtedly be several stages in its development over the years.

The first stage involves a basic document which provides for the care of your children and contains directives for the transfer of your property. This simple instrument avoids the possibility of your children's becoming wards of the state, and it prevents your money from going into probate court when you die.

Subsequent additions to your will may give greater clarity and direction to the Scriptural functions of inheritance.

Once you have composed the basic content of your will, almost any lawyer is able to adapt it to legal terms and make sure that it contains the necessary items.

One of the unexpected benefits of preparing a detailed will is that potential family disagreements can be anticipated and worked out ahead of time.

Before Abraham died, he gave gifts to the other sons that he had after Isaac, and sent them away to live in the east. (See Genesis 25:5–6.)

Isaac's heritage included a much-coveted verbal blessing which he passed on to his sons. (See Genesis 27.)

Jacob's "will" included a detailed description of what God would do in each son's life, based on their actions, character, and abilities. (See Genesis 49.)

Rechab's last will and testament contained strict guidelines for self-control in living. God rewarded his descendants for obeying them. (See Jeremiah 35.)

6 REJECT RETIREMENT EASE

A retirement to a life of ease and pleasure has been the world's alternative to heaven. It has not worked. Multitudes of retired people have discovered the shocking truth that to lose your usefulness is to invite rejection.

There may be a place in later years for a change in vocation, but never did God intend for there to be a ceasing of labor. This was made quite clear in man's beginning, when God said to Adam that he must work until the day he died. *"In the sweat of thy face shalt thou eat bread, till thou return unto the ground . . ." (Genesis 3:19).*

It is significant that many men who were healthy at retirement have died a premature death just a few years later. Still a larger number of retired men have become disillusioned by the constant routine of idleness. The classic warning on this topic is contained in Christ's parable of the rich fool.

". . . I will pull down my barns, and build greater; and there will I bestow all my fruits and my goods. And I will say to my soul, Soul, thou hast much goods laid up for many years; take thine ease, eat, drink, and be merry. But God said unto him, Thou fool, this night thy soul shall be required of thee . . ." (Luke 12:18–20).

God indicated the propriety of adapting work to the strength and maturity of a man when He commanded that the Levites were to transport the tabernacle from place to place until they were fifty years old. Then, after the age of fifty, they were to serve with their brethren in a supervisory position. (See Numbers 8:23–26.)

This function gave the older men maximum opportunity to counsel, drawing from the wisdom and experience that God had given to them.

To cease from active involvement is to deny your family and others the important lessons that God has taught you.

MAKE WISE INVESTMENTS FOR THE FUTURE

The most important investments that a man can make for his future are in the lives of his family and in the spiritual welfare of others.

A man's investments in his family may involve the development of marketable skills, the resources to profitably use those skills, and assistance in securing and maintaining homes for his married children.

Additional investments should be in functional assets, such as land and equipment, which insure freedom of operation during lean financial times. A functional asset is an item that is useful to you now, but could be easily traded for other items when your needs change.

As a general rule, do not invest money in things which you cannot control, such as stocks, gold mines, and oil wells. Rather than expecting others to manage your investments, buy only those things that you can care for and which will enhance the freedom you have to carry out the work that God has given to you.

Investments should be made from abundance and not from needed family or business income. It must be a separate program, and it must in no way put pressure on the family.

Wise investments involve using God's money to advance His kingdom. His money is not to be a hoarded resource, but a ready reserve. Investments must never violate Scriptural principles. If we are faithful stewards, we can look forward to hearing God say, *". . . Well done, thou good and faithful servant: thou hast been faithful over a few things, I will make thee ruler over many things: enter thou into the joy of thy lord"* (Matthew 25:21).

GOD'S WARNING AGAINST HOARDING:

"Your gold and silver is cankered; and the rust of them shall be a witness against you, and shall eat your flesh as it were fire. Ye have heaped treasure together for the last days" (James 5:3).

BECOME RICH TOWARD GOD BY GIVING

By far, the wisest and most rewarding investments of all are those that are given to God for the furtherance of His work.

The Scriptures are punctuated with commands, warnings, and promises regarding the need to lay up treasures in heaven rather than on earth. *"Charge them that are rich in this world, that they be not highminded, nor trust in uncertain riches, but in the living God, who giveth us richly all things to enjoy; That they do good, that they be rich in good works, ready to distribute, willing to communicate; Laying up in store for themselves a good foundation against the time to come, that they may lay hold on eternal life"* (I Timothy 6:17–19).

Giving to the Lord, beyond the tithe, will be prompted by Him and confirmed by your wife. The prompting will be completely consistent with Scriptural guidelines. Those guidelines include:

• *Giving to the fatherless and widows*

"Pure religion and undefiled before God and the Father is this, To visit the fatherless and widows in their affliction, and to keep himself unspotted from the world" (James 1:27).

Many people who are rich in this world's goods are unhappy, because the pursuit of pleasure and fulfillment through monetary means leads only to frustration and disappointment.

- ## *Giving to needy Christians*
  "Distributing to the necessity of saints; given to hospitality" (Romans 12:13).

- ## *Giving to the poor*
  "He that hath pity upon the poor lendeth unto the Lord; and that which he hath given will he pay him again" (Proverbs 19:17).

- ## *Giving to Christian leaders*
  "Let the elders that rule well be counted worthy of double honour, especially they who labour in the word and doctrine. For the scripture saith, Thou shalt not muzzle the ox that treadeth out the corn. And, The labourer is worthy of his reward" (I Timothy 5:17–18).

In addition to giving to individual Christian leaders, we can also contribute to groups that have united to accomplish a particular ministry. In the day of Paul, an inter-church ministry was commissioned by the Holy Spirit and the church leaders to collect an offering from the Gentile Christians for the Jewish believers. Gentile Christians were urged to give to this fund, and many did so sacrificially. Also, the house of Stephanas had a special ministry to the saints, and Christians were urged to support them. (See I Corinthians 16:15.)

There are several important criteria which should be used to evaluate the worthiness of giving to such a ministry.

1. Is the ministry and its leadership under the spiritual authority of a local church which honors the Word of God?

Paul carried on a ministry outside of the local church, yet he was sent out by a local church and remained under its spiritual authority. He also reported back to his local church. (See Acts 13:1–3; 14:27.)

2. Is the ministry strengthening the local church?

God's agency to carry out His program during this age is the local church. Every Christian ministry which is worthy of support will strengthen both church leaders and members to fulfill their God-given responsibilities. *"And he gave some . . . For the perfecting of the saints, for the work of the ministry, for the edifying of the body of Christ"* (Ephesians 4:11–12).

3. Does the ministry teach and maintain Godly standards?

Many ministries allow themselves to be squeezed into the mold of the world. Their worldly appearance and approach is an attempt to identify with the world in order to reach them. However, this philosophy is unscriptural and leads to destructive temptations. (See Romans 12:2.)

"For the grace of God that bringeth salvation hath appeared to all men, Teaching us that, denying ungodliness and worldly lusts, we should live soberly, righteously, and godly, in this present world" (Titus 2:11–12).

4. Is there evidence of God's supernatural workings?

God is a supernatural God. He confirms His ministries by demonstrating His supernatural power through them.

The evidences of God's power should include genuine lasting conversions, Christians freed from the power of sin, broken marriages restored, and God's provision in answer to prayer. *". . . My preaching was . . . in demonstration of the Spirit and of power"* (I Corinthians 2:4).

5. Is the ministry based on sound doctrine?

Sound doctrine begins by acceptance of the verbally inspired Word of God. It recognizes that Jesus Christ is perfect God and perfect man.

Doctrinal error is usually a symptom of deeper problems which will eventually diminish or destroy the potential of a ministry. *"Beloved, believe not every spirit, but try the spirits whether they are of God: because many false prophets are gone out into the world"* (I John 4:1).

Wise, generous, and Spirit-directed giving brings multiplied dividends for you and your family, both in this life and the one which is to come. (See Mark 10:29–31.)

UNDERSTAND THE PRINCIPLES OF INSURANCE

The basic concept behind insurance is sharing the loss. In itself, this is a sound Scriptural principle. *"Bear ye one another's burdens, and so fulfil the law of Christ"* (Galatians 6:2).

However, there are several possible dangers and abuses in insurance programs:

• *Trying to insulate yourself from any loss*

This leads to being overinsured and missing the lessons that God wants to teach through loss. It also may cause bitterness and disillusionment when insurance companies do not pay what you expected, or when they point out the fine print which you failed to notice.

• *Attempting to use insurance as a savings program*

As long as inflation is a reality of life, whole life policies that promise end-of-life dividends may be a very poor savings program. In most cases it is wise to buy term insurance and put the difference into other investments.

• *Insuring away personal responsibility*

Automobile liability insurance is a lawful, proper, and wise expense. However, we must not allow dependence on insurance to decrease our personal responsibility.

A Christian who obeys the laws of God and the laws of the highway can rest assured that he will avoid accidents, unless God has bigger lessons that He wants him to learn. (See Matthew 10:29.)

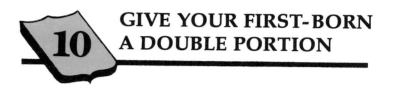

GIVE YOUR FIRST-BORN A DOUBLE PORTION

In God's ideal society, the first-born son received a double portion of the inheritance.

With this double portion came special responsibilities to carry on the goals of the father within the family. The first-born was responsible to provide for his mother until her death, and for his sisters until their marriages. Special training was given to the first-born to do this effectively, and explanations were given to other family members to prepare them for his leadership.

If the first-born son rejected God's leadership before the father died, the double portion was awarded to the next son who qualified. Where there were no sons, the first-born daughter was to receive the double portion.

Reuben was Jacob's first-born son. However, because he defiled his father's wife, he failed to receive a double portion of the inheritance. Instead, it was given to Joseph.

Joseph then carried out the responsibilities of burying his father and looking out for the welfare of his family.

Esau was Isaac's first-born son. However, he was rejected by God because he despised the spiritual responsibilities that came with being the first-born son. (See Romans 9:13; Hebrews 12:16–17.)

TRANSFER WISDOM WITH YOUR WILL

The grief that follows the death of a loved one is often compounded by disillusionment and bitterness because that loved one failed to make a will, or because he failed to design a will that would preserve and transmit character and wisdom.

☐ **1.** Do you have a will?

☐ **2.** Do your wife and family know where it is?

☐ **3.** Do you have a good name to pass on to your descendants? Is there something that you can do right now to improve that name?

☐ **4.** Do you have a carefully prepared book of family records, valuable lessons, rich Scriptural insights, and significant family history that you can entrust to your children?

☐ **5.** Have you acknowledged the sins of your forefathers, and have you established appropriate disciplines for your children to avoid them?

☐ **6.** Have you explained the Scriptural purposes of an inheritance to your family?

☐ **7.** Have you rejected the philosophy of a retirement of ease?

☐ **8.** Have you evaluated your investments and provided clear records and wise counsel for your heirs?

☐ **9.** Have you made rich investments with God that will bring His reward to your family and last for eternity?

☐ **10.** Have you prepared your firstborn son for leadership, and have you prepared the rest of your family to accept his leadership?

Personal Commitment to a Wealthy Heritage

I purpose, by God's grace, to raise up the foundations of many Godly generations. I plan to do this by preparing an inheritance according to the above guidelines, and making sure, as far as possible, that the wisdom, money, and possessions which I pass on will illustrate God's ways and His supernatural provision.

Date my life notebook was begun _____

DO YOU KNOW THE SIGNIFICANCE OF A FATHER'S BLESSING?

THE PATRIARCHAL BLESSING (OR CURSE):

1. It was a verbal statement of the father's approval or disapproval.

2. It was based on past obedience or disobedience.

3. It visualized future success or failure.

4. It contained great authority and influence.

5. It was given by the father to his children and grandchildren.

6. It is based on God's promise to cause things to go well with those who honor their parents and cause reproofs to those who dishonor their parents.

"Honour thy father and mother... That it may be well with thee..." (Ephesians 6:2–3).

Isaac could not detect Jacob when he posed as Esau to get the blessing. (See Genesis 27:6–29.)

Can you detect seven changes in this picture?

Answers: These items are missing: 1. Pitcher 2. Isaac's finger 3. Jacob's foot 4. Jacob's cape 5. Camel's saddle 6. Palm tree 7. Window

WHAT LESSONS DOES GOD TEACH THROUGH INHERITANCES IN THE BIBLE?

Match the lessons to the people who learned them.

A. PRODIGAL SON
(See Luke 15:11–32.)

B. JONADAB
(See Jeremiah 35:6.)

C. LABAN
(See Genesis 31:14–15.)

D. GIDEON
(See Judges 8:24–27.)

E. ESAU
(See Genesis 25:29–34; 27:1–29; Hebrews 12:16–17.)

F. COMPLAINING BROTHER
(See Luke 12:13–15.)

G. RICH YOUNG RULER
(See Mark 10:17–22.)

H. BOAZ
(See Ruth 4:6.)

1. I learned the hard way that you cannot separate the double portion of the firstborn's blessing from its spiritual responsibilities.

2. I demanded my inheritance before my father died. I learned that money without maturity leads to moral and financial ruin.

3. I learned that the price of a spiritual heritage is humility and self-sacrifice. I was unwilling to pay the price.

4. I learned that you lose the loyalty of family members when they cannot look forward to receiving their share of the inheritance.

5. I learned that an inheritance is more than property. It involves personal responsibility for family members.

6. I was bitter because I did not get my share of the inheritance; but my bitterness revealed that I had the problem of covetousness.

7. I left a valuable inheritance to my children. I learned that my early retirement and family wealth were very destructive to my family's future.

8. I had neither houses nor land to give to my children, but I learned that a greater inheritance was the convictions which I instilled in their lives.

Answers: 1.E 2.A 3.G 4.C 5.H 6.F 7.D 8.B

WHAT DOES GOD WANT US TO LEARN FROM HIM?

Use the words at the right to complete each verse.

1. "Ask of me, and I shall give thee _____ for thine inheritance . . ." (Psalm 2:8).

2. "_____ is the portion of mine inheritance . . ." (Psalm 16:5).

3. "House and riches are the inheritance of fathers: and _____ is from the Lord" (Proverbs 19:14).

4. "The wise shall inherit _____: but shame shall be the promotion of fools" (Proverbs 3:35).

5. "I lead in the way of righteousness . . . That I may cause those that love me to inherit _____; and I will fill their _____" (Proverbs 8:20–21).

6. "Blessed are the meek: for they shall inherit _____" (Matthew 5:5).

7. "And every one that hath forsaken houses, or brethren . . . for my name's sake, shall receive an hundredfold, and shall inherit _____" (Matthew 19:29).

8. "That ye be not slothful, but followers of them who through faith and patience inherit _____" (Hebrews 6:12).

9. "Blessed be the God and Father of our Lord Jesus Christ, which according to his abundant mercy hath begotten us . . . To an inheritance _____, and _____ . . ." (I Peter 1:3–4).

10. "He that overcometh shall inherit _____; and I will be his God, and he shall be my son" (Revelation 21:7).

A. The Lord

B. Glory

C. Everlasting life

D. All things

E. A prudent wife

F. Substance, treasures

G. The promises

H. Incorruptible, undefiled

I. The heathen

J. The earth

INDEX OF QUESTIONS ON FINANCES

FINANCIAL REPROOFS

GIVING

INHERITANCE

LENDING

PARTNERSHIPS

PRAYING FOR MONEY

PURPOSES

RESOURCES

RICHES AND POVERTY

SLOTHFULNESS

SWINDLERS

TITHING

WORKING MOTHERS

NOTES

NOTES

NOTES

NOTES

INDEX OF SCRIPTURE REFERENCES